THE
MENTAL - CURE,

Illustrating the
Influence of the Mind on the Body,
Both in Health and Disease, and the Psychological
Method of Treatment

With an Essay on
The New Age By William Al-Sharif

By

REV. W. F. EVANS

AUTHOR OF
Mental Cure

First published in 1869

This edition published by Read Books Ltd.
Copyright © 2019 Read Books Ltd.
This book is copyright and may not be
reproduced or copied in any way without
the express permission of the publisher in writing

British Library Cataloguing-in-Publication Data
A catalogue record for this book is available
from the British Library

THE NEW AGE

An extract from the essay,
The New Age by William Al-Sharif

The 'industrial revolution', the 'Enlightenment Age' and colonialism had strengthened the power of the British Empire. Britain, in the second half of the nineteenth century, was probably the most powerful and influential empire in the world. The power of the empire, accompanied with the processes of modernisation and secularisation, created a new religious and cultural mental space. A 'New age' became part of cultural, religious and romantic imaginaire and represented a new era in which religion and culture would evolve in the favour of the empire and its British subjects. In 1843, The New Age was established in London. It proposed a society 'for the promotion of humanity and abstinence from animal food'. This society would also disseminate 'correct principles on universal peace, [and] health of soul and body'.

Christianity, in the age of the empire and missionary expansion, was influenced by the cultural aspirations for a 'new age'. Christian thinkers began to talk about a new age for 'the Lord' and Christianity. This 'new age' would fulfil biblical prophecies and embody new opportunities and truths for the Christian faith. Rationalist intellectuals imagined a new age for progress and science.

The philosophical and scientific criticism of Christianity, the elaboration of 'holistic' practices and theosophical ideas, the British colonialism of India and romantic Orientalism had all provided an inventive climate for the promotion of spiritualistic ideas. The process of modernisation and secularisation diminished the traditional authority of social and religious structures and shaped the transformation from the idea of destiny to choice and from providence to progress. Yet, there were individuals who opposed the religious hegemony of missionary societies and the hierarchal 'church religion' and sought spirituality in holism, occultism and esotericism. The individualised conquest of spirituality, which later influenced the New Age discourse, was formulated by modernism which invented 'the conception of a unique self and private identity, a unique personality and individuality, which can be expected to generate its own unique vision of the world'.

In the US, the 'New Age' imaginaire represented a new spiritual consciousness of the human self and was transformed by the ideas of Spiritualism, Transcendentalism, New Thought, Theosophy and Millenarianism. People such as Woodbury Melcher Fernald (1813-1873) and Warren Felt Evans (1817-1889) spoke of the coming of 'new age' spirituality. A weekly journal, New Age, was issued in San Francisco in 1865. The foundation of the Theosophical Society in 1875 in New York was significant for articulating theosophical concepts. This Society, which established its international headquarters in India, romanticised the religions of India and declared to challenge dogmatic religious authority and scientific materialism.

Despite the emergence of Christian evangelism and fundamentalism, the first three decades of the twentieth century witnessed numerous attempts by 'spiritual seekers' to create new spiritualities and seek new 'truths' for the 'new age'. Henry Jenkins says that the period between 1910 and 1935 was 'the first new age' and 'the period of emergence'.

PREFACE.

The design of the following treatise is to explain the nature and laws of the inner life of man, and to contribute some light on the subject of Mental Hygiene, which is beginning to assume importance in the treatment of disease, and to attract the attention of physiologists. We have aimed to illustrate the correspondence of the soul and body, their mutual action and reaction, and to demonstrate the causal relation of disordered mental states to diseased physiological action, and the importance and mode of regulating the intellectual and affectional nature of the invalid under any system of medical treatment. We have also endeavored to demonstrate the value, as remedial agencies, of those subtle forces, both material and spiritual, which the improved science of the age is beginning to recognize, and to explain the laws of our interior being which render the so-called magnetic treatment so efficient in the cure of diseased conditions of the organism, and which bids fair to supplant the current and longer established therapeutic systems. We have pointed out the laws that govern the action of mind upon mind, and the transmission of vital force from one person to another, and the potent influence of our inward states in the generation of pathological conditions of the body, and in its restoration to health. While it does not profess to be a work on mental philosophy, some discussion of the nature and laws of the mind seemed to be necessary to a proper understanding of the general

PREFACE.

subject of the volume. We have endeavored to prove the essential spirituality of human nature, to elucidate its hidden, undeveloped powers, and its vital and sympathetic relations to an ever-present world of spirits interfused within this outside circumference of being. This latter idea is beginning to be looked upon as something more than a traditionary theory, an item in a creed, by a large and rapidly increasing number of intelligent persons in all countries of the world, and is a demonstrated fact that is taking its proper place in the positive science of the day. It is to be hoped the volume may prove acceptable and useful to all who feel an interest in the imperfectly explored region of human knowledge into which it attempts to penetrate with the light of philosophy. It was far from our design to present to the public an exhaustive treatise on the subjects discussed, but to give, with as much brevity as was consistent with perspicuity, fruitful hints and suggestions, to stimulate thought and lead to further inquiries. The author had but little in works on mental and physiological science to guide him in his investigations, but was under the necessity of following the light of his own researches, experiments, and intuitions. He claims no infallibility for his opinions and conclusions, but submits them to the candid judgment of all men who love truth for its own sake.

CLAREMONT, N. H., FEB. 22, 1869.

CONTENTS.

CHAPTER I.

THE RELATION OF THE HUMAN MIND TO GOD.

Importance of a Knowledge of God. — The Central Life. — Ubiquity of it. — The whole Idea of God included in Love and Wisdom. — He is the Primal Cause. — The Divine Unity. — Tri-personality impossible. — Man a Divine Incarnation. — God in Christ. — Humanization of Deity. — All men Sons of God. — Teaching of the Oriental Philosophy. — Evolution of the Divine Element. — Jesus introduced a Higher Type of Humanity. — The Allness of God. — His Personality and what is meant by it. — His Omnipresence. — Where to find Him. — Madam Guyon. — The two Aspects of Human Nature. — Medical Science Superficial. — The Root of our Maladies. 19

CHAPTER II.

THE MIND IMMATERIAL, BUT SUBSTANTIAL.

What is meant by Immaterial Substance. — What by Matter. — The Properties of Matter are reducible to the Idea of Force. — Mind the Exhibition of a higher Force. — All Force is Spiritual. — It Originates in God. — Love and Wisdom the First Substance and Force.—Immortality.— The Ground of it. — Life a Persistent Force. — Its receptive Forms Evanescent. — The Brotherhood of Man. — Universal Fatherhood of God. — Moral Influence of such an Idea. 27

CONTENTS.

CHAPTER III.
ON THE FORM OF THE MIND.

Mind not a mathematical Point nor a Monad.—The Relation of Substance and Form.—Perfection of Form belongs only to the Realm of Spirit.—The Soul the inner Manhood.—Humanity of Angels.—Disembodied Souls in the Human Form.—Proved by its being a Necessity of Thought.—Formlessness and Nonentity equivalent.—The Spirit an Organization.—Omnipresence of it in the Body.—Platonic Idea of it.—Pythagorean Conception of it. . 34

CHAPTER IV.
THE DIVISION OF THE MIND INTO TWO DEPARTMENTS.

The two primary Faculties.—The Love.—The Intellect.—All Love and Truth Divine.—Why they appear our own.—The Divine Nucleus of our Being.—Twofold Division of the Mind.—The Will and Love identical.—Motive Power and the Love.—The self-determining Power.—The only Life.—What is it to will a thing?—Practical Value of the Doctrine. 39

CHAPTER V.
THE RELATION OF THE INTELLECT TO THE LOVE.

Derivation of the Intellect from the Love.—Importance of this Truth in Philosophy.—Swedenborg.—G. H. Lewes.—Love the Center of our Being.—The Will and Understanding are like Substance and Form.—Relation of Thought to Affection.—Reaction of the Intellect upon the Love.—Correlative Spiritual Forces.—Freedom is Harmony.—Spiritual Health and Disease.—Relation of our Mental and Physical States.—Importance of regulating

CONTENTS.

the Loves. — Solifidianism based on a wrong Conception
of our Mental Nature.   45

CHAPTER VI.

THE DOCTRINE OF DEGREES.

Three distinct Planes of Mental Being. — Difference between
this and the Common Trichotomous Division of the Mind.
—Each Degree a distinct Mental Nature.—The Outermost
Range.—The Senses. — Animality.— The Psychical man.
—The Spiritual. — Consciousness.— Second Degree. — The
Rational Mind. — Emancipation of the Intellect from the
Dominion of the Senses.— Somnambulism.—Clairvoyance.
— Cognition of Spiritual Things.— Progress an Evolution.
— Education an Educing of what is within.— The Phe-
nomena of the inmost Degree. — Perception or Intuition.
— All truth self-evident to it. — The Divine Internal. —
The Conjunction of the Divine and Human. . . .   50

CHAPTER VII.

THE SPIRITUAL BODY—ITS NATURE AND USE.

The mind the real Selfhood. — Intermediate Essences.—The
Spiritual Body a Mediating Principle. — The Proof of its
Existence. — Testimony of Paul. — Of Swedenborg. — Neither insisted upon.— Objection answered. — Shown to be
the Seat of Sensation. — It is the prior seat of all Pathological States of the external Organism. — Testimony of Clairvoyance. — Of Conscionsness. — The Mental Phenomena
following Amputations. — Explanation of them. — Proof
of Immortality from this Source.—A Succession of Organized Forms in Man.— The Osseous System. — The Muscular. — The Venous and Arterial. — The Cerebro-Nervous.
— Being is real and vital as it becomes Interior. .   58

CONTENTS.

CHAPTER VIII.

ON THE EMANATIONS OF MIND, OR SPIRITUAL SPHERES.

Material Effluvia. — Odorous Particles. — Evaporation. — The mental Sphere a Vibrating Force. — Importance of the Doctrine in Mental Science. — The Sphere the outgoing of the Love. — Mental States Contagious. — What is Influence? — What is Divinity? — Sympathy and Antipathy explained. — Spiritual Remoteness and Propinquity. — Pathological States of Mind and Body traced to the Susceptibility of the Patient. — Subtle Forces of Nature as Therapeutic Agencies. — Connection of the Mental Sphere with the bodily Emanations. — The Imposition of Hands not a mere Symbol. — The Breath. — The Source of our Mental Disturbances. — How to be Useful. . . . 68

CHAPTER IX.

OF THE DOCTRINE OF INFLUX, AND THE RELATION OF MAN TO THE SPIRITUAL WORLD.

The Nature of Influx. — The Unity of Life. — The Mind not self-moved. — Thought not self-originated. — Teaching of Paul. — Of John the Baptist. — Doctrine of Innate Ideas overturned by Locke. — Truth transmissible. — Man's Vital Relation to the other World. — Quotation from Swedenborg. — All Knowledge an Inspiration. — Modern Spiritualism. — How the Old Testament Scriptures were given. — The Demon of Socrates. — Jesus on the Mount. — John in Patmos. — Swedenborg's Intercourse with the Spiritual World. — Sensational Philosophy Unsound. — Locke's Essay. — Condillac. — Original Suggestion. — How Knowledge is Communicated. — Propagation of Mental States. — Mesmeric State how produced. . . . 76

CONTENTS.

CHAPTER X.

THE RELATION OF SOUL AND BODY, AND OF THE MATERIAL TO THE SPIRITUAL REALM.

Three Theories respecting the Connection of the Body and the Spirit. — Aristotle. — Cartesian Doctrine. — Leibnitz. — Man a Microcosm. — The Body an Effect. — The Face and our inward Feelings. — The States of the Mind affect the Body. — Fear and Asthma. — Disease originates in abnormal Mental States. — Chemical Preparations inadequate to a Cure. — Quotation from Dr. Taylor. — Mind the organizing Force. — Relation of the Visible to the Invisible World. — Where is the Spiritual Realm? — Material things inclose a Spiritual Essence. — Pneumatopathy or Mental Hygiene. 87

CHAPTER XI.

CORRESPONDENCE OF THE BRAIN AND THE MIND.

The Brain the Organ of the external Manifestation of the Mind.—Its Extension into the Body.—Its two Substances and their Correspondence. — The Positive and Negative Forces.—The Brain first formed in the Fetus.—Plurality of its Organs. — Sympathetic Connection of the Bodily Organs with it. — The three Brains. — Their Relation to the Degrees of the Mind. — Their independent Action. — The Cerebrum and its Correspondence.—The Cerebellum. — Sleep-Waking. — Mental Exaltation. — Freedom from the bodily Senses.—The Medulla Oblongata.—State of the Mind and Body in the Trance.—Scientific View of Death. 99

CHAPTER XII.

THE HEART AND LUNGS, AND THEIR RELATION TO THE LOVE AND INTELLECT.

Two Universals of the Mind. — Answering Organs of the Body. — The Extension of the Heart into the System. — The Veins and Arteries. — The Heart corresponds to the Affectional Nature. — Proof. — Influence of our Emotional States upon its Action. — And upon Secretion and Nutrition. — Subtle Element of the Blood. — The Diffusion of the Pulmonary Substance. — The Lungs derived from the Heart. — They Answer to the Intellect. — Effect of the States of Thought upon Respiration. — Relation of Respiration to Voluntary Motion. — To the Sensibility of the Nerves. — Influence of Anæsthetic Agents. — How the Mind can increase or diminish vital Action. — Sympathetic Movement of the Heart and Lungs. — How to regulate the Action of the Heart. — How to change our Emotions. — Influence of our Mental States upon the vital Functions. — True Method of Study in Natural Science. — The New Age. — Immanence of the Spiritual World. . . . 109

CHAPTER XIII.

CORRESPONDENCE OF THE STOMACH AND THE MIND.

The Office of the Stomach. — The Digestive Process. — What answers to it in the Mental Economy? — Therapeutic Influence of new Ideas. — Mental Medicine. — Two Stomachs. — Dual Nature of Memory. — Common Forms of Speech Recognizing the Relation of the Stomach to the Memory. — Mental and Bodily Growth. — Mental Vigor necessary to Digestion. — Perpetual Spiritual Adolescence. — What is Old Age? — How to be always Young. — Diseases which are attended with a Loss of the Power of Attention and Memory. 120

CONTENTS.

CHAPTER XIV.

THE REFLEX INFLUENCE OF THE STOMACH UPON THE MIND.

Sensitiveness of the Epigastric Nerves. — Seeress of Prevorst. — Reading with the Pit of the Stomach. — The interior Essence of things. — Their Influence. — Psychometry. — Effect of Medicines held in the Hand. — Philosophy of Amulets. — Action of the hidden Properties of things upon the Reticular Membranes of the Stomach. — Effect of Food upon the Mind. — The Philosophy of Dieting. — Mental Stimulus necessary to Digestion. — The Condition of the Stomach and our Feelings. — Action and Reaction. — The Law of Sympathy between us and those in the Interior Realms. — Effect of happy Frames of Mind upon the Epigastric Nerves. — Mental States attending Various Conditions of the Stomach. — Hunger and its Mental Effects. — The States of the Stomach and Crime. — Hygienic Value of Cheerfulness and other Affectional States. . . .   132

CHAPTER XV.

EXCRETIONS OF THE BODY AND THE MIND, AND THEIR RELATION.

The Excreting Organs and their Use. — Their irregular Action a fruitful Source of Disease. — Influence of the Mind upon them. — The Lower Intestine and the Brain. — Influence of certain Mental States upon it. — Diseases of the Rectum and their Mental Cause. — How Cured. — Office of the Liver. — Chemical Nature of the Bile. — Sympathy between the Liver and Kidneys. — Connection of the Liver with the Brain. — Correspondence with the Mind. — Influence of Conscience upon the Hepatic Functions. — State of the Mind in Duodenitis. — The Cure. —

Melancholy and the Liver. — Elimination of the effete Products of the Mind. — Mental Influence upon the Renal Functions. — Diabetes. — The Connection of the Kidneys with the Brain. — Causality. — Excretory Action of the Intellect. — Renewal of the Spirit. — Perpetual Progress.
. . . . , ... 144

CHAPTER XVI.

THE SKIN. ITS CONNECTION WITH THE INTERNAL ORGANS, AND CORRESPONDENCE WITH THE MIND.

Structure and Functions of the Skin. — Amount Secreted by it daily. — The Period in which the Body is renewed. — The Chemical Laboratory of the System. — Unrecognized Sources of Nutrition. — How prolonged Abstinence has been sustained. — Effect of Medicines applied to the Skin. — Psychological Remedies. — Cellular Tissue. — Mucous and Serous Membranes. — The Physiological Condition in a Common Cold. — The Action of the Mind upon the Skin. — A Psychological Sweat. — Effect of Sleep. — State of the Mind underlying Consumption. — Control over the Action of the Skin by the Magnetizer. — Mind the only Causal Agent. — The Ablutions of the Jewish and Mohammedan Laws. — Spiritual Effects of Bathing. 161

CHAPTER XVII.

THE SENSES. THEIR CORRESPONDENCE, AND INDEPENDENT OR SPIRITUAL ACTION.

Sensation a Spiritual Phenomenon. — Vision without the external Eye. — Somnambulism. — Independent Clairvoyance. — The Relation of the Eye to the Intellect. — Sympathy of the Eye with other Organs. — The Spiritual Eye can discern Material Things. — The Sense of Hearing. —

CONTENTS.

The Mental Act underlying the Sensation of Sound.—Different Forms of Deafness. — How to Treat them. — The Connection of Voluntary Hearing with the Organ of Cautiousness. — The seat of Otalgia. — Clairaudience or Spiritual Hearing. —The Sense of Touch.— Its general Diffusion. — Its Relation to the Love. — Communication of life by the Hand. — The sense of Smell. — Its Spiritual Action. — Taste. — Its Use. — The Spiritual Senses. — How they are opened. — Diseased Conditions in which the Inner Senses are emancipated 176

CHAPTER XVIII.

THE MYSTERY OF LIFE EXPLAINED.

Theories Concerning the Nature of Life. — Not the Result of Organization. — The Mosaic Theory. — Electro-Biology.— The Nervous Fluid. — Definition of Life by Bichat.— Coleridge. — Schelling. — De Blainville. — Comte. — Herbert Spencer. — Swedenborg. — Its inmost Degree is Love. — Organic and Inorganic Forces. — Life a Force. — Correlation and Equivalence of Mental Forces.—Influence of the Emotive Life upon the Intellect. — Relation of Vital Force and Animal Heat. — Health is Equilibrium.— Disease an Inharmony.— Source of Animal Heat.—Heat a Form of Motion. — The Vital Movements. — The Heat of the Sun the Living Force of Nature. — God's Love an all-pervading Life. — The External lives from the Internal. — Effect of Sensation upon the Body. — Influence of the Emotions and Affections upon the organic Functions.— Secretion. — Muscular Contractility.—The Sexual Instinct. — Its Influence upon the Involuntary Physiological Processes. Importance of Regulating the Affections. — Impartation of Life. — Disease and Selfishness. — The Divine Order of Human Existence. 193

CONTENTS.

CHAPTER XIX.

MENTAL METAMORPHOSIS; OR HOW TO INDUCE UPON OURSELVES ANY DESIRABLE MENTAL STATE.

Relation of Mental Disturbance to Disease. — Therapeutic Spiritual Forces.— Our Emotions involuntary.— Self-Conversion. — A General Law stated.— Relation of Form to Internal Character. — The Lesson taught us by the Stage. — Expression of our Inward States by the Face.— How to effect a Change in our Feelings. — Hygienic Value of the Law. — Inspiration and Respiration.— Soul and Breath. —Peculiar Sensation attending Psychological Influence.— Nearness of the Inner Realm. — How to be Inspired.— Breathing of the Soul. — The Respiration peculiar to all depressing Mental States. — How to relieve ourselves of them. — Usefulness of the Swedish Movements. . . 222

CHAPTER XX.

THE COMMUNICATION OF LIFE AND OF SANATIVE MENTAL INFLUENCE.

The Primal Source of Life. — Man imparts life to all below him.— Vital Force Communicable. — How Jesus gave his Life a Ransom for Many. — His cures not Miraculous in the Theological Sense. — The royal Touch for Scrofula. — Sanative Influence of the Hand.— Knowledge is Power. — Mental Conditions necessary to a Cure. — Faith a Spiritual Force. — Its Therapeutic Influence. — The Cure of a Paralytic by Davy with a Thermometer.— Effect of Fear. — Case of Hydropobia caused by it. — Experiment with four Russian Criminals. — The Rose-water Cure. — Vital Force and animal Heat correlative. — How Heat is generated and transmitted.— Therapeutic Influence of Friction. — Compression. — Percussion.— Motion.— Adaptation of the

Hand as an Instrument for Communicating Life. — Efficiency of the Duplicated Movements accounted for. — How to Induce upon a Patient the proper State of Mind. — Polarity of our Feelings. — Inverted Action of the Cerebral Organs. — Restoration of the Equilibrium. — Mental Vibration. — How Jesus healed the Sick. — Health is Contagious. — Spiritual Inoculation. — Mental Leaven. . 237

CHAPTER XXI.

THE MIND NOT LIMITED BY SPACE IN THE TRANSMISSION OF PSYCHOLOGICAL AND SANATIVE INFLUENCES.

Freedom of the Mind from Spatial Restraint.— Spiritual Presence.— Mental Locomotion.— Physiological influence of Psychological Impressions. — Transmission of Mental Force.— The Model Man and Great Physician.— His Freedom from Material Limitations.— The Interior State intensely Positive.— The Prayer-Cure. — The Laws governing it.— Love the Healing Power. — The Mind to be first Healed. — The Mystery of the Cures wrought by Jesus explained.— How to Convert Souls without a Miracle. — Nature of the Mental Sphere.— Healing at a Distance. — The Laws by which it is Effected. — Directions given in regard to it. — Communication of abnormal States by Sympathy. — Practical Value of the Law. . . .   259

CHAPTER XXII.

APPETITES, INTUITIONS AND IMPRESSIONS, AND THEIR USE.

Essential Spirituality of Man.— The *Vis Medicatrix Naturæ* is a Mental Force. — The Fetal Growth. — Incubation. — The Nature and Office of the Appetites.— Their Prescriptions. — Illustrations. — Nutriment for the Mind. —

Spiritual Starvation. — Gibeonitish Crusts. — Voices without a Sound. — Spiritual Impressions. — A deep and calm Revealing. — A Law of the Spiritual Life. — The Communion of Saints.—Education of our Intuitions. — The Inner Language.—The Cogitatio Loquens. — Intuitional Prescriptions. — Mental Telegraphing. — Madam Guyon and her Confessor.— Development of our hidden Powers.
. . . , ... 278

CHAPTER XXIII.

THE SANATIVE POWER OF WORDS.

The Words we utter embody our Mental Force. — They are the Index of Character. — How our Mental States affect our Words. — Their Permanence in the Memory.— Their lasting Influence. — Fact given by Coleridge. — Dr. Rush. — The Power of Written Words.— Books have Life. — Effect of it upon the Pyschometer. — Prescriptions of Frederica Hauffe.— Psychical Remedies. —The Creative Utterances of Jesus.—Frederic Von Schlegel's Philosophy of the Communicated Word. — Therapeutic Force of Kind Words. — Testimony of Baglivi. 296

CHAPTER XXIV.

THE RELATION OF MENTAL FORCE TO PHYSICAL STRENGTH AND HOW TO CURE GENERAL DEBILITY.

The Amount of Force generated in the System. — Whence Produced. — The Abnormal State called General Debility. — What is Strength ? — Case cited to show its Mental Origin. — The Mental Faculties that influence the Will-Force. — Their Importance. — The Cerebral Organ of Muscular Motion. — The Relation of respiration to Muscular Force.—What is Swooning ?—The Force of the Bodily Movement proportioned to the Mental Energy.—The

CONTENTS.

Effect of Respiration upon the Vital Processes.—Nervousness a Mental State.— Its cure. — Relaxation of the Abdominal Muscles. — Misplacement of the Internal Organs. — Depressing Mental States the Cause.— How to get rid of the Supporter and Body Brace. — Relation of the Mind to Diseases of Diminished Vitality. — Dr. Combe. . 309

CHAPTER XXV.

SLEEP AS A MENTAL STATE, ITS HYGIENIC VALUE, AND HOW TO INDUCE IT.

Sleep Defined. — Its Influence upon the involuntary Physiological Processes. — Nutrition. — Circulation. — The Excreting Organs. — Its Remedial Value. — The Obstacles to it. — Cold Feet. — Tea and Coffee. — The Law that Governs in inducing it upon Ourselves. — Position of the Eye. — Its Effect upon the Cerebrum. — The Respiration in Sleep. — In the Magnetic Trance. — The moral Influence of Sleep. — The Order in which the Senses lose their Susceptibility to Impression. — Practical Directions based upon this Law. 325

CHAPTER XXVI.

THE WILL-CURE, ACTIVE AND PASSIVE.

Connection of the Organs with the Mind. — How to affect their Functional Action.— The Will-Force and the Stomach and Intestinal Canal. — Cause of Coldness and Weakness. — The Cure. — The Passive Will-Cure.— A General Law of Health Stated.—Voluntary Movements Fatiguing. — The Involuntary Actions not so. — How to take up thy bed and walk. — How to walk a hundred miles a day. — The Interior State. — Its healthful Influences. — Passive Knowledge. — Influx of better Emotional States. — The Spirit with which to approach the Inner World.—Importance of our Relations to it. 335

CONTENTS.

CHAPTER XXVII.

THE INFLUENCE OF THE SPIRITUAL WORLD UPON MENTAL HEALTH AND DISEASE.

A Self-Evident Truth. — The Law of Sympathy. — How Jesus bore Men's Sicknesses.— Obsession. —Its Influence in causing Disease. — How cured. — Experiences of Swedenborg. — What is a Demon? — Psychological Laws stated. — Scriptural Statements respecting destroying Angels. — They could save Life as well. — The Medium through which Mind acts upon Matter. — Ponderable Bodies moved by Spiritual Forces. — The Release of Peter. — Paul and Silas. — The Rolling away of the Stone at the Entrance of the Sepulcher. — The Availability of such unseen Forces. — Their Useful Employment. — The Plates of Copper and Zinc. — Positive and Negative Mental Forces. — Angelic Influence in the Cure of disordered Spiritual States. — The Nature of Goodness.—The Angelic Ministry.—Vital Connection with the other World. — Nearness of the unseen Realm. — Longfellow. . . 347

THE MENTAL-CURE.

CHAPTER I.

THE RELATION OF THE HUMAN MIND TO GOD.

Importance of a Knowledge of God. — The Central Life.— Ubiquity of it. — The whole Idea of God included in Love and Wisdom. — He is the Primal Cause. — The Divine Unity. — Tri-personality impossible. — Man a Divine Incarnation. — God in Christ. — Humanization of Deity. — All men Sons of God. — Teaching of the Oriental Philosophy. — Evolution of the Divine Element. — Jesus introduced a Higher Type of Humanity. — The Allness of God. — His Personality and what is meant by it. — His Omnipresence. — Where to find Him. — Madam Guyon. — The two Aspects of Human Nature. — Medical Science Superficial. — The Root of our Maladies.

ALL TRUE philosophy must begin and end in God, the fountain of all life, and love and truth. A correct knowledge of the soul involves of necessity a true conception of the Divine Being. To sunder the human mind from him, and then study its phenomena, is to discern only effects, without rising to the higher and more satisfying knowledge of things in their prime causes. The latter alone constitutes true science and real philosophy. God is the First and the Last, the Alpha and Omega, the Beginning and the Ending of all finite things. In him is life. He alone has life in himself unoriginated and self-derived. All else lives from him and in him. Every thing, from the insect to the angel exists by virtue of a life proceeding from him. We live because he lives, our life being the stream of which he is the fountain, or it is a ray of which he is the central sun. This central life is every where and in all. It is diffused through all space and all worlds. It is the inmost essence of all created things. But God's life is love. All that we can think of him is included in the terms Love and Wisdom. This bounds and terminates our conception of Deity. All other attributes, properties, qualities, and powers of the Divine Mind must be referred to one or the other of these, and are only modifications or manifestations of these universal principles. His love is the *esse* of his being, as the schoolmen would have called it, or that which lives in and by itself. His Wisdom is the *existere* thence derived, the term being used in philosophy to denote manifested or derived being. The divine intellect goes forth from the divine love, as light from fire.

This conception of God is a first principle in philosophy, of which we must never lose sight. It is a fundamental verity, without which we can neither know ourselves nor him. It is a self-evident truth, that nothing finite can exist from itself, but from something prior to itself, and this from something primal, which brings us as far as our limited powers of thought can carry us—to the *causa causarum*, the great first cause, whom we call God.

But this divine being is One. This grand truth was long ago announced in the deserts of Arabia, by the Jewish legislator, and proclaimed anew by Jesus of Nazareth. "Hear, O Israel: the Lord our God is one Lord." (Deut. vi. 4; Mark xii. 29.) Three self-existent individualities cannot be conceived. Such a proposition, as Herbert Spencer would say, is unthinkable. Two of them must derive their existence from the first, and that which has not being in itself is not God. It does not answer our conception of Deity.

Man is a finite image of God, or in other words, he is a created form recipient of the one only Life. He is a manifestation and in a mitigated sense, an incarnation of the Divinity. This constitutes the true dignity of humanity. The inmost essence of every human soul is divine, using the word to express that which goes forth from God. Deeply hidden beneath all our external and sensuous coverings, and all our moral and intellectual disorders, is the inextinguishable divine spark, sometimes concealed, like a gem in the ocean abyss.

God was in Christ. In him God was *manifested* in the flesh, as never before in the history of the race. The Father was in him and he was in the Father. This vivid consciousness of the indwelling divine principle, was the marked characteristic of the man Jesus. In him God became man, and the humanity divine. He seemed to himself and has so seemed to others, as the God-Man and the Man-God. In his personality there was a humanization of the Divine, and a deification of the human. But the Deity was thus manifested in Jesus, in order that through him he might be incarnated in all humanity, so that every man might walk forth consciously to himself as a son of God and say, "I and my Father are one." Then every human nature will be viewed as affiliated with Divinity. Then will be realized the full import of the words of Jesus: "He came unto his own, and his own received him not. But as many as received him, to them gave he power to become the sons of God." (John i. 11, 12.) Then will be fulfilled the dream of the Oriental Philosophy, which has haunted the Eastern mind from the remotest ages.

"The idea of God's becoming man," says Dr. Turnbull, "and man becoming God, is the mystic circle in which all their thoughts revolve. Nothing is more familiar to their minds than the possibility of divine incarnations, and the consequent possibility of human transformations. Somehow, God and man, the infinite and finite, must become one."

To evolve and to bring forth to freedom this hidden divine element in human nature is the true aim of all philosophy, and should be of theology. This will add no new property to the soul, but only bring out to our consciousness what lies concealed within. The antagonism between the inmost divine essence in man, and the selfhood, or the blinded and disorderly activity of the mind, either acquired or hereditary, is the secret spring of all our mental and physical unhappiness. When the inner divine life pervades, appropriates, and controls, the more external degrees of our nature, man then returns to God, as did the humanity of Jesus. This is the hour of our glorification. This is the end of our creation, the appointed destiny of every created soul. After the lapse of ages of darkness, the son of Mary appeared in Palestine as the type and model of a new and higher development of humanity. What human nature was in him. it is the design of the infinite Love it should be in all, if not fully, at least in a degree.

God is all and in all, but all things are not God. All things, singular and together, are finite or limited, and the finite cannot be the infinite, for this, to our intuitive and rational thought, is contradictory and impossible.

But is God personal, or an indefinitely diffused principle? In a certain sense, he is both one and the other. He is love and wisdom. These are the essential properties of personality. They are essentially human. An impersonal affection or intelligence is an impossible conception. He is an infinite Man, and we are men by virtue of our derivation and conception from him. But his divine life goes forth everywhere. The sphere of his love and wisdom extends beyond the bounds of creation. The universe of mind and matter is but its ultimation or visible manifestation. The Divine Being is in all things, the least and the greatest, but in the human soul in the highest degree. Here we may seek and find him, as Madam Guyon and the mystics of all ages have averred. She declares the source of the disquietude, the unrest of religious people to be, that they seek him where he is not to be found. "Accustom yourself to seek God in your heart, and you will find him," was her advice to the Franciscan monk, who complained that he could not attain a satisfactory consciousness of God. This pregnant utterance was only a ray of the inner light and life. May it come to every man who reads it, with the force of a new revelation.

We can study human nature under two aspects or points of view. 1. As it was designed to be, and such as it is when it exists and acts according to the divine order of its creation, and stands forth an image and likeness of the Divinity. Such a study, alas, could only create an ideal model, like Plato's perfect man. Or we should be obliged to confine our investigations to the character and state of Jesus of Nazareth, of whom men, in all ages, have said in adoring wonder, "Behold the man." 2. We may view it as we unfortunately find it generally, in a state of moral, intellectual, and physical disorder. This is one of the most prominent facts of consciousness. The geologist, as he surveys the wreck of former generations of animals, studies them as they are, in order to find what they were. By the scicnce of Comparative Anatomy, and under the light of his intuitions, he is able to restore the imperfect and decayed animal frame-work, and show us what it was when it moved, a thing of life, in an age of the globe long since passed, and which presents only broken relics of its living inhabitants. It belongs to a true mental philosophy to discover the source of our unhappiness, and to point out the way in which we may rise from our inharmony of mind and body to that divine and celestial order, into which the Divine Love longs to introduce us. All medical science that does not penetrate with its light to the root of our physical maladies and sufferings, but applies its remedies only to visible effects, and to the removal of temporary symptoms, is superficial and unphilosophical, and "heals the hurt of the daughter of my people but slightly." True science is a knowledge of things in their causes, and an intelligent system of medication aims to remove the source of our suffering. This done, the effect ceases of its own accord. This will be the honest aim of this necessarily imperfect treatise on Mental Hygiene. "Philosophy is a futile, frivolous pursuit, unworthy of greater respect than a game of chess, unless it subserve some grand practical aim— unless its issue be in some enlarged conception of man's life and destiny."

As our prescriptions will be more of a spiritual character, than is common in medical science, it will be needful to enter into some discussion of the general nature of our inner being, whose varying states are the body's health or malady.

CHAPTER II.

THE MIND IMMATERIAL, BUT SUBSTANTIAL.

What is meant by Immaterial Substance. — What by matter. — The Properties of Matter are reducible to the Idea of Force. — Mind the Exhibition of a higher Force. — All Force is Spiritual. — It Originates in God. — Love and Wisdom the First Substance and Force. — Immortality.— The Ground of it. — Life a Persistent Force. — Its receptive Forms Evanescent. — The Brotherhood of Man. — Universal Fatherhood of God. — Moral Influence of such an Idea.

THERE ARE two distinct substances in the universe. One we call mind or spirit, the other matter. It is difficult for some to conceive of a substance without attaching to it some material properties, for, to most persons, in consequence of the senses having a controlling influence over their conceptions, that which is not material is as nothing. Their thoughts seldom rise above the range of the external or sensuous degree of the mind's action. All spiritual realities are in their thoughts materialized. The common idea of spirit is that of refined, etherialized matter,—a matter so subtle as to be imponderable, and almost without reality. But we must learn to think of spirit and matter as discrete or distinct substances, that is, as real being, but having no properties in common. When we assert that mind is immaterial, we do not weaken the conception of the reality of its being, but we simply mean that its essence is invested with properties entirely unlike those by which matter is manifested to our senses. Yet it is the most vitally real thing in the universe. Matter is known to us by a certain combination of properties, cognizable to our senses; mind by other and distinct properties or powers, known only to our consciousness or inner perceptions. Yet our knowledge of the latter is as certain as that of the other.

Persons are apt to think of matter as something solid and tangible to the senses, but of spiritual substance as an etherialized, volatile essence, destitute of these qualities, and consequently of reality. But what we call solidity is only force. It is simply resistance, and is more a sensation in us than a property of matter. Taking this view of it, spirit may be as *solid a reality* as anything in nature. Anything that causes in us the proper sensation of resistance is as solid to us as gold, or platinum. For all that we know, or can know of hardness, firmness, compactness, impenetrability, or gravity, is a force occasioning in us a particular sensation. The world of spirit is as real in itself, and to the sensations of its inhabitants, as this outside range of created things.

All that we know of matter is force, as all its properties are only modifications of force. Its inmost essence may be spiritual, and what we call matter may be only the outward clothing, or ultimation, or external manifestation of some spiritual reality. The properties of matter are reduced to the single idea of force. Mind is a higher and diviner force, approaching many degrees nearer the Central Life. All force, in its origin, as well as all causation, is spiritual. Mind is a manifestation of force entirely distinct from that we call matter. Between color and thought, there is a broad distinction. They are not identical. One belongs to matter, the other to mind. One is a material, the other a spiritual property or force.

We have seen that God is the Central Life, the first and only life. All life in the universe is a derivation from him, and a manifestation or modification of this primal vital force. But his life is love. Hence his love is the first and only substance, whence all other substances emanate. Every thing, from the atom to the world, from the animalcule to the angel, has the root of its being in him. He is Love and Wisdom, two divine forces, like positive and negative. But love and wisdom, or affection and intellect, are the essential properties of personality. The divine love is not a mere idea, or an emotion, but a substance from which, by creative influx, has gone forth all other being. If we can accustom ourselves to think of Love and Wisdom in God, and will and understanding in man, as substance, an important point will be gained. But we must carefully subtract from our conception of that substance all the properties or forces of matter, such as divisibility, impenetrability, and weight. The essential conditions of all material existence are time and space. All matter exists in time and fills space. Mind or spirit is not in time, and is not limited by space. To raise the thoughts above time and space is to think spiritually. Until we can do this, all our ideas of God, of the human soul, and of spiritual and heavenly things, will be material, earthly, and sensual.

Whether the soul of man be destined to endless existence, is a question that is not affected by its materiality or immateriality. The ancient-philosophers, as Plato, and after him, Cicero, endeavored to maintain the doctrine, that mind in its own nature was indissoluble and indestructible. But this is not true of any finite thing in the universe. Nothing has life in itself, but all live from God. He alone has immortality or life in himself, eternally springing from the depth of his own being. Immortality depends upon the will of God. The immutability of that will is the ground of its certainty. It is true now and always will be so, that because he lives, we live also. We live by virtue of our being finite receptacles of the one and only Life.

But why is not animal life, which must be referred to the same primal source, also immortal? We do not hesitate to affirm, that no life will ever be annihilated. It is the conclusion of the improved science of the day, that all force is perpetual and indestructible. What we call life is a force, a vital force. The quantum of life in the universe will never be diminished, but the forms receptive of it may change. Man is the recipient of the divine life in the highest degree. The human soul exists in three degrees, whereas animals possess only the lower or external degree. The life of animals is indestructible, but their *individuality* is not equally stable. The latter may cease, while the former goes forth to animate other forms. The vital force is persistent, but the external shell that contains it, is evanescent. There is no real death anywhere. The boundless universe is life. But man retains his individual and personal existence. His inner life is not only a persistent and imperishable force, springing perpetually from out the depths of the divine existence, but his affectional and intellectual nature ultimate themselves in an outward form that constitutes his everlasting identity or individuality.

If it be true, that all men live from the one and only Life, and that the father does not create new life in his offspring (for he has no life in himself), but that life is imparted to the receptive germ in the womb from the Lord alone, then, as Des Guys has truly shown, all men are brethren, children of a common Father. It matters not whether there was only one created pair, from whom the race has sprung, or a thousand, the brotherhood of men, and the fatherhood of God are established on an unshaken basis.

And moreover, all men, of every clime and color, are sons of God and incarnations of the Divinity. All conception is an operation of the central living Force, whether in the womb of Mary or any of the millions of the daughters of Eve. In all men the Divinity becomes finitely human. The consciousness of this grand verity would be a living moral force to elevate the debased populations of the globe. Self-respect is one of the safeguards of virtue. To think meanly of human nature has a depressing moral influence. To entertain noble thoughts of the real dignity of man, ourselves and others, becomes an interior *conatus* or endeavor to act worthily of our divine origin, and "to do the works of God."

CHAPTER III.

ON THE FORM OF THE MIND.

Mind not a mathematical Point or a Monad.— The Relation of Substance and Form.— Perfection of Form belongs only to the Realm of Spirit.— The Soul the inner Manhood.— Humanity of Angels.— Disembodied Souls in the Human Form.— Proved by its being a necessity of thought.— Formlessness and Nonentity equivalent.— The Spirit an Organization.— Omnipresence of it in the Body.— Platonic Idea of it.— Pythagorean Conception of it.

IT HAS been one of the vagaries and fantasies of the philosophy of Mind, that it has sometimes taught that our interior being which we call the soul or spirit, was without form. The mind has been taken to be a formless, unsubstantial something of which no definite idea could be conceived. It has been reduced in the conceptions of certain metaphysicians to something like a mathematical point, which is defined to be position without magnitude. Such a thing, if it be not absolutely nothing, is next to nonentity. It is at least on the dividing line between entity and nihility.

We have seen that mind is a real and positive substance. That which is not substance is nothing. For in order to be a something or a somewhat, it must be a substance or essence. And it is self-evident that a substance cannot exist without a form, nor can a form be conceived without substance. By the constitution of our minds, and the necessary laws of thought, we are compelled to connect the ideas of substance and form. By form we mean the external manifestation of a substance, or it is the boundary of an essence. It does not belong merely to matter. Material things have *shape*, but perfect form does not exist in the realm of matter. The geometrical figure we call a circle is not found except in the world of mind. There is not a straight line, nor a perfect square, nor a cone, nor a cube, in the material universe. These exist only in the world of spirit. We may find in nature rude approaches to these mathematical forms, but under a powerful combination of lenses they are found not to answer the definition of those geometrical figures. They are purely mental creations, and can never be realized in the outer world.

The shape of the body is a resemblance, or an external manifestation of the spiritual form, the inner man. Matter has no definite form or shape of its own. The shape it assumes is always an effect, the result of the action of some spiritual cause. In the case of the body, its form is an effect of which the soul is the cause.

That the soul or mind of man is in the human form, we might prove from several considerations. The divine Being is an infinite Man. This is an intuitive truth, for it is the idea that all men instinctively form of him. Love and Wisdom are the necessary elements of personality. But a formless personality is impossible to thought. As our bodies receive their shape from the indwelling soul, so this receives its form from the Divinity within. Because God is the Divine Man, and all things have gone forth from him, they exhibit a *conatus* to assume the human shape. The higher they rise in the scale of life the more manifest this tendency becomes.

We might show that angels are in the human form, and that they are only the spirits of men, who have graduated to the inner world, and passed into the heavens. This is the unmistakable teaching of the Scriptures, and also commends itself to our intuitive reason. But we will not insist upon this.

That the spirit, which may be properly called the *interior man*, as has been done by Plato and Paul (Rom. vii. 22; 2 Cor. iv. 16; Eph. iii. 16), is in the human form, is an intuitive truth, and a necessity of thought. Our minds are so constructed by the Creator, that we cannot think otherwise of our departed friends than as existing still in the human form on the plains of immortality. This enters necessarily into our conception of them. That such is the truth, is a perpetual revelation from God, as it is not supposable that he would so constitute our minds that they must of necessity conceive a falsity. We always view our friends after death, or their emancipation from the material body, as *persons*, and the human form enters into our idea of personality. Subtract from the conception of them this element of form, and it is equivalent to their annihilation. If the soul is not in the human form, after the dissolution of its mortal covering, if it exist at all, it is dissipated into an indefinable and formless principle, which cannot be an object of thought. For of that which has no form, it is not possible for the mind to gain any idea. That the spirit is the inward man, as Paul and Swedenborg denominate it, is a truth constituting the foundation on which alone rests an intelligent belief of its immortality. Remove this, and faith in our personal existence hereafter falls to the ground.

The mind being the interior man, is not confined to the brain, nor, as Descarte supposed, included in the Pineal gland. But it pervades and is interfused through the whole body. This is a truth of vital importance in the system of Mental Hygiene. The body is not merely an external robe, the outward shell of the living soul, but the mind interpenetrates every atom of it. This was a Platonic form of speech, and many, following in the wake of the Grecian philosopher, have represented the body as the vestment of the soul. But it does not express the true analogy, for the spirit is coëxtensive with the physical organism. It thrills in every nerve, and pervades every fibre. The same objection lies against the Pythagorean form of speaking of the body as the tent or habitation of the soul. A man does not fill the house he lives in, but the spiritual principle pervades the whole outward organism. The latter is but the echo of the former. It corresponds or answers to it in every part. This idea we shall unfold more fully hereafter.

CHAPTER IV.

THE DIVISION OF THE MIND INTO TWO DEPARTMENTS.

The two primary Faculties. — The Love. — The Intellect. — All Love and Truth Divine. — Why they appear our own. — The Divine Nucleus of our Being. — Twofold Division of the Mind. — The Will and Love identical. — Motive Power and the Love. — The self-determining Power. — The only Life. — What is it to will a thing? — Practical value of the Doctrine.

MAN IS endowed with two primary faculties, or powers of reception, called the Will and Understanding, or the love and the intellect. These together constitute what we call the mind. All the mental operations and phenomena may be classed under the one or the other of these two general divisions. They contain the whole interior life. Either one of these faculties may predominate in its action, but they cannot be separated, though in thought they may be viewed as *distinct*. The will, which includes our whole affectional or love-nature, with all the desires and emotions, is our inmost being, and the understanding or intellect is that through which the love manifests itself and acts.

We have seen that the whole divine nature is included in Love and Wisdom. The will of man is the created and finite receptacle of the divine Love, and the understanding, of the divine Wisdom and the ideas of the uncreated Mind. All love, in its origin, is from this supreme fountain, for, as John avers, "Love is of God." In its purity, and unperverted, it is the divinest and most vital thing in the universe. All the truth that is contained in our intellectual nature, or that our powers can grasp, is a ray from the abyss of light, the infinite circle in which the thoughts of God move. Love and truth have no other origin and paternity, yet it is according to appearance that they are our own, being self-originated. Why is this? That all the movements of our love-nature, and all the knowledge in our understanding should *seem* our own and self-derived, is owing to the nature of the divine Love, which gives birth to every good. This love is an infinite and irrepressible inclination to make its own good the possession of others made capable of receiving it. Hence when admitted to the human mind, it carries with it the appearance that it is ours, and that it is eliminated or evolved by the action of our spiritual powers. But its genesis is divine. It is ours, not in its origin, but as a divine gift. But the boundless love of God imparts good to us so freely and fully as to cause its *seeming* to be ours,—the absolute property of our own minds. It is a fundamental principle, of which we must never lose sight, that all good and truth in the universe of created mind are from God alone. We cannot become too fully confirmed in this great truth. It is the corner-stone on which the whole temple of angelic wisdom rests. Our will is a faculty or created organism, made to be admissive of the divine life or love, and the intellect to receive the light of the infinite wisdom. These flow from within outward, as the nucleus of every soul is a germ of the divine nature.

In most systems of mental science, we find a threefold division of the mind, or what is technically called Trichotomy, and all the mental operations are classed under the three general designations of Intellect, Sensibility and Will. But a careful examination and thorough analysis of the phenomena of what they call the will, discloses the fact that they are only some form of the love. What a man loves he interiorly wills, and what he wills he loves. Volition is

a movement of the affections. If one does what he
loves not, if he pursues a course of action repugnant
to some love, it is in obedience to some stronger affection.
Motive, which is supposed to influence and
sometimes control our volitions, is always some form
of love. And an act without a motive, or an impulse
leading to it, and lying behind it, would be like the
motion of machinery without any mechanical force.
It would be a self-originated movement. When we
wish to influence the mind of another to some action
or conduct, or to bring that mind to some desired
determination, we always appeal to some love, and
there is nothing back of that of which we have or can
have the least consciousness, which acts in the decision.
We may act from an interior love contrary to
an exterior one. The spiritual degree of the mind
may and ought to control the mere animal instincts.
But it is always the love that decides. It is important
to define the distinction between the love and
affection. The latter is external to the former, or
what amounts to the same, it is the love passed outward
into the region of the emotions or feelings.
There may be love that influences and controls the
whole outward activity, that is attended, at least
sometimes, with no conscious emotion. We may
from the love of our family and friends labor all day

solely for their good, without once feeling any excitement of the emotions. In this case the love is interior, and beyond the perception of the external consciousness. But to assert that there is some principle behind and beyond that love, and further inward, is an assumption without evidence. If it exist at all, it lies beyond the soul's inmost perceptions, and of which we can have no possible proof. The love is the life of man, as it is of God. If we act from life, we are moved by love. There is no other life in the universe of sentient existence. This is the moving force in soul and body, the hidden spring that moves life's machinery. This is one of the most important and far-reaching principles in the spiritual philosophy of Swedenborg. The life of an animal is some form of *affection*, with the instincts that arise from it, and this controls their whole being and its activities. That love is the only life is a fundamental truth, and ever to be borne in mind.

Among some of the older metaphysicians, as well as in the Scriptures, where we find many correct principles in the philosophy of mind, the will and the love are used as identical. The term *thelo, to will,* always implies an action of the love. It is generally used in the sense of *to wish*, which implies *desire*, and this is only a mode in which love is manifested.

When it is used in the sense of *arbitrium* or determination, it is only the same love or affectional tendency toward a thing or particular result, heightened into an endeavor (conatus), or an effort of the love to ultimate itself in the outward act.

That the love is the life of man, and that the love and the will are identical, we shall find to be of much practical value, in Mental Hygiene, or the cure of diseased conditions of the body through the mind. It may become the fountain of health, or the hidden spring of deranged physiological action.

CHAPTER V.

THE RELATION OF THE INTELLECT TO THE LOVE

Derivation of the Intellect from the Love. — Importance of this Truth in Philosophy. — Swedenborg. — G. H. Lewes. — Love the Center of our Being. — The Will and Understanding are like Substance and Form. — Relation of Thought to Affection. — Reaction of the Intellect upon the Love. — Correlative Spiritual Forces. — Freedom is Harmony. — Spiritual Health and Disease. — Relation of our Mental and Physical States. — Importance of regulating the Loves. Solifidianism based on a wrong Conception of our Mental Nature.

WE KNOW of no principle in the philosophy of mind, attended with more far-reaching consequences than that the intellect is derived from the will or love, as taught originally by Swedenborg, but now adopted by some of the leading thinkers of the age. One has remarked: "That the intellectual aspect is *not* the noblest aspect of man, is a heresy which I have long iterated with a constancy due to a conviction. There never will be a philosophy capable of satisfying the demands of humanity, until the truth be recognized that man is moved by his emotions, not by his ideas: using his intellect only as an eye *to see the way*. In other words, the intellect is the servant, not the lord of the heart." (Comte's Philosophy of the Sciences, by G. H. Lewes, p. 5.)

As in the divine Being, Wisdom is evolved from love, as light from heat, so in man, made after a divine type, the understanding is derived from the will, truth from goodness, thought from affection, faith from charity. It must be acknowledged that this is contrary to the first appearance arising from a casual glance at the subject. The reason why it appears that thought is not generated by affection is, that the former comes more distinctly under the observation of consciousness than the latter. The love is nearer the center of our being, and is hence more concealed from our perception. Yet it is easy to conceive, that if our love-nature were annihilated or suppressed, all life, all thought, all consciousness would perish with it. The will and the understanding sustain the relation of substance and form. Our thoughts are the boundary of our affections, and give them coloring or quality. It is also a matter of consciousness, that our thoughts are always busy with the objects of our affections. That which we love is spontaneously and perpetually recurring to our thoughts. What we love the most, fills the largest place in our thoughts. If love is not the ruling element of our life, why is this so? Our system of truth or faith will always exhibit a tendency to adjust itself in harmony with the nature of our ruling love. If we are confirmed in the love of what is evil or what is morally disorderly, the truth we receive is thereby changed to falsity.

We do not deny that the intellect may have a certain reflex influence upon the love. They may be the correlative forces of our spiritual organism, like action and reaction, or heat and light, or like the positive and negative principles in magnetism. One cannot exist without the other. They should mutually balance each other. This is a state of spiritual harmony and freedom. For freedom and harmony are the same, being the perfect equilibrium of the two forces of will and understanding, or sensibility and intellect.

This is also a state of spiritual health. The fundamental idea of mental disease, is a loss of balance between the intellectual and affectional departments of the mind. Such is its origin and nature. Some false idea is pushed to undue prominence, or some feeling becomes inordinate and predominant. To restore the balance, the lost harmonious equilibrium, is to effect the cure of the soul. To restore the lost harmony should be the steady aim of him who ministers to a mind diseased. To maintain it in ourselves, should be our constant study.

Such is the mysterious relation of the soul and body, that every mental condition records itself in the bodily organism,—first in the brain, and then in the organs that have sympathetic connection with those parts of the cerebral system. The healthy and happy equipoise in the mental powers, can be effected by magnetizing away the false notion, or the disorderly feeling, by a judicious and intelligent treatment of the part of the brain where it is recorded.

If love is the inmost essence of our being, and the fountain in us of all vitality and activity, if it be "a well of water in us, springing up into everlasting life," then to regulate our loves is the great object, the grand result, we should study to achieve. It also follows from this doctrine that every man's interior character is shaped by his prevailing affectional states, for the ruling love is the impelling force in the mental economy. It makes the laws for the intellectual powers to execute. A genuine faith, instead of producing love or charity, is generated by it. This view of the mind and its invisible subtle forces, overturns from its foundations the great error of the religious world in all ages, that salvation is by faith alone. A man is saved, not by the belief of a tenet, but by a predominant holy love. His restoration from a state of moral, intellectual, and bodily disorder, commences not so much in the credence given to a dogma, as in the first dawning of a proper state of the affections. And when this condition becomes confirmed by the law of habit, a soul is saved either in the church or out of it. No faith can save us if it has not its vital root in love. The doctrine of this chapter is not an idle speculation, without practical value, but there is inclosed in it the principle that shall issue in the highest well-being of the race here and hereafter In this world even, our ruling love is our life, and a knowledge of it is the key that may open to our perception, our whole interior character, and to a great extent, our physical condition.

CHAPTER VI.

THE DOCTRINE OF DEGREES.

Three distinct Planes of Mental Being. — Difference between this and the Common Trichotomous Division of the Mind. —Each Degree a distinct Mental Nature. — The Outermost Range. — The Senses. — Animality. — The Psychical man. — The Spiritual. — Consciousness. — Second Degree. — The Rational Mind. — Emancipation of the Intellect from the Dominion of the Senses. — Somnambulism. — Clairvoyance. — Cognition of Spiritual Things. — Progress an Evolution. — Education an educing of what is within. — The Phenomena of the inmost Degree. — Perception or Intuition. —All truth self-evident to it. — The Divine Internal.— The Conjunction of the Divine and Human.

IN THIS chapter we approach an important and interesting subject. The doctrine of the three distinct degrees or planes of mental being is characteristic of the philosophy of Swedenborg, who has thrown more light upon the subject of our inner self, than any other writer. The doctrine of degrees, in the form in which he presents it, is entirely new, not being found, nor any thing but a distant approach to it, in any of the older philosophers. It is true, we often meet with a three-fold arrangement or classification of the mental powers, as into intellect, sensibility, and will. But this is a widely different conception from the doctrine of degrees, as unfolded in the writings of the Swedish seer, and northern Apocalyptist. In the prevailing systems of mental science, the intellect is not viewed as a complete mind, having all the powers and faculties of mind, but is simply intellect, no more nor less. The same may be said of the sensibility. It is not conceived to be a complete mental organism. It is only one branch or department of the inner nature. And so of the will. But in the spiritual science of Swedenborg, each degree of the mind is complete in itself, rounded out to the full proportions of an interior manhood, with nothing wanting to complete the fullness of a distinct mental existence. It has will and understanding, affection and thought, memory, reason, and imagination. Each lies within the other, like concentric circles, and the more external is evolved from the internal.

The lowest or outermost degree is called the external or natural man, or what amounts to the same, the external or natural mind, as we make no reference to the material body. This is the degree of mind we have in common with animals, and might with propriety be denominated the animal mind, though it is found in man more complete than in the lower orders.

So far as any one lives only on this plane of mental life, he is only a higher animal, having the same desires, affections, and appetites, as control the lower orders. To this degree belong the senses. This external mind is well defined to consciousness. Its phenomena come distinctly under the cognizance of the higher or interior range of the soul's action. Each interior degree is endowed with a power of perceiving what transpires in the next outer circle of existence. The animal desires and appetites, and the external thoughts stand out with prominence, and are as distinctly seen by some power lying further inward, as the material objects around us are by the senses. What we call consciousness is but the observation the inward degrees of mind take of what transpires in the plane external to them.

But is this a distinct and complete degree of the mind, or, in other words, is it a mind by itself? A little reflection will convince us that it is so. There are those in the world (and they are not an exceptional few), in whom no other range of mental life has been unfolded. The spiritual mind is still in its chrysalis state. They are sensual and corporeal, mere fleshly men. All their thoughts and desires and enjoyments are material and sensuous. They believe in nothing that is not apprehended by the senses. The world of infinite reality lying further inward, is to them a *terra incognita*, an unknown land. The spiritual, the supersensuous, is beyond their mental grasp, and to them unreal and intangible. They are described by Paul in the following passage: "The natural man receiveth not the things of the Spirit of God: for they are foolishness unto him: neither can he know them, because they are spiritually discerned!" (1 Cor. ii. 14.) This degree of the mind is called in the New Testament psychology, the *flesh*. The Greek philosophers, as Plato, denominated it *psyche*, and those who were in that degree only, were called *psychical* men, in opposition to the *pneumatikoi* or spiritual men, those in whom the next higher range of mental existence had come to be developed. When one lives only on this lower plane, the other degrees are closed, or are in a state of quiescence. They are like the unborn fetus. These embryonic powers await a birth to a higher and diviner life.

The second or interior degree may be characterized as the rational mind or man. But it does not consist of reason alone, for on the first plane of the mind reason is developed more or less. Even animals exhibit something akin to it. The knowledge of the external mind is sensuous, that of the interior rises above the range of the senses, and is a spiritual intelligence. The intellect becomes emancipated from the bondage of sense, and soars above the limitations of time and space. This degree of the mind comes into activity in the somnambulic or clairvoyant state. New powers of sense, that act independently of the bodily organs, are opened. There is vision far-reaching, and penetrating, when the outward eye is closed. There is hearing, when the natural ear receives no impression. The sounds of the inner world are borne by a more refined medium than the atmosphere we breathe, and affect the inward auditory sense. The eye is illumined with a purer light than emanates from the sun. Spiritual realities to this degree of the mind, become as objectively real as the outward scenes of beauty and grandeur are to our ordinary vision. This spiritual mind is at home in the higher clime, the land of perpetual spring. Sometimes these spiritual senses and powers are developed normally and by a gradual unfolding, and a man exhibits the phenomena of a double consciousness and existence. He becomes an inhabitant of two worlds at the same time, and is as much at home in one as the other. Supersensuous things are not creations of fancy to him, but vitally real. In such a state was Swedenborg for twenty-six years of his life. The solid realities of another and higher sphere of life were as familiar to him as the landscapes of his native land. The external mind, through the sense of vision, sees things in the material universe—the sun, the stars, the clouds in the atmosphere, also the trees, fruits and flowers. The interior mind, the spiritual man, takes cognizance of a diviner creation, and a world that is a blank to the outward senses.

It is to be observed that this degree of the mind is complete in itself. There are loves and affections that belong to it. In the natural mind there is the love of food; in the spiritual mind, the love of truth. These are entirely distinct, and perfectly defined to the consciousness.

All genuine progress is an *evolution*, a bringing out of what is within men. There is in every man the unfolded germ of all that is good and true. Great futurities are hidden in the mysterious depths of our inner being. The divine life itself is there. Progress is an education of our powers, using the word in its radical sense, of the *educing*, or drawing forth of what is within. When the highest or inmost degree of the mind has come to conscious activity and freedom one attains to angelic perception. Higher and diviner powers are unfolded. All knowledge and truth become self-evident, and the slow and tardy process of reasoning is exchanged for intuition. The arcane powers of nature and hidden properties of things are brought distinctly to view. Such a one has risen above the control of the selfish animal instincts to a state of self-forgetting purity of love. He walks in the mild radiance of the celestial light, and has attained to a fellowship of life with the angelic heavens. He reads the characters of men by a sort of spiritualized instinct. All deception is impossible in his presence. He gains knowledge, not from books, but drinks in the living light of heaven, as a flower imbibes the light of the sun. He is conscious of intellectual perceptions, and states of feeling, beyond expression in any external language. He sees and feels unutterable things. He comes to a conscious knowledge of the Divinity within. "The Father is in him, and he is in the Father." He has communication with the indwelling divine light and life. He walks and talks with God, and receives truth from its sempiternal source. For it is this degree of the mind that has fellowship with the Divine. The Light itself is now revealed, and he walks in it. It may be difficult to believe there are such men, but human history has been able to give the world a few examples, so as to disclose the undeveloped possibilities of our nature. But these have towered so far above the sensuous populations, among whom they dwelt, as to be misunderstood in the generation in which they lived, but attained the honors of divine worship in subsequent ages. It is remarked by one, in whom these hidden powers were evolved, and who has been accepted by some as a "man sent from God," "The internal of man is that principle by virtue of which man is man, and by which he is distinguished from brute animals. By this internal he lives after death, and to eternity; and by this he is capable of being elevated by the Lord among the angels: it is the very first form by virtue of which he becomes, and is, a man. By this internal, the Lord is united to man." (Arcana Celestia 1999.) By it, the Infinite Life, comes to finite limitations, and God is manifest in the flesh.

The unfoldment of these interior degrees of spiritual life and light, it is devoutly hoped, will not be infrequent in the New Age, now in the order of Providence dawning upon the world. We are in the feeble light of a higher day, the opening morn of the "good time coming" which kings and prophets waited for, but died without the sight.

CHAPTER VII.

THE SPIRITUAL BODY—ITS NATURE AND USE.

The Mind the real Selfhood. — Intermediate Essences. — The Spiritual Body a Mediating Principle. — The Proof of its Existence. — Testimony of Paul. — Of Swedenborg. — Neither insisted upon. — Objection answered. — Shown to be the Seat of Sensation. — It is the prior seat of all pathological states of the external Organism. — Testimony of Clairvoyance. — Of Consciousness. — The Mental Phenomena following Amputations. — Explanation of them. — Proof of Immortality from this source.—A succession of Organized Forms in Man. — The Osseous System. — The Muscular. — The Venous and Arterial. — The Cerebro-Nervous. — Being is real and vital as it becomes Interior.

WE HAVE seen that the mind or soul is the real man, and exists in the human form. The external body is not the living self. Its curious and wonderful structure and mechanism only render it a form in the lower degree of created things receptive of an animating principle from a higher range of being. It receives its life and moving forces from the indwelling spirit. But between the mind and the outward organism, there is an intermediate and substantial form, called by Swedenborg and Paul the spiritual body. Between all discrete creations in the universe, there are such intermediates, through which influx descends from the higher to the lower, or, what means the same, from the interior to the external, and by means of which connection is formed and communication is effected. So between the interior soul and the outward material body, there is such an organism. It spans the discrete chasm between mind and matter, connects the two links in the chain of our being, conjoins the soul and body into a unity, and through it they mutually act and react upon each other. It is composed of a substance intermediate between pure spirit and matter, a sort of *tertium quid*, as the schoolmen would call it, a third something, through which the spiritual principle enters into the grosser body.

But have we any evidence of its existence in our complex being? Is its existence a mere conjecture, an hypothesis, a bold assumption, destitute of any solid proof? Is it a thing taken for granted, and incapable of demonstration? I will not dwell upon the intuitive reasonableness of recognizing such an intermediate substance coming between mind and matter. Nor will I insist upon the plain and positive averment of Paul that, " there is a natural body, and there is a spiritual body." (1 Cor. xv. 44.) Nor need we quote Swedenborg to prove it. The demonstration does not rest upon the authority of any great name. No array of authorities, or long line of unbroken traditions, no marshalling of opinions or personal beliefs, ought to make us give credence to what is not inherently rational, and does not come within the grasp of our intuitions. Modern science does not deal with hypotheses,—that stage of mental growth has passed, —but with positive facts. It is with such solid verities that its temple is built.

It has been objected that the anatomist has never detected the existence of any such organism. Neither has anatomical science, even when aided by microscopical investigations, been able to discover the mind, with its thoughts and affections. Yet there is nothing whose existence is more certain or real. There is a good reason for both these failures. Where a thing is not it cannot be found. This is self-evident. If a man is not in his house, he cannot be discerned there, though we search never so long and sharply for him. The anatomist studies the *dead* body, the cast off and decaying shell of our being. In this there *is* no spiritual body. Hence none can there be found. The living inhabitant has vacated his former mansion.

But may we not discover it in the living body? Effects reveal the presence and action of adequate causes. We affirm that it is the seat of all sensation. If we establish this point, the existence of a spiritual body is susceptible of positive demonstration. The material body is destitute of feeling. That it feels is only an appearance which an examination by the light of consciousness shows to be not the real fact. Sensation belongs somewhere to our inner nature. This is admitted in all systems of mental science. We occupy here undisputed ground. The eye does not see, but something sees through the eye. The outward ear does not hear, but it is only an organ through which something within is affected by the vibratory waves. Nor is the sensation of feeling located in the substance of the brain and nerves. The brain itself is destitute of sensibility, and it has been cut and removed as far down as the *Corpus Callosum*, without the least pain. The optic nerve, at its base, has been shown to be insensible to light. These are unquestioned truths. But it is equally certain that pure mind cannot be affected by the direct contact of matter. This is also admitted. Fire will not burn it, nor does it feel the thrust of a sword. The two substances are discrete. They have unlike properties. So far is sensation from belonging to the interior mind, that the mind perceives it in something external to itself. Consciousness assures us of this. But if sensation, as for instance feeling, is not in the mind, and it is admitted that it is not in the outward body, where must it be placed? Most certainly in an intermediate nature or substance coming between the two, and through which the outward world acts upon our inner being, and mind communicates with and affects external things. If the anatomist would discover the spiritual body, let him apply the dissecting knife to his own flesh, and the pain he feels reveals it to his consciousness. In this way the scalpel proves the fact of its existence. The prick of a needle reveals it. Puncture the flesh with a lancet, and where the pain is, there it is. For all sensation belongs to this region of our complex being. This explains the reason why, after a limb is amputated, the patient feels a pain in the part as before the operation. The unpleasant sensation only continues where it was, that is, in the answering part of the external spiritual organism. This is a simple solution of an otherwise inexplicable fact. The external body corresponds or answers to the interior body. The one is the living substance, the other the projected shadow. The parts of the outer are pervaded by the corresponding parts of the inward man, from the greatest to the least.

The outer depends upon the inner for its life, and when the former drops off, the interior man lives on. In the chemistry of death, the earthly husk remains in the retort, while the volatile essence ascends to the next higher sphere in perfect human form.

This inner form is the prior seat of all diseased disturbance in the body. Any abnormal mental states, that immediately affect this inner principle, and impede its free circulation through the external organs, so as to weaken its correspondence with the parts, and loosen its connection with them, is the primary cause of disease. When this correspondence ceases, the outward body dies. Magnetic manipulations act upon this department of our being, and go to the root of all diseased action. Hence their efficiency as a therapeutic agency. In clairvoyance, somnambulism, and the trance, there is a temporary and partial loosening of the connection between the external and internal man, and the subject becomes invested, to a limited degree, with the powers and perceptions of the spirit-life. He anticipates and antedates the state of man in the world beyond

The reality of the existence of an interior organism within the outward body, has been brought within the range of consciousness in another way. In the case of those who have lost a limb in battle, or otherwise, there remains as vivid a perception of the part as before the mutilation. This is the experience and testimony of all who have lost any part of the outward form, and can be accounted for satisfactorily only on the supposition of an inward body that is not affected by the destruction of the outward organism. Attempts have been made to explain the fact, so familiar to all surgeons, but they are vague and incomprehensible. The solution is more mysterious than the phenomena to be explained. It is a darkening of counsel by words without knowledge. If there be a spiritual body, or as Kerner calls it, a nerve-projected form, which is the subject of all sensation, every thing in relation to the above named fact becomes plain and simple. We may boldly aver, that we have the same evidence of its existence as we have of the material body. In both cases the proof rests upon the testimony of consciousness, beyond which there is no higher evidence, and in which the human mind always rests. It is one of the original laws of belief, and is deemed final in every argument. If we deny its authority, we unsettle the foundation of all evidence, and we may doubt the existence of anything, even of ourselves.

When any part of the external body is removed by disease or accident, there remains the perception of the answering spiritual part, so that after a limb is amputated under the influence of ether, or other anæsthetic agent, on awakening, as it were, to life again, the absent member is not missed, and the person comes slowly to realize that it is gone. But suppose another limb is removed, and still another. Convey them, if you please, to the cemetery. The case remains the same. They are not missed in the consciousness. Go a step further, and suppose the whole outward form to be removed from the spirit. Disrobe the inner man entirely of its fleshly envelope, there remains the same consciousness of a body as before. The man, the conscious self, still lives. Such is the condition of the freed spirit upon its entrance upon the life to come. It is conscious of losing nothing that constituted any essential element of its being. It has parted with no life, for the outward body had none of its own. It has been deprived of no one of the senses, for these belong to the inner and not to the outer man, and when the former passes to the higher realm, it carries with it all that belongs to its nature.

There is in our complex structure a succession of bodily forms, each inclosed, as it were, within the other. First we have the bony frame-work. Taken by itself, it exhibits a rude approach to the human shape. Next comes the motory or muscular system Added to the former, it fills out the outline to a nearer approach to completeness. Then interpenetrating this rough model or cast of humanity, we have the venous and arterial system, with their innumerable minute branches. These are so diffused, that to puncture the flesh anywhere, even with the point of a lancet, we strike one, and the circulating fluid escapes. If we could perfectly abstract this system from the rest, it would be a comparatively perfect human form. But the brain with its continuation into the spinal column, and the nerves ramifying from it, is so interfused through the rest of the system, that by applying the point of a needle to any part, we come in contact with it. Taken by itself it would be a nearly complete human form. But pervading this, and diffused through it, is the spiritual body, the nerve-projected form. With the nerve matter, the outward vision terminates its range of action. But before the unveiled eye of independent clairvoyance, the inner man is revealed. Then comes the mind with its successive degrees of interiority. Within these, in the living center of our being, lies concealed the divine germ, a spark of the infinite Life. As we progress inward, our being becomes more real and vital. The inner, all the way through, acts upon and into the outer

The external lives and moves by influx from that which is interior. The mind affects first the spiritual body, then the nerves, then the external organism. Hence all disease being an outward visible effect, we must search for its cause in something further inward. It is a corollary, or natural inference from the principles already established, that it has its origin in some disordered states of the inner man. For there is a pathology of the mind as well as of the external body.

CHAPTER VIII.

ON THE EMANATIONS OF MIND, OR SPIRITUAL SPHERES.

Material Effluvia. — Odorous Particles. — Evaporation. — The mental Sphere a Vibrating Force. — Importance of the Doctrine in Mental Science. — The Sphere the outgoing of the Love. — Mental States Contagious. — What is Influence? — What is Divinity? — Sympathy and Antipathy explained. — Spiritual Remoteness and Propinquity. — Pathological States of Mind and Body, traced to the Susceptibility of the Patient. — Subtle Forces of Nature as Therapeutic agencies. — Connection of the mental Sphere with the bodily Emanations. — The Imposition of hands not a mere Symbol. — The Breath. — The source of our mental Disturbances. — How to be Useful.

IT IS a truth recognized by science, that every material body is surrounded by an atmosphere generated by a subtle emanation of its own substance. The air enveloping the globe we inhabit is charged with the minute particles proceeding from the various objects of nature. The atmosphere thus becomes the general repository of these visible and invisible effluvia. But what is true of the globe at large, may be affirmed of the smallest thing. There perpetually exhales from it an effluvium of its own corpuscles and atoms, which surround it as the air envelops and pervades the earth. These emanations sometimes become visible and manifest to the senses. The sensation of smell is occasioned in us by an emanation of the minute particles of the odorous body, which impinge against the delicate membrane of the nostrils, as in the case of the rose. These invisible effluvia are often wafted to a great distance. Sailors detect their approach to land in this way, before even the mountains become visible to the eye. The acute sense of smell in animals—as the dog and various beasts of prey—is affected by them sometimes when they are miles away from the object producing them. A familiar illustration of emanation is seen in water, which perpetually emits vapor into the atmosphere, where, if it could all be condensed, there would be enough to form an ocean. The human body is surrounded with a sphere of the substances that compose it, which go forth in the sensible and insensible perspiration. The same is true of all animals, vegetables, and minerals.

This phenomenon, like all the forces and movements of the material universe, is an effect of which something spiritual is the cause. At least, there is something analogous to this in the world of the mind. The mind is a spiritual substance or essence, and there goes forth from it a sphere that surrounds it. It is a radiant force like heat and light. In fact love is spiritual heat, and truth is spiritual light. This doctrine of spiritual spheres is of great importance in mental philosophy, but has been almost wholly ignored. In the system of Swedenborg, it has been given that prominence that belongs to it. Every angel, every spirit, every man, is surrounded by a spiritual sphere of affection and thought, or radiant circles of an emanating force, within which he imparts—often silently and unintentionally—his own feelings and ideas. Just as a heated body, for instance a stove, imparts its heat to surrounding objects, and a lamp its light.

There are persons who exert a secret but powerful influence over those who come in contact with the sphere of their inner nature. This influence is good or bad, happy or depressing, elevating or degrading, according to the confirmed affectional state or ruling love of him from whom it proceeds. For it is to be borne in mind, that it goes forth primarily from the love which constitutes the soul's life. If the mental state be joy or melancholy, gladness or sorrow, meekness or anger, contentment or impatience, faith or fear, it affects others with a like feeling, in a degree proportioned to their impressibility. In this way the mind propagates its own prevailing condition, and all our mental states are contagious. This law of our being operates to bring all into a similitude of spiritual condition. In the heavenly realm, there is a communication of all to each, and of each to all,—a universal fellowship of thought and affection. The sphere of each intermingles with that of the whole in a divine community of life and celestial harmony. The encircling sphere or emanating wave, surrounding every created spirit is more or less extended and powerful, according as the angel or man is more or less elevated in the moral scale or degrees of life. There are those whose influence (from *in* and *fluo*, to flow in) extends to great distances. And mind acts upon mind, so far as we know, independently of spatial nearness or remoteness. The sphere of the Deity is infinite, and is the inmost life of all things. We use the term divine, to express that which goes forth from the Godhead. By divinity, we mean the *radios Deitatis* as Jerome calls it, the radiations of Deity, that which is not, when taken by itself, infinite, but proceeds from God. All our light and love, our good and truth, are an emanation, or undulation from the eternal Goodness. It is somewhat of the Divinity in us, and makes him who receives it, in a mitigated sense, an Immanuel, an individuality which is an outgrowth of the Deity.

The doctrine of mental spheres explains many phenomena in the science of mind, and is of much practical value and comes into constant application, with every one who would cure disease by spiritual remedies. What we call sympathy and antipathy finds here its cause and explanation. When the sphere of two or more persons is homogeneous and concordant, their spiritual emanations meet and mingle without repulsion, like the vibrations occasioned by musical instruments in tune. Their life blends in harmony, constituting nearness, union, and sympathy. The opposite of this is antipathy. All associations and conjunctions in the realm of spirit are thus effected. All disjunction, separation, and remoteness, which are there a *feeling*, rather than distance of space, are the result of discordant spheres. Like joins itself to like, by a law as invariable in the spirit-world, as that of gravitation and chemical affinity in this.

There are many persons of a negative and passive nature, who are easily affected by these subtle influences. There seems to be no reactive force in their mental organism to repel them. They are like a vessel at sea impelled by sails, and at the mercy of every wind that blows, and not like the powerful steamer driven by a force within, and pursuing its course against opposing currents and contrary winds. They become impregnated at once by the influence of more positive minds, with whom they happen to come in contact. There are many disorderly, inharmonious mental states, that affect even the body, that are the result of this peculiar organism and susceptibility of the patient, and they only need the influence of some more positive will, adequate to the casting out of demons, to restore them to mental and moral soundness. Here is the secret origin of more diseases of mind and body than the world at large is aware of. There are many subtle causes at work to generate a diseased condition, which the science of Pathology does not notice. And I believe with the force of a conviction, that within the vast storehouse of nature, there lie concealed very many undeveloped, and unused forces and laws, that are available for the cure of the diseases that flesh is heir to. Science is beginning to turn its attention in that direction and to explore this hitherto unknown realm of spiritual causation. The attempt will be fruitful in results.

It is worthy of observation, before leaving this topic, to remark, that the spiritual emanations, or those that proceed from our affectional and intellectual states, infuse themselves into the natural sphere continually flowing from the body. This latter is poured forth from the palms of the hands more copiously than from any other part of the body, because, as has been demonstrated by the microscope, the pores are there the most numerous. Hence the imposition of hands was not once an unmeaning ceremony, nor a mere sign or symbol. It was an actual communication of spiritual life. Our affectional states, which are our inmost vital force, are communicated by the touch, which is the sense sacred to the love. Hence in blessing others—as Jacob his sons, and Christ little children—the hands were placed upon the head. The mental sphere also goes forth with the breath. Hence Jesus, who perfectly understood these laws, breathed on his disciples, and said, "Receive ye the holy spirit" (Jno. xx. 22), and thus imparted to them, so far as they were recipient of it, his own gentle, loving, and tranquil frame of mind. Thus we have a silent but powerful influence, for good or evil, over those who come within the sphere of our minds. Our touch is morally healthful or poisonous, and our very presence is salutary or noxious. There goes out with our breath a celestial aura, or a hellish miasm. Our spiritual states are contagious, and it is a serious and earnest thing to live and move among our fellows. Many of our troublesome thoughts, and unhappy feelings, are excited in us by the sphere of those around us, and come to us from spirits in the flesh, rather than from those who have passed to the world beyond, to whom they are often unjustly charged. There is a tendency, through the operation of this law of our minds, to make all others like ourselves. This tendency is not originated, but only intensified, by the action of our wills. Even if we are outwardly good, but interiorly selfish and corrupt, our influence will be morally unwholesome and deleterious. Through a beautiful garb of feigned sanctity, the sphere of the real character will penetrate and spread, as the odor of a decaying body will make its way through a shroud of the finest linen. The best way to be useful, is to be inwardly good and true. And it is one of our highest duties to be innocently happy, not merely for our own sake, but for the general weal. For our life will mingle itself with the ocean of created mind, and we should seek so to live, that our tributary stream be not added to it as a turbid element.

CHAPTER IX.

OF THE DOCTRINE OF INFLUX, AND THE RELATION OF MAN TO THE SPIRITUAL WORLD.

The nature of Influx. — The Unity of Life. — The mind not self-moved. — Thought not self-originated. — Teaching of Paul. — Of John the Baptist. — Doctrine of Innate Ideas overturned by Locke. — Truth transmissible. — Man's Vital Relation to the other World. — Quotation from Swedenborg. — All Knowledge an Inspiration. — Modern Spiritualism. — How the Old Testament Scriptures were given. — The Demon of Socrates. — Jesus on the Mount. — John in Patmos. — Swedenborg's Intercourse with the Spiritual World. — Sensational Philosophy Unsound. — Locke's Essay. — Condillac. — Original Suggestion. — How Knowledge is communicated. — Propagation of mental States. — Mesmeric State how produced.

THE WORD influx signifies an inflowing, and is applied to all that in us which is not self-originated, but derived. The doctrine of influx is closely related to that of mental spheres, discussed in the previous chapter.

It is a fundamental truth, that there is one only Life, from which all in heaven and earth receive their

being, but each in a different degree. But life in its
last analysis is love. All the phenomena of our interior nature are referable to affection and thought, or
to will and understanding. The movements of the
love and the intellect generate all the various states
of the mind. But are these self-moved, or do they
act as they are acted upon by some living force applied
to them? That which constitutes our essential life
is momentarily received from its central source, the
Divinity within, or descends to us through the
mediation of angels and spirits, who receive it in
the same way. The first is an immediate or direct
influence, and the latter a mediate influx. There is
nothing that lives from itself except the uncreated
One, though we may *appear* to ourselves to possess
an independent existence, because the influx from
above is continual and uninterrupted. The idea of
the unity of life in all the multifarious forms of
existence, is a basic verity, and its recognition, not
as a theory or an external dogma, but as a vital,
conscious truth, is essential to a genuine spiritual
state. The more fully we come to realize it, the
more receptive we are of an influent wisdom and
love. It is also to be borne in mind, that the inflowing life from God is the same in all, but is varied according to the state of man and the form or quality

of the recipient spirit, just as a fluid receives its form
from the containing vessel, and light is modified by
the substance through which it is transmitted.

All thought, and consequently all knowledge, descend to us from above. Paul declares, "that we are not able of ourselves to think any thing as of ourselves." (2 Cor. iii. 5.) And a greater than he affirms, that "A man can take nothing to himself except it be given him from above." (Jno. iii. 17.) Our ideas must originate somewhere. They were not born in us, but only the faculty to contain them, and the power to be conscious of them. The doctrine of innate ideas has long since been exploded. Since Locke assailed it with a keen and irresistible logic, it has been banished from mental science, though he was not equally successful in settling the question of the real origin of our knowledge. As our thoughts are not innate, there was a time when we had them not. Hence they must have been imparted to us. Truth is the reality of things, it is a *substance*, a spiritual something, that can be imparted from one mind to another, just as really as a fluid can be made to pass from one vessel to another on a lower level, or, to employ a closer analogy, as light can emanate from one body to another. It is a thing, a substance, divinely real. God is truth, and all truth is originally in and from him. But whence does it usually come to us? Swedenborg, whom I quote not as an authority, but as an illuminated mind, whose opinions are worthy of respect and attention, asserts that it flows in from our living connection with the spiritual realm. No individual is an isolated existence, but the whole universe of created minds are bound up in the same bundle of life. The Swedish philosopher observes, "It is in-consequence of this communication that a man enjoys the faculty of perception, and the power of thinking analytically on all subjects; and if this connection were sundered, he would be incapable of any more or other kind of thought than a beast, and also if this commerce with spirits should be taken away from him, or intercepted entirely, he would instantly die." (T. C. R. 475.) For no one can live by himself alone, nor could he have affection and thought, for these are the vital activities of the mind. All our ideas, according to him, flow in from above. There cannot be in us the least excitement of thought, without this influent vital force from the spiritual realm. It logically follows from this that all truth, all knowledge, all light in us is an *inspiration*, and to receive light and love by the commerce of our spirits with the heavens above, is the normal state of the human mind. And what is called modern spiritualism is only an instinctive reaction of the general mind against the unnatural condition it has been in for centuries. According to Paul, the Old Testament Scriptures were given through the mediation of angels. Many of the greatest and best minds of the world's history lived in communication with the inner spheres. Socrates had his demon or good spirit who attended him and admonished him by impression. He respectfully listened to the interior voice. Jesus, on the mount of transfiguration, communed with Moses and Elijah. If this had been contrary to the divine order of our being, would he have set the world so bad an example? To his pure spirit the heavens were continually opened, and his receptive soul was held open toward them. By communication with an angelic human spirit, John received the Apocalypse. If such communication is necessarily wrong in us, it was in him, and we ought to purge the Scriptures of the offensive document. Swedenborg for twenty-six years walked and talked with spirits and angels, and, as he affirmed, in a way perfectly harmonious with the laws of the mind, and without a miracle. It was only a return to the primitive order of our being. And why may not a disciple of his philosophy do the same? Why may not all, if they come to the knowledge of those mental laws that govern in this case? It cannot for a moment be admitted that he obtained a monopoly of this high and holy commerce with the skies. He may have had a distinct use to accomplish in the plan of Providence. But the opening of his inner senses was no miracle. In the progress of the spiritual development of mankind, it may become common. But we are aware of the evil effects of attempting to enjoy an open intercourse with the other world, unless we are normally unfolded to a degree which shall render it natural.

It was for many years a favorite theory that our knowledge is to be attributed in its origin to the action of the senses. But there must be interior sight before there can be outward vision. The senses are all correspondences, that is they are effects, of which something in our spiritual nature is the cause. And the action of that superior or interior power in the mind, to which each of the bodily senses corresponds, or of which it is the outward expression, must be anterior to the action of the sense, for the reason that a cause is prior to an effect. A man may look towards a tree, yet if the *attention* is not directed to it, he sees it not. And how many sounds are unheard when we are asleep or in a revery, yet the atmospheric vibrations are received by the ear. In the sensational philosophy of the seventeenth century, it was asserted that all our ideas have their origin in the action of the bodily senses. The celebrated treatise of Locke (Essay on the Human Understanding) was written as a defense of this theory. It was advocated in France by Condillac, and became the current doctrine of mental science in Europe. The prevailing systems, at the present time, attribute only our *first* knowledge to this source. But there is a class of ideas that are supposed to arise from what is called "original suggestion," which, unless our knowledge is self-created, is only another name for intuition. And this is identical with spiritual influx. All knowledge is from above and cometh down from the Father of lights, and from lesser luminaries enlightened by him, and reflecting to us the effulgence they receive. "With him (and them) are hid all the treasures of wisdom and knowledge." Truth is not to be classed among created things. Creation can only be predicated of the forms receptive of it. The senses may be like the steel that brings the spark from the flint, but the fire was there before the steel brought it out. The latter did not create it. It only came to manifestation through its agency. So the senses do not originate knowledge, but only mark that degree of the mind, which is the first theatre of its manifestation. But its source is not there.

Let us suppose a case that lies within the range of possibility and sometimes of actual fact. A child is born whose outward senses have never been called into action. In its birth, its natural life becomes extinct. The candle is quenched in its lighting. It never saw, or heard, or felt, or tasted. What is to be the condition of such a mind, for no one would affirm that it was a soulless thing? Must it become an eternal blank? Must it remain a created receptacle doomed to be an eternal vacuity and emptiness? According to the current doctrine, such must be its fate, or annihilation. If our knowledge originates with the action of the bodily senses, as these were never called into activity, the mind of such a child must remain empty of all ideas or be exterminated. Such is the necessary inference from the premises. If we are shocked at such a conclusion, it is because of the absurdity and falsity of the doctrine with which we start. That thought is self-originated, is an infinite falsity. The losing sight of God and of our vital relation to the spititual world, has been the perpetual fault of philosophy for ages. If thought can originate in us, why not life as well? If the material world acting upon our bodily senses, conveys to us the first ray of knowledge, why may it not originate our life? Then outward nature becomes to us God, and we plunge into the starless night of materialism. The bodily senses are only organized matter. How can the motion of their fibres create thought? Is knowledge a material emanation? Matter, in all its forms, is in itself dead and passive. It acts only as it is acted upon. It moves only as it is moved. If the motion of matter creates thought, it creates the mind that thinks, for thought is only a state of mind. The material universe may then be supposed to be the creator of the Divine Mind, and God himself becomes a creature. Here, by an easy descent, we fall into blank atheism. Thus philosophy has walked about for ages with its disciples, on the brink of a precipice. By a few short logical steps they plunge into the abyss of a cheerless infidelity. And this descent to Avernus has been found by many too easy.

We have spoken of knowledge received by influx, as an emanation from one mind to another. But we have done so only in the same way as the chemist speaks of light and heat as *radiant* forces, as if particles of a luminous fluid darted off into space. This theory is abandoned, and light is proved to be only a vibration. In its essence it is motion, force. One body illuminates another by communicating its motion to it, and not by pouring into it a luminous fluid. So one mind imparts its knowledge and affectional states to another, by causing it to vibrate in harmony with it. The mind is like a divinely constructed stringed instrument. An angel's intellect may communicate its motion to its harp strings, and a celestial music is the result. Thought and affection are not something that go forth from the mind that thinks and feels. They are states, interior movements of the thinking, feeling substance. And as one vibrating string, will communicate its motion to another in tune with it, so one mind imparts its intellectual life to another. The mind is capable of all knowledge, when it is subjected to the action of divine and celestial forces, just as a musical instrument, properly constructed, is capable of producing the most rapturous sounds, when the hand of a skillful player imparts to it the necessary motion.

In harmony with this law of the action of mind upon mind, we all know how readily our mental states are imparted to others. A state of fear in some one individual, will spread through a whole army in a few minutes of time. One sad person in a company, will throw a gloom over the entire assembly. One cheerful happy soul will communicate its spiritual sunshine to hundreds. The presence of a genial, loving heart, is a treasure to a whole community. A sour, morose, misanthropic mind, in a social assembly, changes the joyful music of all hearts to a funeral dirge. One ruling mind will convert all in its presence to its own modes of thought and feeling. What is called the mesmeric state, is produced by the action of the same law, only the effect is intensified. What are called the magnetic passes are not necessary to its production. We have thrown many persons into this state, some of them miles away, but never once made use of the prescribed passes. It is the action of mind on mind. In the same way, those who revel in the light of a higher day, and the beams of a brighter sun, may impart to us their sublimer thoughts, and their happier affections. Revelation from the inner realm has never ceased, but will be endlessly progressive. The heavens will always speak to man on earth. For it is the established order of creation, that life and light should descend from the higher to the lower, from the interior to the external, from the inner to the outer circles of existence.

CHAPTER X.

THE RELATION OF SOUL AND BODY, AND OF THE MATERIAL TO THE SPIRITUAL REALM.

Three Theories respecting the Connection of the Body and the Spirit. — Aristotle. — Cartesian Doctrine. — Leibnitz. — Man a Microcosm. — The Body an Effect. — The Face and our inward Feelings. — The States of the Mind affect the Body. — Fear and Asthma. — Disease originates in abnormal Mental States. — Chemical Preparations inadequate to a Cure. — Quotation from Dr. Taylor. — Mind the organizing Force.—Relation of the Visible to the Invisible World. — Where is the Spiritual Realm? — Material things inclose a Spiritual Essence. — Pneumatopathy or Mental Hygiene.

THERE HAVE been three theories respecting the relation of our outward organism to the interior spiritual principle. Two of these recognize in their connection the relation of cause and effect, but differ as to which is the one or the other, which is prior and which is posterior. The first theory is that of physical influx, or that matter influences mind. This was taught by Aristotle, and the sensualistic schools of philosophy in all subsequent ages. By some, mind has been viewed as the result of a sublimation of matter. This first theory has *appearance* in its favor—an evidence always unreliable and often deceptive.

The second is, that matter is influenced and governed by spirit, and derives all its life from it. Al its changes, forms, and phenomena, are effects of which something spiritual is the cause. This idea pervades the Cartesian philosophy, and was adopted by Swedenborg.

The third is that of pre-established harmony, or that neither acts upon the other, but both were made to act in concert. This theory was advocated by the celebrated Leibnitz. We are not aware that it is seriously advocated by any one at present, and may be left without further notice. It only belongs to the history of human opinions. In the other two doctrines, we choose between theism and atheism. If there be a God, creation has gone forth from him. But God is a Spirit. Consequently the material universe owes its origin and its continued existence and control, to an all-pervading divine force, distinct from matter, as a cause from an effect. But man is a microcosm, a world in himself, and his body sustains the same relation to the soul that the outward universe does to God. The body without the spirit is dead. Consequently it has no life of its own and in itself. Its vital force is derived from the all-pervading spirit. It is an effect of which the soul is the cause. As some one has said, "The active plastic principle is the soul—the true man, of which the body is but the external expression and instrument." It is not merely the outward envelope of the interior man, but is pervaded by it, as light is diffused through a crystal vase of water. Hence it becomes transparent to all the states of the soul. Every emotion expresses itself in the face. In a countenance that has not been taught to dissemble, all the varying affections and emotions of the mind are there visibly displayed. Every change in our feelings, produces a correspondent arrangement of the moving fibres of the face. Here is a visible effect resulting from a spiritual cause. But every part of the body corresponds to something in the mind —the hands, the feet, the hair, the brain, the stomach, the lungs, the heart, and all the internal organs. These have no vital action except as they receive it by influx from the indwelling soul. And every organ in our bodily structure, is only the outward manifestation of a correspondent part and function of our spiritual nature. Consequently our mental states affect the condition and action of the various organs

—in fact, are the body's health or malady. They first influence the intermediate principle, denominated the spiritual body, then the brain and nerves, and then the various organs. Every abnormal mental state ultimates itself in a correspondent bodily condition. Let us illustrate this by the effect of fear or a sudden fright. It immediately quickens, and at the same time weakens, the action of the heart. Its regular contraction and dilatation are changed to a spasmodic flutter. A nervous thrill is felt in the epigastric region or pit of the stomach. This is in the diaphragm, which loses its contractility, and becomes relaxed, so that the respiration is impeded and oppressed. The blood retreats from the surface inward, and from the extremities upward. Such are its immediate effects. If the mental state producing this order of things should become permanent, in the form of anxiety, the corresponding bodily condition will be chronic. And a common disease, called asthma, is the result. But fear will no more really affect the body than any other disorderly mental state. Melancholy, envy, jealousy, anger, disappointed affection, produce each its specific effect. All diseases originate in some abnormal states of the mind, some disturbance or loss of harmony in the inner man, and are but the ultimation, or passing outward to the region of visible effects in the material organism, of those disordered mental conditions. To ascertain the nature and cause of the disturbed state of mind underlying the physical troubles of a patient, is of greater importance than an examination of the pulse or the tongue. If the action of the heart, the diaphragm, the lungs, or the liver, is not healthy, we desire to know what is the cause of their disordered physiological manifestations. It is of no avail to apply chemical preparations to a cause that chemistry cannot reach. It is of no use to administer stimulants and tonics, when the patient needs only encouragement and sympathy. Why give opium and narcotic drugs, when it is only the excited mind that needs to be quieted, and there needs to be "plucked from the heart a rooted sorrow?" Why give physic to a man who only needs instruction and ideas? Says Dr. Taylor, "Diseases are perpetuated, if not produced, by causes over which mere chemical influences cannot be presumed to exercise any positive control. This fact may be, often is, tacitly acknowledged by the physician, but he declines to investigate its relations, so as to be able to turn them to a useful account. He is unwilling to acknowledge in practice, although he may admit confidentially, that the headache, the nervousness, the heart disease, the dyspeptic qualms which he is called upon to remedy, are only indications of a *peculiar morbid state of the mind or of the emotional nature of the sufferer*, which it becomes him to meet directly, rather than to torment his patient with an eternal round of palliatives. In these cases, every medical prescription must be totally irrelevant (though written in the best Latin), unless it recognizes the operation of causes existing in a sphere quite beyond the reach of the most potent drug."

He further observes, "The jests that used to be hurled at the defenceless head of the practitioner who dared to suggest that the thoughts, and feelings, and mental habits of the invalid might need rectifying as well as his bile and blood, are fast losing their point. We are all beginning to suspect that perhaps, after all, a disease may not be the less a disease because its source happens to lie in an unruly imagination, or in excessive activity, or wrong modes of thought. And gradnally—very slowly to be sure—yet really, we think people are waking up to the conviction that these intangible causes are not irremediable. They are beginning to see and understand that by this close union and coöperation of the material and immaterial natures, remedial agents may possibly find access to either or both these avenues that otherwise could have no existence. We have faith to believe that the time is near at hand when the mental aspects and relations of disease will receive an amount of attention equal to that which has always been given to the pulse and the tongue, the temperature of the skin, and color and consistence of the excretions." (Movement Cure, p. 388, 389.)

The body is an *organization* of material substances, by which we mean the arrangement of its particles so as to form organs or instruments adapted to use. But unless the particles are self-moved, which no one but a disciple of Epicurus would argue, the mind must be the organizing force. The body is only the evolution of the mind, and the means of its external manifestation. The whole material universe is the ultimation of the spiritual world. The spiritual realm is the *animus mundi*, the soul of the outward visible creation, and the latter exists from the former.

If you ask where we locate the spirit-world? we answer, it is where our spirits are, for our inner nature belongs to it and is a part of it. The spiritual world is the interior realm, and it is not separated from this by spatial distance, but it is as near to this as our souls are to our bodies. It is in the center of the universe and in its circumference; it is in the Milky Way, and the fixed stars, and it is here and now. The kingdom of heaven is within. Jesus proclaimed the great truth that it was *at hand*, so near as to be within our grasp. Spiritual substance is the soul of things, and the angel-world is interfused within this. But things become real, substantial, and living, in proportion as they are interior. We may gain some idea of this by observing that all substances that can be perceived by the senses, have other substances more subtle within them. Thus all solids contain water in their interstices or pores, even those that seem the dryest. Suppose the globe we inhabit to be a solid sphere. It contains within and around it water. It is enveloped with aqueous vapor, that surrounds and penetrates it. This is distinct from the solid contents, but is contained within them and around them, and we may conceive it to be a world by itself abstracted from the solid earth. In fact, nearly three-fourths of this earthy system is water. And it was taught by Thales more than two thousand years ago, that the earth was formed from the water. There may be truth in this. But water contains within it and around it, air enough to support the life of fishes, whose gills serve them for lungs where their blood is oxygenated. The atmosphere extends upward to the distance of forty-five miles and more. It penetrates the ocean, and may be viewed as a world or sphere, interior to the earthy solids and the aqueous element. But the atmosphere has three degrees. Within and around the air is the ether, whose vibrations, according to Euler, produce light, and the various phenomena of electricity. The ether contains within it the *aura*, which is not cognizable by the senses. This may be identical with or analogous to the *odylic force* discovered by the Baron Reichenbach. It may be the same as the *animal spirits* of the older physiologists, the nervous fluid, the medium through which mind acts upon matter, as the will upon muscular fibre. It constitutes the boundary line between the natural and the spiritual world. Next to this, but discrete or distinct from it, is the spiritual world in its lowest or outermost degree. Thus in thought we may proceed through the three heavens, each within the other, until we come to the sun of the spiritual world, which is the first substance, and the sphere immediately or proximately surrounding the Lord, the central life. We may conceive of creation as going forth from him in successive waves, and the various degrees may be represented to the eye by so many concentric circles. He is the living centre. Around this is what is called the sun of heaven. Further outward is the celestial heaven, then the spiritual heaven, then the ultimate or lowest heaven, then the world of spirits or the intermediate realm, and then the natural world in its various degrees. This is the outside circumference of being, where the creative wave terminates. It is the furthest removed from the vital center, not by distance of space, but in the degrees of life. It being the furthest from the central life, is what we mean by the term ultimate. The word means the furthest and sometimes the last. Creation in its successive degrees has rolled off in distinct waves of being, like concentric circles, or rather spheres within spheres, and here it terminates. This world is the furthest and last, and is the basis, the continent, and the firmament, of the other degrees.

But is it possible for us to comprehend how natural substance is the ultimation of spiritual substance? There are things analogous to it, which may throw some light upon it, yet they are only remote analogies. Every visible object, or every thing cognizable to the senses, is composed of invisible particles or atoms. These by themselves are so minute that none of our senses are affected by them. It is by their combination that they become visible and tangible. Thus what we call a material object, that is, one that is cognizable to the sight or touch, is composed of a substance that cannot be detected by the senses. A muscular fibre is composed of thousands of fibrils bound together, and each fibril of others still more minute, and these of primary atoms. Water is composed of two gases, hydrogen and oxygen. The diamond is solidified or crystalized carbonic acid gas. Thus the diamond may be called the ultimation of that gas. All vegetable structures and tissues are combinations of various gases, carbon, oxygen, hydrogen and nitrogen, with a small amount of earthy salts. These gases may, and probably do, owe their origin to more subtile substances, and these to others, and they to spiritual substance, which is discrete from them, but may be ultimated in the form we call matter.

There is in every material object a spiritual essence, which is as a soul in its body. The external form which is manifest to our senses, is the correspondent and representation of that invisible and pneumatical substance.

To the everywhere-present spiritual world we sustain a vital relation. All the involuntary functions of the body, as the action of the heart and the lungs, are carried on by a force received thence by influx, though the action of all the organs may be affected by the influence of our own minds and wills.

If the ideas we have unfolded in this chapter are sound, and we think they cannot be succesfully controverted, they constitute a new mode of medical treatment, and may form the basis of a succesful practice of the healing art. It is a law, on the operation of which we may rely, that where a diseased condition of the body is caused by a disordered and morbid state of the spiritual life, if we can induce upon ourselves, either directly or through the medium of others, the opposite modes of thought and feeling as a permanent mental state, it will cure the disease. Hundreds of facts could be given to prove the uniformity of the action of this law. All that is necessary is the power intuitively to detect the morbid state of the mind underlying the disease, and how to *convert* the patient to a more healthful inner life. All disease is, in its cause, an insanity, using the term in its radical or etymological sense, rather than in its common acceptation. Its secret spring is some abnormality, unsoundness of the mind, some departure from that most happy of all earthly conditions, expressed in the terse line of Juvenal, *sana mens in sano corpore*, a sound mind in a sound body. And we think the time is not far distant, when this fundamental truth will be more fully recognized and conformed to by all medical practitioners. The therapeutic systems that acknowledge the influence of the mind upon the body, are the most succesful in the cure of disease, as those of Hahnemann, Ling, and the practitioners of what is called magnetism.

CHAPTER XI.

CORRESPONDENCE OF THE BRAIN AND THE MIND.

The Brain the Organ of the external Manifestations of the Mind. — Its extension into the Body. — Its two Substances and their Correspondence. — The Positive and Negative Forces. — The Brain first formed in the Fetus. — Plurality of its Organs. — Sympathetic Connection of the Bodily Organs with it. — The three Brains. — Their Relation to the Degrees of the Mind. — Their independent Action. — The Cerebrum and its Correspondence. — The Cerebellum. — Sleep-Waking. — Mental Exaltation. — Freedom from the bodily Senses. — The Medulla Oblongata. — State of the Mind and Body in the Trance. — Scientific View of Death.

THE BRAIN is the immediate organ of the spirit of man, or is a mediate substance through which the mind acts upon and into the rest of the body, and through which mind is externally manifested in this lower stage of our being. It corresponds or answers to the mind, as an echo to the original sound. Its sensitive fibres respond to every change in the inner life. It is the veil drawn over the interior man, tremulous and wavy to all its motions. But the brain is extended through the whole body, by means of myriads of white cords or rays proceeding from the cerebro-spinal center, and interfused through all the living textures. So the soul-principle is co-extensive with it, and is everywhere in the organic structure.

All the manifold forms of mental life and action may be arranged into two grand divisions, and are activities either of the love or intellect. In all the endless variety of human character and condition, one or the other of these two departments is uppermost, and rules. What we call the mind is the union of these two into a harmonious unity. The one is positive and the other negative, for polarity is a universal property of things. We have everywhere action and reaction in the outward world, answering to love and intellect in the realm of spirit. All the phenomena of nature are generated by two distinct forces. A large proportion of mineral or earthy compounds are formed by the union of a positive alkali and a negative acid, whose combination produces the endless variety of the salts of chemistry. In the body we have the mucous and serous membranes, with their positive and negative secretions, the harmonious relation of which is necessary to its healthy functional action. So in the composition of the cerebral mass, there are two distinct substances, for the brain is the echo of the mind. There is a greyish, cineritious, or ash-colored substance, and a white medullary or fibrous substance. The ash of the former exhibits an alkaline reaction; that of the latter is acid. The one is positive; the other negative. The cineritious portion is relatively external, and has been called the cortical substance, because it is as the bark or rind of the other. The fibrous portion is below it. The first has been pronounced by some the correspondent of the will or love. It is arranged into clusters like grapes, and the fibres radiate from them as beams of light from a luminous center. The nerves extending from the brain and spinal column, are only fascicles or bundles of these two kinds of cerebral substance, inclosed in a sheath called the *neurilemma*. The lower part of the brain corresponds to the intellect, and is the medium through which it acts upon the body. The brain is first formed in the body of the fetus, and the rest of the organism is an outgrowth from it. The life of man is first in the brain, and derivatively through the nervous system, in the rest of the body. The brain is the connecting link which unites the inner man to the outer. As the mind consists of a pleurality of faculties combined into a harmonious unity, so there is a correspondent plurality of organs in the brain, as was demonstrated by Dr Gall. For distinct functions require different instruments for their performance. But as all plurality proceeds from a fundamental unity, or from one as its root, so this does not destroy the unity of either the soul or the body. The most perfect oneness is that which is made by the combination of the greatest number of various and harmonious parts. The doctrine of a plurality of organs in the brain, and a knowledge of their special functions in the manifestations of the mind, is the science of Phrenology—a branch of human knowledge yet in its infancy and formative stage. There are many discoveries not made by Dr. Gall, in relation to the sympathetic connection of the various organs of the body with particular parts of the brain, whence they receive their vital stimulus, which are of great importance in the system of Mental Hygiene.

The whole body is connected with the brain. By means of the grand systems of ganglionic and sympathetic nerves, every organ is united to every other, as by a sort of spiritual telegraph, and the whole with the mind. This explains a mystery. It is known from experience, and comes under the cognition of consciousness, that particular mental states or faculties act into and affect certain organs of the body. It was given the most remarkable man of modern history, " to know this from much experience." The influx of certain feelings, which was first into the appropriate parts of the brain, was seen to affect the organs of the body that were in sympathetic connection with those portions of the cerebral structure. Those parts are like the key of the telegraph. Place your finger upon them, and your influence sends a message which is at once recorded in the distant organ. Your mind in that way acts upon that part of the cerebrum, and the bodily organ, through the telegraphic nerves, responds with a vibratory motion in harmony with your own mental force. We have a thousand times in this way affected sensibly to the consciousness of the patient the functional activity of any part of the body. But to do this, requires a knowledge of the anatomical structure not given the student in his usual course of medical study. The heart, the lungs, the diaphragm, the stomach, the liver, the kidneys, and the intestinal canal, are all bound by sympathy with certain parts of the brain, and the faculties of the mind to which those parts correspond. Thus we are prepared to see more clearly still, the truth of a statement previously made, that the states of the mind are ultimated, or recorded, in corresponding bodily conditions, and are the body's health or malady.

The mind is not only to be divided into the two distinct departments of the love and the intellect, but there are three degrees or planes of mental life, like the three stories of a palace, or, more correctly, like three concentric circles or spheres, each within the other. The doctrine of the degrees of the mind is imaged in the cerebral system. There are in reality three brains. We have first the *cerebrum*, the large brain, composed of the two kinds of substance of which we have spoken. Then we have the *cerebellum* or little brain, about one eighth part of the former in size, and containing both kinds of cerebral substance; but what is peculiar, the cineritious portion is internal, and the fibrous external. Though smaller in size, it has far more vitality. For these three brains are like the mysterious books of the Sybil—as they decrease in quantity, they increase in value. Next we have the primitive brain, the *medulla oblongata*. It is that which is first formed in the fetus, and the other portions of the cerebral system proceed from it in order. It would weigh but little more than the Koinoor, the mountain of light, the celebrated diamond of queen Victoria, but is far more valuable. To one whose inner vision is unveiled, there dart from it in every direction millions of rays of a pure light into every part of the system. It is much smaller than the cerebellum, but a myriad times more sensitive and vital. These three distinct brains, as we have reason to believe, are correspondences and organs of the three degrees of the mind. Either may act by itself, or our mental activity, our memory and consciousness, and perceptivity, may use either as its organ. In our normal state, and our waking hours, we use the cerebrum as the instrument of our thoughts and volitions. This in sleep becomes quiescent, as we have had occasion to notice. in cases of fracture of the skull, where a portion of the cranium has been removed. Its pulsations cease, and all is still as the tomb. Its vital force has retreated backward and downward to the cerebellum. On the dividing line between sleeping and waking, the mysterious dream-land, the mental powers become greatly exalted and quickened, so that the experiences and perceptions of hours, and even weeks and months, are crowded into moments. The mind breaks loose from its material thraldom, the limitations of time, place, and sense, and asserts its innate freedom. It sees without the external eye, and to distances almost unlimited. It perceives distant objects, persons and things, something as we see the image of an absent friend in the mind, only with more objective clearness, and they do not appear to be in the mind, but external to it, like the scenery around us in our every-day life. There are those who can enter this state at will. It has become, in fact, their normal condition. We have experimented much with it, putting it to severe tests, a thousand miles away, and have found it as reliable as our ordinary vision. The power of thus suspending the action of the cerebrum, possessed by a scientific person, is of great value in the diagnosis of disease. It is a condition of the highest wakefulness, though physiologically it is a state of sleep, and has been denominated somnambulism. It may exist when the external senses are not oblivious to the objects surrounding us. It is a waking up from their usually dormant state of the undeveloped powers of our inner life. Like the apocalyptic angel, it breaks the seals of the closed book of nature, and unrolls the parchment on which are written characters that our usual vision cannot read, and the wonders of an inner world pass in panoramic review. The veil of sense, ordinarily opaque, becomes transparent, and through it the interior man looks out upon the universe. It is a state of *illustration*, or interior illumination, which may be permanent, normal, and attended with no loss of consciousness as to our external surroundings. It is governed by fixed laws, which may be the subject of education, but is none the less a gift of God for this. Blessed is the man to whom it has been given, and who consecrates it, with all his activities, to the good of universal being.

In the trance, both the cerebrum and cerebellum are quiescent (when it is with the individual subject an *abnormal* state), and their vital force has passed to the primitive brain, the *medulla oblongata*. The mind is awakened to the most intense degree of activity and power of which it is susceptible, in the present stage of our existence. Usually, but not *necessarily*, there is a loss of consciousness of the outward world. The pulse sometimes becomes nearly or quite imperceptible. The movement of the lungs is tacit, and the spiritual body only breathes. But these are not necessary concomitants of this interior state, for all the degrees of the mind may be consciously active at the same time. Persons may be developed normally into this almost angelic range of the soul's powers and activities. In this degree of the inner life the heavens are opened, the separating veil is rent if not removed, the curtain is rolled up, the invisible appears in sight, and the soul is transported in its vision to the perception of the solid and enduring *realities* of a world veiled in darkness to our common sight. In this degree of the unfoldment of the soul's life, man possesses in a degree the properties and powers of a spirit, and *may act upon others as our guardian angels do*, and seems to be a messenger from another world, to demonstrate to mortals the reality of its existence. Hidden imponderable forces, to a certain extent, come under his control, and he may appear to a sensuous world as a Thaumaturgus, or wonder-worker, and like a partially developed Messiah, he heals all manner of sickness and disease among the people. Such a mind has blossomed into angelic proportions.

The next step beyond, is what men have called death. In every step and degree of progress towards it, the mental powers become more and more exalted, and their range of action extended. Viewed in this scientific light, death is seen to be only transition to a higher life. It cannot be a punishment for our sins, but a necessary step and normal process in human development. Having finished the work committed to our hands, and accomplished our appointed use here in the plan of Providence, when our friends shall call us dead, we shall have only languished into life.

CHAPTER XII.

THE HEART AND LUNGS, AND THEIR RELATION TO THE LOVE AND INTELLECT.

Two Universals of the Mind. — Answering Organs of the Body. — The Extension of the Heart into the System. — The Veins and Arteries. — The Heart corresponds to the affectional Nature. — Proof. — Influence of our Emotional States upon its Action. — And upon Secretion and Nutrition. — Subtle Element of the Blood — The Diffusion of the Pulmonary Substance. — The Lungs derived from the Heart. — They Answer to the Intellect. — Effect of the States of Thought upon Respiration. — Relation of the Respiration to Voluntary Motion. — To the Sensibility of the Nerves. — Influence of Anæsthetic Agents. — How the Mind can increase or diminish vital Action. — Sympathetic Movement of the Heart and Lungs. — How to regulate the Action of the Heart. — How to change our Emotions. — Influence of our Mental States upon the vital Functions. — True Method of Study in Natural science. — The New Age. — Immanence of the Spiritual World.

EVERY THING that can be predicated of the mind has relation either to the love or the intellect. The reasons on which this classification of the mental powers rests, have been given in a previous chapter. The will and the love are identical and it is an interesting fact that the two words are from the same root. Their radical sense is the same. The love and the intellect are the two *universals* of the mind, by which we mean something that enters into the whole and every part of a subject or thing. Since these are the universal and everywhere-present principles and elements of our inner organism, and since the body has correspondence with the mind, and is only the external or ultimate expression of it, we should reasonably expect to find in it the echo of our spiritual structure in two universal organs. Such in fact are the heart and the lungs. An advanced state of anatomical science, the result of more accurate microscopic and chemical investigation, we doubt not, will show that these two organs are in the whole and every part of the body. Though located primarily in the thorax, by derivation and ramification they are present in the whole organism. Such is demonstrably true of the heart. The minutest veins and arteries which permeate every part of the system, all proceed from it and maintain an unbroken connection with it. They are continuations of it, and interpenetrate even the bones, so that the point of the finest needle cannot enter the flesh without coming in contact with fibers and tubes proceeding from this central organ, and by means of which it maintains an omnipresence in the body. Its action must affect the condition of every part.

The heart corresponds or answers to the affectional nature of man. This is recognized in all languages, and unconsciously confessed by all men. It is an intuitive truth. Everywhere we speak of a man of a kind heart, of a friendly heart, or a warm heart. A lack of benevolence and sympathy is denominated hard-heartedness. It is a fact also well known that the various affections, desires, emotions and passions, which are only forms or states of the love, affect the systolic and diastolic action of the heart, or its contraction and dilatation. This is discernible in the pulsations of the arteries and veins, whose motions are synchronous with the parent organ from which they procced. Fear, anxiety, anger, grief, melancholy, joy, contentment, hope, and all the affections, are responded to by the motions of the heart. There is no truth of science capable of a more satisfactory demonstration than this. But as the blood contains the elements of nutrition, and supplies the means of growth and the particles necessary to repair the waste of the various tissues, so that they can be maintained in their integrity, whatever affects its action must modify these physiological processes.

The blood contains a subtile vitalizing element and stimulus that chemistry is not adequate to detect. It is only the unveiled eye of independent clairvoyance that can perceive it, yet it is as necessary to the healthy functional action of every organ as sunlight to a flower. Without it the organs droop and die, like plants smitten with an autumnal frost. It is the due supply of this subtile element, the soul-principle of the blood, something like the animal spirits of the old physiologists, that occasions the healthy glow of warmth in an organ, far more than what we call the blood. Its absence in the feet occasions their coldness, even where they are crowded with blood. Its accumulation is the hidden cause of inflammations and congestions. No organ can perform its functions without a due supply and harmonious distribution of it, any more than the body can move without the spirit. It is the *blood* of the spiritual body, answering the same purpose and accomplishing an analogous use in the interior form, that the blood does in the outward man. We do not call this principle electricity, or magnetism, only for the want of a better name. It is certainly governed by different laws. It is the living aura of the blood, and may be identical with the *odyle* discovered by Reichenbach. But by whatever name we call it, the states of the mind immediately affect it, and mediately through it the rest of the body.

As the heart is everywhere present in the body by its radiation into the venous and arterial systems, so the same is true of the lungs, though in the present state of anatomical science it is not so clearly discernible. The heart is first formed in the fetus, and the lungs are an outgrowth from it. The six millions of blood-cells are only the terminations of the branches of the pulmonary veins and arteries proceeding from the heart. The air-cells, so numerous as to contain a surface of one hundred and forty square feet, when taken together, flow together into the bronchial tubes, and these unite to form the trachea. But they are all formed from the pericardium, the membrane investing and interpenetrating the heart, and which surrounds and lines every vein and artery. The heart and lungs, thus connected in their origin, sympathize in their actions. The more rapid the respiration, the faster beats the heart, and *vice versa.*

As the one corresponds to the love, so the other responds to the action of the intellectual nature. We are assured by our consciousness that our thoughts influence the movement of the lungs. We may be as certain of this as of our own existence. The more

interiorly and intently we think, the less we breathe.
When our thoughts are involuntary and passive, our
respiration is involuntary and tacit. In certain states
of mental abstraction, the breathing is almost or quite
imperceptible, as in the trance. When our thoughts
are concentrated upon some vigorous muscular motion, as striking or lifting, we instinctively precede
the effort with a deep inspiration, which is a hint of
great practical importance. As every state of the
affections influences the movements of the cardiac
system, so every condition of the intellect affects the
action of the lungs. These are primary vital motions
in the organism, whence, by derivation, all other motions exist, the involuntary from the heart, and the
voluntary from the lungs. As involuntary movements
are attended with no fatigue, or loss of nervous force,
as the heart is never tired; so our respiration, when
not the result of our volitions, never wearies us, however long and incessantly it is continued. But voluntary and artificial breathing is the most exhausting
movement we are capable of making. To rest ourselves, is to cease from the latter, and to subside into
the former. An entire cessation of the contractions
of the muscular tissue of the heart, suspends the
movements of the involuntary vital organs, but a suspension of respiration, so that the breathing becomes

tacit, only takes away the power of voluntary muscular motion, and many persons can do it for hours, as the Fakirs of India. It is attended with great intellectual elevation. In proportion as the breathing is diminished or suspended, the body becomes insensible to pain. Surgical operations, in this state, would be less painful, in fact this suspended respiration and consequent insensibility, is what is affected by chloroform. There have been persons who could induce upon themselves this state without the use of any anæsthetic agent. To direct the attention to a part, increases its vital action, and its sensitiveness. To abstract the mind from it, deprives it of feeling in proportion to the degree of mental absent-mindedness. To keep our thoughts from an inflamed and painful organ, is antiphlogistic, or cooling. The vital action is lowered. To direct the mind and will to a negative part, as cold feet, a paralytic limb, or wherever there is a lack of vital force, infuses life into it. Thus the mind contains in itself, when its spiritual forces are intelligently directed to a given aim, more potential virtues than can be found in a drug shop. It can take away or add to the vital action of any organ, and what more do the advocates of drug medication profess to do, from their *heroic practice*, which borders on man-slaughter, to the homeopathic and

infinitesimal doses, that are next to nothing, if not
an absolute nihility. But all these results in Mental
Hygiene, are accomplished by the mind through its
influence upon the action of the heart and lungs.

A careful study of the connection between the
heart and the lungs, their relations to each other,
their reciprocal influence, and their correspondence
with the two general departments of the mind, would
be fruitful in results. The heart is a muscle whose
contractions and relaxations are not subject directly to
our control. The action of the lungs is both voluntary
and involuntary, as they are supplied with both kinds
of nerves. When we control their movement, they
receive the necessary stimulus from the cerebrum,
which is the organ of our voluntary life. When their
movements are passive, the nerve-force comes through
the cerebellum, the organ of our involuntary life.
Harmonizing with this action of the pulmonary system, there is active and passive thought. Our affections and emotions are not directly under the control
of our volitions. We cannot love or hate, be joyful
or sad, at the nod of the will. We have emotions
and feelings at times, from which we would gladly
be delivered, and there are other affectional states we
would fain possess, but they will not come at our call.
The affections may be indirectly influenced by the

intellect. So the action of the heart may be changed through the lungs. There is a sympathetic influence of the one upon the other. The heart and lungs do not contract and expand synchronously, but in the ratio of three to one, or the movement of the heart may be represented by a measure in music composed of three notes, while that of the lungs is a measure containing one long note. But this does not destroy the harmony of the rhythm. As there is a sympathetic connection between the motions of the two organs, and as the lungs obey the behest of the will we are furnished with the means of indirectly affecting the action of the heart. If the heart beats too quickly and feebly, we have only to breathe more slowly and deeply, and the heart will adjust its systolic and diastolic movements in harmony with the respiration, so as to preserve the ratio of three to one. If the pulsations of the cardiac system are too slow, then breathe faster, and the heart will conform to the action of the lungs. They are like two horses harnessed together to draw the chariot of life, but only one of them obeys the rein, yet they feel an impulse to act in harmony. If one starts ahead, the other soon follows. The reins are attached to only one. If you wish to change the movements of the other, you must do it through the one connected with your hand. So if we wish to change our emotions and feelings, we can do it through the intellect. Change the direction of our thoughts, and the affections will follow. How to induce upon ourselves any desired mental state, will be the subject of consideration hereafter.

In what has been said in the brief limits of this chapter we may see more clearly the influence of the states of the mind over the vital functions and processes of the body. Any system of medical practice that does not recognize this great truth, is fundamentally and radically defective. Physiology and anatomy must be unsatisfactory and superficial, while they ignore the spiritual organism of man. The true method of study in Natural Science is to investigate the phenomena of the outer world in relation to the inner realm, of matter in its connection with spirit. When we rise to the perception of things in their causes, we can then understand effects. We believe without a doubt, and affirm without hesitation, that there has been introduced among men a new and better method of philosophizing, of greater value to the world than the Organum of Bacon. It is destined to revolutionize the sciences, and lead to a reconstruction of their systems. The science of the correspondence between the material and the spiritual departments of nature, stretches in an endless and ever-widening perspective into the dim distance of futurity, which is closed to all but prophetic intuitions. We live in a transitional era. Old things are passing away, and a New Age has come to the birth. But we now perceive only the first feeble rays of the opening morn, which shoot into the solid darkness of the past, that still settles heavily down upon the mind of the race. The chilling fogs will gradually lift, and show the willing feet of coming generations the way to mountain summits. The spiritual world is drawing nearer and mixing itself with human affairs. The heavens are opening and their living light is falling upon the sightless eyeballs of our hitherto blind guides. The door of the upper realm of being stands ajar, and the uncreated light, in which angelic mind delights to bathe, is leaking through. It is a knowledge of spiritual things that illustrates nature. When we understand the soul of things, we shall be prepared to comprehend more of its outward manifestations. Already has the angel-world given us the thread of Ariadne, to conduct philosophy out of its labyrinth. A new spiritual science has been born in a manger, but, thanks be to God, cannot be led to the cross by a pharisaic church or learned bigots. The infant in his swaddling-cloth has in him a germ of Divinity, and the feeble pulsations of an immortal life.

CHAPTER XIII.

CORRESPONDENCE OF THE STOMACH AND THE MIND.

The Office of the Stomach. — The Digestive Process. — What answers to it in the Mental Economy ? — Therapeutic Influence of new Ideas. — Mental Medicine. — Two Stomachs. — Dual Nature of Memory. — Common Forms of Speech recognizing the Relation of the Stomach to the Memory. — Mental and Bodily Growth. — Mental Vigor necessary to Digestion. — Perpetual Spiritual Adolescence. — What is Old Age ? — How to be always Young. — Diseases which are attended with a Loss of the Power of Attention and Memory.

EVERY PART of the body has correspondence with the spiritual nature of man, and is the ultimate expression of some mental faculty, from which it exists and derives its stimulus, or the force that enables it to accomplish its appropriate use in the animal economy. The stomach performs an important function in the vital machinery, answering to certain mental powers and processes. In it, the food we eat undergoes a chemical change to fit it to be appropriated by the various organs, and its nutritive elements to be assimilated into the several tissues. When it performs its functions faithfully, the body is kept in a healthful condition, and the proper balance is maintained. When in an abnormal state, it affects every other organ, and the body becomes unfitted for the uses of the mind. The process of digestion, or the reduction of the food to a substance containing the elements of the blood, is a triple one. The aliment is first received by the mouth, where it is masticated and mixed with the secretion from the salivary glands, which seems to be a preparatory process without which digestion is imperfect. The saliva is slightly alkaline, and has the power of changing the amylaceous or starchy elements of the food into grape sugar, and sugar into lactic acid. This is the commencement of the digestive process. By the act of deglutition or swallowing, it then passes into the first stomach, where it is agitated by a vermicular movement of the organ and is subjected to the action of a peculiar solvent called the gastric juice. Here it is reduced to a uniform pulpy mass denominated chyme. It then passes through the pyloric orifice on the right side into the duodenum or second stomach. Here the contents of the gall cist are emptied into it, and also the pancreatic juice which contains some important vital or nerve stimulus. It is now reduced to a milky substance called chyle, which only awaits the change effected in it by the lungs to transform it into arterial blood. After leaving the duodenum, it enters the intestinal canal, some twenty feet in length, which is lined by the mesenteric glands that drink it up and it is conveyed into the subclavian vein, whence it passes to the heart and lungs. It receives the influx of spiritual life by the action of the pulmonary organs. If these processes have been complete, it becomes healthful blood, from which every organ selects what it needs for its nutrition. Such is a brief account of the important process of digestion, so needful to the normal functional activity of the various members and organs of the body.

But we are to bear in mind that everything in the external organism has correspondence with and a vital relation to some part of the spiritual nature, on which its existence and power to act depends. "The body without the spirit is dead." All its vital processes have a mental origin. The stomach and its use in the animal economy have a spiritual correspondence and significance. But what is there in the mental organism answering to it as cause to an effect? The memory performs an office in the interior man analogous to that of the stomach in the outward bodily structure. It is the first receptacle of all knowledges—a word we use in the plural as well as singular form, after the example of Lord Bacon. It is the only entrance into the mind of truths from without, and is as the courtyard and portico of a house. Through it all those truths which we receive by instruction and reading, and which are our spiritual food and drink, enter into the interior man, where they are appropriated and serve to nourish the hidden life. Thus in its spiritual use the memory answers to the stomach. The one acts on a spiritual, and the other on a material plane. Genuine truth is the proper nutriment of the mind. Sometimes the reception and appropriation of a new truth by a patient excites his whole being, mental and physical, to a higher and healthier activity. The addition of a few new ideas have a hygienic and therapeutic influence far beyond that of the most potent drug. The gateway over the entrance to the famous Alexandrian library bore the expressive inscription, " Medicine for the Mind." "And certainly many books," remarks Mr. Alger, deserve to be so characterized. Many a mind has found books charged with sanative influences. Their contents have proved a spell to release the spirit from the brood and harassment of its cares, to allay its heat, lessen the throbbing speed of its emotions, cheer its depression, counteract its delusions, distil blessed anodynes into its hurts, and feed its exhausted energy with restoratives." But truths received by influx from the spiritual realm, and from angelic mind, need not, like those from books and tutors, pass through a process of mental digestion. They enter at once into our life, like the infusion of a healthy arterial blood from one person into another.

We have noticed a fact generally overlooked, that there are two stomachs. Answering to this, there are two memories, an external one that receives and retains simple facts or the record of things done, and an internal one which contains the registry of the ends, motives, or loves from which we act. The one is the recollection, or at least, the record, of truths received, the other of the loves from which all thought and external activity proceed. The latter or interior memory is the mysterious book of our life, for every thing which a man ever did, thought, spoke, or felt, and all that he has heard and seen, is indelibly inscribed upon this imperishable tablet, and may become perceptible to angelic intuitions. For every thing proceeding from the love is a manifestation of the life of man, and is inscribed upon his inmost being, and must be as lasting as the life itself. Thus our inward history is written in a book more durable than the Ararat or the Andes. Before a truth can nourish our spiritual life, and minister to the growth of the mind, it must not only be intellectually received, but embraced by the affections. This is as necessary as that food should undergo the second part of the digestive process, before it is fitted to be appropriated into the organic structure. The distinction of memory into external and internal, is not common in systems of mental science, where its dual functions are generally overlooked, but it is based upon the nature of the mind, and imaged and echoed in the bodily organism.

The correspondence of the stomach and the memory is recognized unconsciously by certain forms of speech in common use. There lies hidden in the words that men instinctively use much genuine philosophy. Many intuitive truths are seen here struggling for utterance and desiring recognition. The word digestion comes from the Latin *dis* and *gero*, the supine of which is *gestum*, and signifies both to distribute, to reduce to order, as a *digest* of statute or common law, and also to dissolve. And we are urged sometimes to mark and inwardly digest certain truths, as a homily or discourse. Truths received into the external memory are digested when they are reduced to order, embraced by the love, and appropriated by the mind as principles of life. Then they contribute to the nourishment and real growth of the mind, just as healthful food, when dissolved in the stomach and fitted to be taken up by the lacteals, furnishes the elements necessary to repair the waste of the tissues and to supply the materials of growth. And we firmly believe that a healthy mental nourishment and consequent progress, is essential to the vigorous functional activity of the digestive apparatus. But we are to avoid overeating and cramming, in the mind as well as the body. Intervals must be given between the introduction of great truths to afford time for *rumination*, which is a spiritual chewing the cud. One great and living verity will afford nutriment for a week or a month sometimes. If there be a real connection between a healthy mental progress and a vigorous digestion, it may be asked, why it is that literary men have weak stomachs? The shortest way to explain this, would be to deny the fact. When it is demonstrated to be a truth, we will take the time to show the cause. We challenge the world to prove that there is any necessary connection between literary labor and dyspepsia. One thing we know, that the period of life when the memory is usually the most active and tenacious of truth is that of youth. Then also the digestive organs are the most vigorous. And we have had occasion to observe many times in our dyspeptic patients, that there was a loss of power in the memory. There was at the same time a mental and bodily indigestion, and there is here the relation of cause and effect, but which is antecedent and which posterior we leave every one to decide for himself. Youth is more a mental state than a condition of the body. Adolescence, a term used to denote this stage of human life, (from the Latin verb *adolesco*, to grow), may be predicated of the inner man as well as of the outward form. And youth is really a state of mental and spiritual growth, resulting from the desire of knowing and becoming wise, and lasts as long as that progression continues, and ever ultimates itself in the bodily organism. For a proper exercise and vigor of the mental powers is necessary to the most healthful state of the outward man. It is only when a state of spiritual adolescence ceases, that we begin to grow old. But the Creator manifestly designed that the youthful condition of the interior man should never end, in this world or the next. It is well known that a tree never ceases to grow while its life continues. Every new leaf and twig it puts forth furnishes it with the means of future enlargement. Thus the Washingtonia Gigantea of California, though it has continued for more than twenty centuries, leaves the record of its yearly growth in a new layer of woody fiber added to its circumference. Thus man should grow spiritually by adding some new truth every day to the sum of his knowledge, and applying it to the practical uses and charities of life. The first few years of our existence is not the only time to do this; but every age is the appropriate period for storing the mind with living verities. However old we are, however numerous are the days of the years of our earthly pilgrimage, we are only in the infancy and formative stage of our being. Our earth-life in its whole duration is the seed-time. The future harvests the germs our hands have sown. Life is probationary, and always will be so, that is, our present state is the chrysalis to be unfolded into our future condition. Every subsequent state will be born from the present, and the morning of every new day will issue from the womb of the preceding evening. Thus through the endless cycles of the eternal future, life will be a succession of seed-time and harvest, sowing and reaping, evening and morning. The coming age, however far off, has its roots deep-set in the present. Every passing moment contains in its bosom, if we but fully understood its influence and import, an unerring prophecy of what the next shall be. Perpetual progress is the law and normal condition of all created mind. Without this perpetual development of our mental powers, there can be no perfect health of spirit or body.

It is proper to remark that memory is a general property of the mind, and belongs to all the faculties, intellectual and affectional. Each cerebral organ or instrument retains, and, under certain conditions, reproduces the impressions made upon it. A loss of this property of our spiritual organism, indicates a want of tone and vigor in the mind. And this torpidity of the mind enfeebles the action of the organs concerned in the digestive process. And there can be no healthful vigor of the mental powers, without that intellectual progress which we have characterized as perpetual youth. The confirmed dyspeptic is prematurely old, and exhibits all the signs of senility. There is no hope for him, until his affectional and intellectual nature is rejuvenated. If they can be restored to the normal youthful state of the inner man, and his "youth be renewed as the eagles," and this not as a transient, momentary mood, but a confirmed spiritual condition, we will warrant it to cure the worst form of indigestion with all its horrors.

And such a mental metamorphosis can be effected upon the patient in harmony with certain laws which we hope to be able to unfold. Persons can be made to feel young at the age of threescore years and ten. For youth is an affectional and intellectual state that ought to be perpetual. It is our normal condition in earth and heaven.

In the remarks made above, it has been stated that there is a correspondence between the stomach and the memory, or a sympathetic connection between the digestive organs and that intellectual faculty. They mutually act and react upon each other. But memory depends, to a great extent, upon the power of directing the mind to a fact or object, so as to gain a distinct and full perception of it. It has long ago been observed by physiologists, that all those diseases which affect the digestive organs, are attended with a loss of the power of directing the mind steadily and for any length of time in a particular direction, and there is consequently a weakened state of the memory. This takes place in the earlier stages of all febrile diseases. It also occurs in persons broken down by intemperance, and in the first approaches of old age. It is observed in a remarkable degree in connection with all disordered states of the stomach. This shows the vital relation between the faculty of memory and the stomach. The latter receives from the former the spiritual stimulus that is necessary to its vigorous and healthy action. And an intelligent application of the principles of Mental Hygiene will be found a far more efficient agency in the cure of all forms of dyspepsia, than the administration of drugs and medicines.

CHAPTER XIV.

THE REFLEX INFLUENCE OF THE STOMACH UPON THE MIND.

Sensitiveness of the Epigastric Nerves. — Seeress of Prevorst. — Reading with the Pit of the Stomach. — The interior Essence of things. — Their Influence. — Psychometry. — Effect of Medicines held in the Hand. — Philosophy of Amulets. — Action of the hidden Properties of things upon the Reticular Membranes of the Stomach. — Effect of Food upon the Mind. — The Philosophy of Dieting. — Mental Stimulus necessary to Digestion. — The Condition of the Stomach and our Feelings. — Action and Reaction. — The Law of Sympathy between us and those in the interior Realms. — Effect of happy Frames of Mind upon the Epigastric Nerves. — Mental States attending Various Conditions of the Stomach. — Hunger and its Mental Effects. — The States of the Stomach and Crime. — Hygienic value of Cheerfulness and other Affectional States.

THE STOMACH, in consequence of its delicate net-work of nerves, supplied from the ganglionic system, is one of the most sensitive and easily affected organs of the body. It may with some show of propriety be denominated another brain. The more a person's spiritual nature is developed, the more susceptible it becomes of impression from the semi-spiritual and generally unrecognized properties of things. In the Seeress of Prevorst, the phenomena of whose life have been so accurately and scientifically delineated by Dr. Justinus Kerner, we have a striking instance of the extreme sensitiveness of the nerve-center in the epigastric region, and of the reticular membranes of the digestive organs. She was able to read writing when laid upon the pit of the stomach. In fact she averred that she made no use of her brain, but lived wholly in the epigastric region. And an old philosopher gravely and seriously maintained, that the soul was located in the pit of the stomach. This is partly true and partly false. The mind is there, but it is also in every part of the body. In the case of the seeress, it is undoubtedly true, that the cerebrum, the organ of our voluntary life, was quiescent. But the cerebellum, which affords the peculiar brain-stimulus to all the involuntary vital processes and movements, was the organ of her thoughts and feelings. The nerves of the stomach, in her case, were extremely, and perhaps morbidly acute and sensitive. But it was only a larger degree of what really exists in every human body. It was only the intensity of this property of the epigastric nerves that was peculiar to her.

Before speaking of the states of the stomach in their influence upon the manifestations of the mind, it will be well to observe, that in all material things there is a spiritual essence. There is a sort of half psychical principle in all the objects around us through which mind acts upon them, and they react upon the mind. This interior principle is the life of the outward objects of nature, as is implied in the term essence (from the Latin *esse*, to be), and external things are only its manifestation to the sensuous degree of the mind. In stones, metals, plants, and animal substances, there exist many subtle, but important and influential elements and forces, that elude the grasp of our ordinary senses, and only become perceptible to those whose minds are elevated above the sensuous plane to a more interior range of action. These invisible forces act with greater power upon some than others, owing to their peculiarly impressible organization. But all human bodies are like a delicately constructed Eolian harp, moved by the lightest airs that blow upon it: and our varying moods and frames of mind, our shifting joys and sorrows, and often even our volitions, are under the influence of powers to us altogether imperceptible, but whose subtle effects we cannot escape. Dr. J. R. Buchanan made the discovery in 1840, that certain persons possessed so acute a sensibility to these invisible effluvia and influences, that they were able to distinguish and name the different metals, and various substances, as sugar, salt, pepper, and acids, when inclosed in paper and brought in contact with them. Out of a class of one hundred and thirty students at the Eclectic Medical College of Cincinnati, forty-three of them signed a statement, that when various medicines were enveloped in paper, so as to be wholly unknown to them, by holding them, for a length of time, in their hands, the peculiar effects were produced upon them that would have followed their administration in the ordinary way. When an emetic was the subject of experiment, the individual was able to avoid vomiting only by removing the medicine. There are those so sensitive that even the sight of certain drugs affects them. It is on this principle that amulets have been worn through the whole history of mankind. Their effects are not purely imaginary, but upon susceptible persons vitally real, though the law that governs their influence has but recently been made known to science. There are numerous individuals, who would declare, under oath if necessary, that a horse-chestnut carried in the pocket, is a preventive of piles. We know those who assert, that whenever they lose their precious amulet, they experience a recurrence of their hemorrhoidal difficulties. If this is a wild fancy, and only acts upon the body by the faith of the patient in its potent virtues, such a remedy is a medicine not bad to take. Frederica Hauffe, the Seeress of Prevorst, whose opened interior perceptions detected the hidden subtle properties of various substances, and their influence upon the mind and body, often prescribed the wearing of different things as amulets about the person. She made much use of laurel leaves, as their effects were such as to open more fully her inner vision, and this may account for their use in the temples of Delphi and of Esculapius. She also found the hazel-nut tree, which has long been used among the people for purposes of divination, to produce a powerful magnetic effect. Here is an interesting field for scientific investigation. It is to be hoped that some one adapted to such inquiries will enter the already opened door, and take possession of the long hidden treasure. If any one will carefully read the work of the pious and amiable physician of Weinsburg, together with Denton's 'Soul of Things,' he will gain some light upon the relation we sustain to external nature, and will find in many mysterious frames of mind and states of body, the conscious effects of unseen causes.

The membranes of the stomach, so highly nervous in their structure, are extremely susceptible to the influence of the hidden properties of things. Substances coming in contact with its reticular membranes, affect the mind immediately, and long before they have been changed by the digestive process. Thus morphine is no sooner swallowed, than the spiritual essence it contains affects the mind. The same is true of tea, coffee, alchohol, and all other narcotics, and in fine, all articles of food and drink. The eating of some forbidden fruit by Eve, may be a myth that has some scientific meaning after all, and may have had something to do with her backsliding and mental deterioration. There are substances, which through the stomach, or rather its nerves, affect the manifestation of the amative, or combative, or destructive propensities. Some, as rice, affect the reflective powers, others the powers of volition used in muscular movements, others still are anti-spasmodic in their effects. It is said of wine that it " maketh glad the heart of man." But its exhilarating effects are more mental than physical, or rather, it affects the body through the mind. There is no doubt that the flesh of animals is pervaded to some extent with their peculiar spiritual properties. The Ichthyophagi, or fish-eaters, were sensual and stupid. The modern

Esquimaux are widely different from the rice-eating Hindoos. Carnivorous human beings, as well as animals, are unlike the herbivorous and graminivorous races. It is our conviction that no one can attain to a highly spiritual state who makes much use of a flesh diet. The state of the stomach, and what we place within its sensitive cavity, are not a matter of indifference. And yet nothing but the most general rules can be given as to the diet of patients. There are idiosyncracies, or peculiarities of mental and bodily character, that must not be overlooked. That diet must be recommended which is adapted to the peculiarities of the case, and this can properly be done only by an intuitive perception of what the person needs, and of the adaptedness of certain things to meet the special want. The presence of food or medicine in the stomach excites or reacts upon the mind, and before those substances can be anything more than a lifeless, putrifying mass, it must receive the influx of those mental states and be animated by them, and be prepared to diffuse them with the circulation of the new particles through the whole physiological domain. Fermentation is not digestion. The gastric juice of the dead subject in the dissecting-room will digest nothing, because the influx of the spiritual principle has ceased. The living mind has much more to do with the mysterious chemistry of digestion, than is generally apprehended. All negative and depressing mental states, fear, grief, anxiety, melancholy, interfere with the healthful action of the digestive organs, while persons of a prevailing mirthful disposition, are seldom found in the number of dyspeptic patients.

We sustain a living connection with the spiritual world, and the men and women who have gone to inhabit it, and certain states of the stomach render us peculiarly receptive of influences from that realm of being. They constitute a plane into which influx naturally descends, and a form or attitude of the outward man that attracts the feelings of which they are the physiological manifestation—a law we shall more fully explain hereafter. Every abnormal state of mind, by an invariable law of our being, constitutes a bond of sympathetic and living connection with similarly diseased mind in the interior world. A stomach overloaded, and holding an indigested and putrifying mass, affects the diaphragm by drawing away from it its nervous force and thus destroying its contractility. The diaphragm losing its convexity, or falling down, the lungs are not emptied in expiration, and the chest feels oppressed and heavy as well as the mind. But this is a physiological expression of the sentiment of fear, of which anxiety and melancholy are modifications, and consequently those feelings flow into this receptive form and aggravate the pathological state that already exists. For between the inner and outer man, there operates the law of action and reaction. A distinguished seer and philosopher has said, "When anxieties occupy the mind, the region about the stomach is tightly bound and sometimes pain is perceived there, also anxieties appear to arise thence; and hence also when a man is no longer solicitous about the future, or when all things go well with him, so that he is no longer afraid of any misfortune, the region about the stomach is free and expanded, and he experiences delight." A happy state of mind, as every one knows, occasions a pleasant thrill in the epigastric nerves Ask any man you meet, where he feels happy, and in ninety-nine cases out of a hundred he will put his hand over the region of the stomach, supposing perhaps that he is putting it on his heart. Ask a child the same question, and he will give the same answer. It is, in fact, the seat of our pleasant emotions, or the point where, more than in any other, they ultimate themselves in the body. But unless this region is kept in a condition to receive the influx of such feelings, it becomes admissive only of the opposite, which arise from beneath, like vapors from the sulphurous waters of an extinct volcano.

When the mucous surface of the digestive apparatus is inflamed and dry, it is attended with an irritable, impatient, excited, and hurried state of feeling. This hurry of spirits, so common in most chronic diseases, especially those of a nervous character, has its seat in the brain in or near the organ of individuality. And magnetism applied here affects the stomach. To induce upon ourselves the opposite state of feeling, as an habitual spiritual condition, will cure the disease. The cravings of hunger create a temporary inflammation of the kind just mentioned. And every one must have observed both in himself and others, that when feeling the demands of appetite, he is more impatient and irritable. Animals of prey are also more fierce when their stomachs are empty, and they feel the pangs of hunger. It is not unreasonable to suppose, that many crimes, especially those of violence and assault, which constitute a large fraction of those before our police courts, find here their secret spring. It is a disease of mind and body, and the unfortunate beings should be sent to the hospital, rather than to prison, or rather, our penitentiaries should be turned into hospitals for the souls of men. No dynasty in France could stand a week against the furious hunger of the Parisian masses. This the reigning powers have long known, learning the lesson from Roman history, and have always aimed to regulate the price of breadstuffs, so as to bring the necessaries of life within the reach of all. Inflamed stomachs and violence in the social body go together. Hunger, by the heat it occasions in the mucous surface, excites both combativeness and destructiveness— a hint it would be well for that respectable, impersonal, and collective man we call society, to heed. A congested, heated state of the mucous membrane of the stomach, and impatience, irritability of temper, an instinctive tendency to attack, and to destroy, and a headlong hurry to do something, no matter what, are not accidental coincidences, but are cause and effect. One is action and the other reaction, one prior and the other posterior. There is here the relation of cause and effect, but an effect may become in turn a reactionary cause. He who adopts the principle as an axiomatic truth, that all causes are spiritual, will not hesitate in deciding which is prior and which is a sequence. Of one thing we may be assured, that the opposite state of the affections, one of calmness, patience, loving gentleness, cheerful contentment, and an innocent mirthfulness that leaves no regret to cast a gloom over its spiritual sunshine, will avail more in the cure of this form of dyspepsia, than all the drugs, pills, powders, and potions, that would be necessary to fill the gulf of Mexico. We have seen that all diseased conditions connect us with disordered and unhappy mind in the other world. To cure disease is to "cast out devils" or to break our sympathetic consociation with undeveloped spirits. But the demons that revel in the emanations of a diseased stomach, like vultures in the odor of a dead and decaying buffalo, will fly at the approach, or the return to the patient, of the playful innocence of restored childhood and youth. He who is so benevolently happy, that he longs to share his bliss with the whole realm of created mind, can put them to rout like the sword of Michael in the battle of the angels, that felled squadrons at a blow. An undeveloped spirit will fly from the loving joyfulness of the soul, like a bird of night from the light of the sun, or will quietly and harmlessly stay to warm himself in its heavenly radiance.

CHAPTER XV.

EXCRETIONS OF THE BODY AND THE MIND, AND THEIR RELATION.

The Excreting Organs and their Use. — Their irregular Action a fruitful Source of Disease. — Influence of the Mind upon them. — The Lower Intestine and the Brain.— Influence of certain Mental States upon it. — Diseases of the Rectum and their Mental Cause. — How Cured. — Office of the Liver. — Chemical Nature of the Bile. — Sympathy between the Liver and Kidneys. — Its Connection with the Brain. — Correspondence with the Mind. — Influence of Conscience upon the Hepatic Functions. — State of the Mind in Duodenitis. — The Cure. — Melancholy and the Liver. — Elimination of the effete Products of the Mind. — Mental Influence upon the Renal Functions. — Diabetes. — The Connection of the Kidneys with the Brain. — Causality. — Excretory Action of the Intellect. — Renewal of the Spirit. — Perpetual Progress.

THERE ARE several organs whose physiological use is to separate from the blood the worn out, broken down, and devitalized particles, which can be of no further use in the system, and whose continnance there is positively injurious to the vital functions.

If left to accumulate, the body becomes so far dead, as those corpuscles are no longer capable of receiving and retaining the influx of vital force from the animating spirit. Their connection and correspondence with the soul-principle is already sundered. The healthful state of the general system requires that they should be expelled from it, and their place supplied by new particles. A great proportion of the diseases, for which the medical profession are called upon to prescribe, can be traced, in their secondary causes, to a want of proper action in the excretory organs, whose duty it is to throw off the effete and poisonous matter. A scrofulous diathesis or disposition, which is the root of numerous acute and chronic ailments, is nothing but an imperfect action of the excreting organs, which are five in number,—the liver, the kidneys, the lungs, the perspiratory glands of the skin, and the large intestine or colon. If any one or all these discharge their functions imperfectly, disease, and finally death, is the result. The dead and the living atoms cannot mingle in harmonious fellowship. One or the other must be predominant. The devitalized particles must be eliminated before the new and vital corpuscles can take their place. There are diseased conditions where the accumulation of effete matter gradually increases, and a person dies, atom after atom, until all vital action ceases.

It is to be remembered that every physiological process is but a correspondence or effect of some psychological action. The latter is prior, and the former is an established sequence. And if that mental state which sustains a causal relation to the healthy tone of the excreting organs can be discovered, and is capable of being induced upon a patient, it will be of more value in the healing art than all the drugs and patent nostrums in the universe. Can we discern the connection of the spirit's movements with these organs? It is well known that grief induces an inflamed condition of the intestinal canal. A fit of weeping is followed by thirst, which is only the system calling for water to quench the inward fire. A constipated condition of the bowels is a universal accompaniment of insanity and of most melancholic patients, while an over-excitement of the intellectual powers produces the opposite pathological result. Some of the most vigorous thinkers whom we have known were invariably attacked with diarrhea after a lecture or sermon. These phenomena are sufficient to establish a sympathetic connection between the states of the mind and the physiological action of the lower intestine. A despairing habit of mind, and a tendency to forebode evil, will generate a weakened action of the bowels, while the opposite mental state will give to them a healthful vigor and tone. The bowels receive their cerebral stimulus from a part of the brain situated between hope and veneration. And in constipation, when long continued, we have often observed a congested and inflamed state of this portion of the brain. An abnormal or inverted action of hope is communicated to the part of the cerebrum adjacent to it, from which the bowels derive their power to act. By magnetic manipulations of this point of the brain, removing the unnatural heat, and stimulating the organ of hope to a boundless faith in the "good time coming," and thus infusing a healthy mental stimulus into the bowels, will produce all the good effects, with none of the evil reactive results, of cathartic medicines. Such drugs, through the spiritual essence they contain, act upon the mind and this part of the brain. A very moderate dose of rhubarb will sometimes lift the mountain of despair temporarily from the most gloomy patient. But this can be done more effectually and permanently by a psychological influence intelligently applied. All diseases having a mental origin, require spiritual remedies.

There are certain affections and painful derangements of the rectum, that indicate the connection between certain abnormal conditions of the body and their accompanying disordered mental action. Among these are hemorrhoids, sometimes ultimating in an ulcerous condition of the rectum. We have had occasion to observe many times, that this troublesome and painful affection is attended with great irritability of temper and impatience, and there is always in this disease a tendency to that spiritual state. Let us see if we can trace any necessary connection between such a mental state and the disease under consideration. Is there here the relation of cause and effect? In this disease there is always an abnormal state of the liver. Impatience, irritability, and fretfulness exhibit a morbid excitability of what is called combativeness. Now the liver receives its nerve-stimulus from a part of the brain between combativeness and caution. There is often a severe pain here in the headache occasioned by a derangement of the hepatic functions. The excited state of the so-called organ of combativeness robs the point of the cerebrum, with which the liver is in sympathetical connection, of its vital force. When the patient is irritable or fretful, opposed to everything, and contented with nothing, the organ in the brain, through which these feelings are manifested, draws into itself the nerve-life from the adjacent parts of the brain that supply the peculiar force necessary to the healthy action of the liver. Thus our pettishness and peevishness rob the liver of its vital power, and this occasions our hemorrhoidal troubles.

To cure this painful complaint, the patient's attention should be directed to the spiritual cause. The root of the trouble should be shown him, and he should induce upon himself the opposite mental state. If one would be his own physician, and cure himself, let him lay aside all nostrums—which only aggravate the trouble in their final results—and attend to his feelings. The cause being removed, the effect will cease. If he has not sufficient mental control to do this, he should permit the magnetic or psychological healer to induce upon him a calm, gentle, and patient frame, and to *convert* his soul to a meek and quiet spirit.

The office of the hepatic apparatus is to separate from the blood a certain portion of the waste, worn out particles, which are collected into the gall-cist, from which they are emptied into the contents of the duodenum or second stomach. All that can be worked over into healthy blood passes with the chyle into the general circulation. The remainder is ejected from the system with the excrementitious matter of the rectum. The bile is alkaline in its chemical nature, while the urinary secretion contains an acid principle. As there is an affinity between an acid and an alkali, so there is a sympathetic connection between the liver and kidneys, and both are usually diseased together. The careful student of human nature will not fail to observe, that the organs are connected in pairs in the discharge of their functions. We have already spoken of the heart and lungs, and shown the dual nature of the brain. The liver and kidneys act in concert. The same is true of the spleen and pancreas. As the mind is composed of the two distinct departments of the love, or affectional nature, and the intellect, so the organs of the body receive the influx of spiritual life from the one or the other. The liver corresponds to the emotions or feelings, and the kidneys are influenced indirectly by these or through the intellectual principle. As every affection has its correspondent or harmonious mode of thinking or intellection, so the action of the liver is attended with an answering or echoing movement of the kidneys. If the one is torpid, the other is inactive. The mental states that influence the one, act upon the other. This concordant movement of the two organs deserves to be noted, as it is certain that every morbid spiritual state that occasions a deranged action of the hepatic functions will indirectly affect the renal action.

As an evidence that the states of the mind affect the chemical action of the excreting organs, we have the demonstrated fact, that the effete products separated from the blood by the kidneys vary in character with the amount of cerebral action. Excessive activity of the mind is uniformly accompanied by the excretion of an unusual quantity of the alkaline phosphates. All abnormal nervous excitement produces the same effect, rapidly using up the element of phosphoric acid in the brain. Every one must have noticed the 'peculiar odor of the insane," implying certain morbid products in the perspiration, and showing the influence of unsound mental conditions upon the action of the perspiratory glands. No organ can, in a healthy manner, perform its appointed use in the human body, unless it is preceded by an equally normal state of the part of our mental nature to which it belongs and of which it is the external manifestation. The office of the excretory organs is to throw off the worn out material, preparatory to the introduction of new particles, so that the body is actually renewed many times during our earthly existence. But the mind should also be renewed. The idea of spiritual renovation is no modern discovery. Paul even speaks of the inward man being renewed day by day, and enjoins upon us the duty of putting off the old man, or our worn out states, and of being renewed in the *spirit* of our minds, or our affectional nature and its emotions. There are faculties of the mind whose office is excretory. It is the office of what men call conscience to give us an instinctive perception of what is good and evil, and to influence us to receive the one and reject the other. By good we mean that which affords us delight, and by evil that which is undelightful. We have nothing to do with that which bears these names in the current theologies. Every healthy mind possesses in itself, and as a part of its organism, an intuitive perception of what is needed for its happiness, and an instinctive repugnance to what seems undelightful. Call it by what name you will,—intuition, perception, an internal dictate, or conscience,—in the spiritual nature it performs an office similar to the hepatic functions in the bodily organism. It rejects what it deems evil, and incites to what seems to us our good. That the correspondence of the liver and conscience is not imaginary, nor merely the expression of analogy in their action and use, but is vitally and sympathetically real, is made manifest from this—that in certain derangements of the liver we often witness a similar abnormal state of the faculty of conscience. It is sometimes morbidly sensitive, at other times it may be torpid and indifferent to good or evil. Its organ in the brain is also affected with inflammation and congestion. The unhappy patient suffers a constant sense of self-imposed condemnation. He imagines that the theological scare-crows, hung up by the pulpit, are, in his case at least, living realities, that he is the most wicked of men, has blasphemed the Holy Ghost, committed the sin unto death, is obnoxious to the wrath of God, and is guilty of all manner of imaginary evil. Such persons suffer untold misery, seeming often to their friends as unnecessary, from the diseased sensitiveness of the conscience, and are overwhelmed with a sense of guilt, though the outward life is not disorderly. We have noticed this state of mind to underlie that worst form of dyspepsia known as *duodenitis*, which involves a too sensitive state of the mucous surface of the duodenum, and a derangement of the biliary secretion. And we have known the whole disorder of body and mind to be removed, in an exceedingly brief time, under a judicious magnetic treatment. Every observing physician will have frequent opportunity of witnessing this state of body and mind, and of testing the correctness of the theory. And he will find that the shortest way to a cure of the body is by relieving the mind of the patient 'rom this morbid action. The soul must be delivered from the "body of this death," before any remedial agents in the form of medicines will be of any avail. If this be done by his own psychological influence in his office, or at the anxious seat by the prayers of those who feel called to save "immortal and never-dying souls," which is only the influence of happier minds upon the sufferer, it matters not, if it only be well and effectually done.

An habitually gloomy state of mind, and dejection of spirits, which is, as Cullen observes, a partial insanity, has received the expressive name of melancholy, from two Greek words, signifying *black bile*. Such a state of mind was intuitively perceived to be connected with a diseased liver. But what is melancholy but a clinging to old and worn out enjoyments, that now belong to the past? The melancholic patient, instead of finding his happiness in the living present, tries to feed his hungry affections with the memory of dead joys. A state of mind that sees in the divine arrangements of the present moment, all that is necessary to constitute our highest good, and turns no longing look to the past, nor anxious gaze into the unknown future, is one that assures a healthy activity of the liver. Old enjoyments and worn out delights, that have subserved their use, should be cast off, to make way for new and more vital pleasures. "Very often," remarks a writer in the Christian Examiner, "the cause of mental disease is an abnormal adhesiveness of certain states, an involuntary pertinacious retention of the effete products of the spirit. Dreams, superstitions, imaginary conceptions, differentiated and offcast acts, old emotions, the clogged-up perspirations of sentiment,—the excrementitious stuff of the mind—which should be regularly deported by the active excretories of thought and feeling, are sometimes unduly detained in consciousness, producing anxiety, fastening attention, and resulting in the most deadly disturbances of mental equilibrium and health. In the subjects of excessive melancholy, how often old joys, to be known now no more, and which should therefore be cheerfully dismissed, with sickly persistence float back over the memory in strains of elysian sadness to break the heart!" It is precisely this state of the inner man and the interior life, that lies at the bottom of most forms of liver disease. And the best medicine for the patient is some new and living enjoyments. This will operate as a specific upon the biliary secretion, and obviate the use of all mercurial preparations. Magnetize the patient into the supreme bliss of the present moment, so that he shall feel that he has found the *summum bonum*, and need no longer to search for it among the decaying relics of the past, and you have loosened, at once, the grasp of the disease.

The corresponding state of the intellectual principle, the same ideas being retained in the thoughts, the brooding perpetually over old troubles and old delights, occasions a diseased action of the kidneys. In many nervous derangements, as they are falsely called, there is a tendency to frequent urination, the discharge being small in quantity sometimes and highly colored, as if the kidneys were trying to do the work of the liver, but usually the discharge is limpid as pure water. This is occasioned by the perpetual thinking of the patients. He sits for hours like a marble statue, his mind moving in the same old channels of thought, and his breathing in these morbid reveries almost imperceptible. It is the office of the lungs, as an excreting organ, to eliminate the worn out hydrogen and carbon of the blood. It combines with the oxygen of the air and forms the watery vapor that goes forth with the breath. This in twenty-four hours amounts to no inconsiderable quantity, if it could all be condensed and preserved. In the patient's state of perpetual thinking, the lungs perform this office only to a limited extent, and their work is thrown upon the kidneys. Hence the increased watery and saccharine excretion of those organs. Sugar contains the elements of water, oxygen and hydrogen, and also carbon, combined in definite proportions. This should pass off from the body through the lungs, and not through the kidneys. To change the fixed habit of thinking, and educate the respiration of the patient, is the most efficient remedy for diabetes and other kidney diseases, which are confessedly difficult to manage by the ordinary systems of medication.

The kidneys were supposed by the ancients to be the seat of the intelligence. This arose from a vague apprehension of their correspondence with the intellectual principle. The heart was thought to be the seat of the affections, and the reins of the reason. And it is an interesting fact in this connection, that the part of the brain whence they receive their cerebral stimulus, is situated on each side of the organ of causality. In their diseased condition, attended also with a morbid state of the liver, there is often felt a severe pain, commencing here and apparently extending through to the opposite pole between combativeness and caution. The kidneys correspond in their use in the outer man, to the judgment or reason in the mental economy. They separate from the blood the uric acid, which if allowed to remain would poison and pollute the life of the body. This acid is an expressive symbol of devitalized truths, and truth without vitality is falsity. Acids are usually generated by certain putrefactive processes and fermentations. And the secretion of this waste and worn out material by the kidneys, and its elimination from the organism through the bladder and ureters, answers to the function of the judgment or the reason in the soul-principle. The Greek word which is usually translated by the English term judgment, primarily signifies to separate, and to reject. The reason is that faculty of mind by which we distinguish truth from falsity, a living verity from a devitalized notion, and separate the latter from the former, or cast away the one to make room for the other. There can be no perfect health of mind, nor genuine spiritual growth, without this excretory action of the intellect. Defunct ideas should be laid aside, stereotyped and fixed modes of thinking exchanged for new methods of intellection. Monomania, a form of insanity not uncommon, is only the fixedness of an idea, the petrifaction of a thought, and a calculus or stone in the mental bladder. Old and worn out dogmas, when they have accomplished their use and lost their life, should be rejected, that the intellect may become receptive of new and vital truths. The dead past should be decently buried, to make room for a future and better generation of youthful and living verities. If the excretory organs eject from the system vital particles, disease is the result. The new supply does not balance the waste, and the bodily tissues are diminished, and their substance impaired. So we should be careful lest we too hastily put away the truths of a former dispensation before they have lost their vitality to us, and ceased to be of any further use, for fear that spiritual leanness and mental emaciation should result. But our greater danger is found in the reluctance with which we part with old and worn out truth, and the pertinacious adherence of the mind to its fixed modes of thought and feeling. We cling to them after we are conscious they are dead, and mourn over their loss, like Rachel weeping for her children, and refusing to be comforted because they are not. Or we are too often like Rizpah, the daughter of Aiah, who took the bodies of her seven sons, slain in the beginning of the barley-harvest, and, spreading sackcloth upon the rock, seated herself upon it, and guarded them day and night, lest the birds of the air, or the beasts of the field, should consume them. Thus we cleave to the defunct and decaying truths of a past age and bygone era of human development, until their putrid exhalations corrupt the spiritual air we breathe, and poison our intellectual life. The prophets and apostles of the New Age are the best physicians for such a scrofulous diathesis of the interior man. It is not lifeless mineral or vegetable compounds their case requires, but living ideas, that shall act as alteratives in the mental organism, changing the fixed direction of their thoughts and feelings into other channels, that they may be renewed in the spirit of their minds.

CHAPTER XVI.

THE SKIN. ITS CONNECTION WITH THE INTERNAL ORGANS, AND CORRESPONDENCE WITH THE MIND.

Structure and Functions of the Skin. — Amount Secreted by it daily. — The Period in which the Body is renewed. — The Chemical Laboratory of the System. — Unrecognized Sources of Nutrition. — How prolonged Abstinence has been sustained. — Effect of Medicines applied to the Skin. — Psychological Remedies. — Cellular Tissue. — Mucous and Serous Membranes. — The Physiological Condition in a Common Cold. — The Action of the Mind upon the Skin. — A Psychological Sweat. — Effect of Sleep. — State of the Mind underlying Consumption. — Control over the Action of the Skin by the Magnetizer. — Mind the only Causal Agent. — The Ablutions of the Jewish and Mohammedan Laws. — Spiritual Effects of Bathing.

THERE IS no organ of the body more skillfully and wonderfully constructed, and whose normal action is more necessary to our physical well-being, than the skin. The substance of which the various tissues are made, are being constantly changed. It has been stated that once in seven years, the whole bodily structure is renewed. But there are satisfactory reasons for believing that complete renovation is effected in a much briefer period, perhaps as often as once a year, if not once a month. The time necessary for this change in the organic elements, is that which is required for an amount of worn-out material, equal to the weight of the body, to pass off through the appropriate channels, and an equal amount to be received and appropriated. Every day new matter is supplied from the food, and particles of every tissue are dislodged and carried out of the system by the excretory organs, one of the most prominent of which is the skin. The waste, worn-out particles pass off from the skin invisibly, in the form of *insensible* perspiration, and visibly, and in appreciable quantities, in sensible perspiration or sweat. This useless matter is eliminated from the system through what we call the pores of the skin, which are crowded together upon the entire surface of the body, and are the terminations of millions of minute spiral tubes, proceeding from the membranous envelopes of the internal organs. They are not mere punctures or holes in the cuticular covering, but are the outlets of a grand system of drainage, and of pipes conveying nutritious elements into the body. In this way, and by means of nervous fibers which proceed from the various organs, and are spread out into a nexus or network in the *cutis vera*, the skin has connection and communication with all the internal organs, and is their ultimation or external boundary. These pores or tubes are more numerous in some places than in others. There are more of them in the palms of the hands than in the heel of the foot, there being in the former about *three thousand five hundred twenty-eight* to the square inch, and in the latter *two thousand two hundred sixty-eight*. The general average has been estimated in Wilson's Anatomy, to be *twenty-eight hundred* to the square inch. The number of square inches of surface in a man of medium size, is twenty-five hundred. This would give *seven millions* as the whole number of pores. These tubes are estimated to be only one fourth of an inch in length, which falls greatly short of the truth, but this gives the number of inches of perspiratory tube as *one million seven hundred fifty thousand*, or nearly twenty-eight miles. But this is some six times too small in relation to the length of each tube, and at least five times less than the real number of pores to the square inch. If so, there would be *eight hundred and forty miles* of these minute draining pipes terminating in the skin.

Physiologists have computed, that through these

channels there are excreted about two and a half pounds of waste matter every day, or seventy-five pounds a month. A large proportion of this is mere watery vapor, but holding in solution minute quantities of solid matter, which once composed the muscles, nerves, and other tissues. If this were left to accumulate, it would aggregate in such quantities as to interfere with the healthful and vigorous functional action of all the organs, and fevers and other morbid conditions of the system would be the inevitable result. This passes off from the body through the skin, and is lodged in the clothing, or surrounds us as a sphere or atmosphere of its own exhalations. This perspiration is attended with a sensible odor, different in various persons, and in the same person at different times. To keep these pores open and in proper action is as necessary to the health of the internal organs as it is to that of the surface. And to ascertain what spiritual states and influences affect their action, is not merely a matter of curiosity, but of practical hygienic value. We shall endeavor to show this in as clear a light as we are able.

The investing membranes are the grand chemical laboratory of the living system. The secretory and perspiratory glands, and the absorbents, are the apparatus nature uses in her chemistry of life. The one throws off the diseased and worn-out particles, the other imbibes them. We are satisfied "that the spring of all nourishment and abundance, whether of the inner or outer man, is not to be found where we seek it: it lies deep in the spirituality of our nature, there where no external evils can reach, to trouble or dry it up." It was the opinion of Paracelsus, that man is not only fed through his stomach, but through all the membranes of the body by drawing in nutriment from the elements surrounding us. We drink in life from the viewless air, and from the unseen and all-surrounding spiritual realm. There are well-authenticated cases of persons passing long periods without food or drink. But undoubtedly the *spiritual elements or essences*, contained in our ordinary diet, were received from other sources. Thus man may eat angels' food. Elijah in this way passed forty days without other nutriment than the spiritual world supplied. Thus Moses on the mount, and Jesus in the wilderness of Bethsaida, sustained life for more than a month without material food. We imbibe from the atmosphere much that is essential to life and health, not merely through the lungs, but like the leaves of plants from the air in contact with us. Hence the hygienic value of both the air-bath, and the sun-bath, in which the whole surface of the body is exposed to the unobstructed action of the atmospheric elements and the influence of light. The parts of the body least covered by the clothing, are always in the healthiest condition. All the internal organs may be affected by an application of medicines and various substances applied to the surface, as we have previously shown. And it is better to apply medicines here, than to the stomach and intestinal canal. The latter is the common sewer of the body, and is the last place in the world in which to put medicinal compounds. We have often known a cloth wet in a solution of sulphate of magnesia, to cause a movement of the lower intestine, in a costive state of the bowels, and that without inflaming the whole alimentary tube, as when administered through the stomach. Any organ may be thus affected, for when there is in it a lack of any element, it has a hungry affinity for it, and attracts it to itself, when the substance containing it is applied to the skin over it. Our experiments with medicines thus applied have satisfied us that they possess efficiency, without the usual morbid results attending their administration in the ordinary way. An application of common salt to the lumbar plexus, will relieve an inflamed state of the kidneys, indicated by an excess of saccharine matter in the urine. But an intelligent application of spiritual or mental force, may produce all the effects that can be produced by medicines. We have thrown persons into a gentle perspiration in five minutes, without touching them, and sometimes when they were miles away. *For let it be remembered that a psychological influence can affect the physiological action of any organ in the body.* But it is in this, as in everything else,—knowledge is power. To know how to do any thing, is to be able to do it. The laws that govern in the production of such results we hope to explain hereafter. But what can be done by one mind acting upon another mind, and through this upon the body, can be effected in a still higher degree by angels and spirits. If they can move ponderable bodies, as a stone at the entrance of a sepulcher, or articles of furniture, or a man's hand, and these are established facts of science, and demonstrated truths, they can certainly just as well affect the physiological activity of any organ in the body, by an intelligent employment of spiritual and imponderable forces. We have the means of knowing, or at least of believing, that there are associations of spirits in the other world, whose use and happiness are found in ministering to minds diseased. There are many Raphaels, or divine physicians there. And the laws that govern the production of healing effects by sanative spiritual influences, are subjects of earnest investigation. Hereafter the world will receive higher light on this important and interesting subject, than has ever dawned upon us from the serene and lucid depths of the angelic heavens. A calm clear light is already breaking in the east. It will be seen by coming generations, that all the therapeutic effects that we aim to produce by medicines, but often fail in our attempts, can be unerringly caused by psychological forces. The spiritual world contains, and perhaps is made up of, the invisible essences of material things. All the sanative virtues of plants and minerals are to be attributed to the spiritual forces of which they are only the ultimate expression. It has been established by experiment, that pure water, in the hands of a good magnetizer, can be made to produce the specific effects of any medical preparation. But it is only the action of his mind upon it, for our inner being inherits from the central Life a sort of creative force. The so-called miracle, in Cana, where Jesus made water into wine, was performed in harmony with this law; for all miracles that are historically true, are only the *exhibition of higher laws of nature* than those men usually avail themselves of. If by the employment of un recognized spirit forces, such a result was effected in an obscure village of Galilee, cannot spiritual beings impart a sanative principle to any thing we take into the system, or that comes in contact with us? And cannot the human mind here learn to do it? If the account of the pool of Bethesda be accepted as literally true, an angel imparted sanative virtues to its water, so that whoever stepped in was made whole of whatsoever disease he had. (Jno. v. 2—9.) There is nothing contrary to the known laws of nature in this. Facts go to show that the manipulation of medicines by the physician, and his mental states while compounding them, produce psychometrical effects upon a sensitive patient.

All chemical changes in the body are effected by the action of the cellular tissue, which composes the membranes that surround and interpenetrate all the organs, and the entire system. These membranes are mucous or serous, positive or negative, like the copper and zinc in an electro-magnetic battery. All positive substances give off a negative magnetism, and all negative substances absorb and throw off a positive electrical force. Any influence that stimulates to excessive action the mucous surfaces of the body, throws it into a negative state, and closes the pores of the skin. This is the case in a common cold, which is only an infant fever. All the mucous membranes or tissues exhibit an increased action, and the serous surfaces are correspondently inactive and dry. There is a loss of vital harmony. Before the pores can be opened, and the febrile symptoms relieved, the bodily organs must be rendered more positive by an excitement of the serous membranes. The dryness of the surface is only what is seen everywhere in the serous tissue of all the organs. The question now arises: What spiritual states, or forces, will excite to action the appropriate membranes, and increase the serous secretions, and open the pores of the skin, and what mental states will so act upon the mucous surfaces, as to close the mouths of the spiral draining tubes, and check or suspend all perspiration? It is an interesting fact in this connection, that certain animals never sweat, however much they may be heated. This is true of the dog, the goat, the cat, and all animals of the feline species, and the hog. In the animal races that never exhibit any sensible perspiration, we find prominently developed some one or more of the selfish propensities that have their organs in man in the base of the brain. Occasionally a human being is found who never exhibits much, if any, sensible perspiration, while others in the same atmosphere, the same temperature, and the same employment, may appear to have been immersed in water. It seems to be his normal state, a peculiarity of mental and physical organization. But it will be found that some one or all the organs at the base of the brain are predominantly active. To lower the action of these organs by demagnetizing them, by sending their vital force down into corresponding organs of the body, or up to the region of the intellectual and spiritual faculties, is the *modus operandi* of giving a patient a psychological sweat. The more the mind is elevated above the animal and sensuous range of action, the more active are the perspiratory glands of the skin. In sleep this region of the brain is usually quiescent, and an increased perspiration is the result. One of the first symptoms exhibited in that exalted state of the mind's action characterizing the magnetic coma or trance, is the unusual moisture of the hands and the surface of the body. In consumption there is invariably exhibited a loss of harmony between the intellectual and affectional departments of the mind, the former predominating. They are affectionally cold and *think* more than they *feel*. This predominance of the intellectual over the emotional, affects the amount of the respiratory action, and also the state of the skin. They often exhibit a morbid tendency to undue perspiration. And they never can be relieved of the disease, until the lost harmony of the mind is restored. It is well known that unusual muscular exertion induces an increased perspiration, and by magnetizing the part of the cerebrum which is the organ of all voluntary movements, the same effect can be produced upon the perspiratory glands. Thus the action of the skin is under the control of the intelligent magnetic healer. A certain mental force, brought to bear upon some parts of the brain, will send a glow of heat over the whole surface of the body, producing a transient febrile state. By another action of his mind and will, he can produce almost instantly the opposite physiological condition, and throw the patient into a gentle perspiration. Are there any drugs that can equal the living force of a mind made in the image of God, and which incloses in its hidden depths a germ of the one and only Life? We have known fevers, in their incipient stage, to be cured by a psychological force in less than five minutes. In one case a person connected with the War Department in Washington, was thrown into a profuse perspiration, while the operator was quietly seated in his library in New Hampshire. Many facts and testimonials could be given to confirm the statements we might make in relation to the wonderful effects produced by the simple force of the mind. But they would not seem credible to those who do not understand the spiritual laws that govern in such cases. We are apt to forget that mind is the only causal agent in the universe, and that all effects and phenomena in the realm of material things owe their origin to the action of spiritual forces. The sublime movements of the universe are all effects of a divine and self-sustaining force whose name is the I AM, the Living One, and whom the philosophic Greeks called Zeus, from a verb meaning to live. The whole realm of nature is subordinate to spirit, and controlled by it. All physiological action is only an ultimation of psychological forces. All vital movements are a display in the realm of organized matter of spiritual dynamics. And sufficient hints and glimpses of truth have been afforded us in this chapter to warrant the belief, or at least, the hope, that the time is coming when all cutaneous diseases, and febrile states of the system— and their name is legion—will be under the control of an intelligent use of the living powers of the human spirit. Jesus cured Peter's wife's mother of a fever by taking her by the hands, and we have seen a person thrown into a healthy perspiration in the same way. The arms are the chief instrument of muscular motion, and all the voluntary strength of the body can be concentrated in them. They have sympathetic connection with the point of the brain where muscular force has its seat. And an excitement of this part of the brain acts upon the perspiratory glands.

We have before remarked that our physiological and pathological states render us receptive of a corresponding spiritual influx. The various ablutions of the Jewish and Mohammedan laws have not only a hygienic value, but a real spiritual use. The washing of the body not only purifies the skin, and whitewashes the outside of the sepulcher, but purifies the internal organs, and the spiritual man as well. It is a law that the influx of life from the realm of spirit, is modified by the quality and condition of the recipient form. Hence when the body becomes foul by the retention of worn-out material, which accumulates on the surface and in the interior of the structure, it becomes a cage suitable only for the dwelling of unclean birds, and no others will descend and make their nest in it. It is a vessel fitted to receive only the lower passions and feelings of human nature. Such mental states, ultimated in a correspondent bodily condition, are the spiritual causes of fevers and many loathsome and unclean cutaneous diseases. External cleanliness is not only next to godliness, but may be viewed as a part of it. Public bathing houses are as important a means of grace as our poorly ventilated churches, and many an unhappy soul would be brought nearer to heaven by a judicious application of soap and water, than he could be by listening to a sermon about things of which he comprehends little and cares less. If we purify the external body, it prepares a recipient vessel for the influx of pure affections and of truths in agreement with them. To bring the external nature into correspondent harmony with the higher and diviner sentiments and powers, should be our steady aim. For the soul not only acts upon the body, but the latter reacts upon the former.

CHAPTER XVII.

THE SENSES. THEIR CORRESPONDENCE, AND INDEPENDENT OR SPIRITUAL ACTION.

Sensation a Spiritual Phenomenon. — Vision without the external Eye. — Somnambulism. — Independent Clairvoyance. — The Relation of the Eye to the Intellect. — Sympathy of the Eye with other Organs. — The Spiritual Eye can discern Material Things. — The Sense of Hearing. — The Mental Act underlying the Sensation of Sound. — Different Forms of Deafness. — How to Treat them. — The Connection of Voluntary Hearing with the Organ of Cautiousness. — The seat of Otalgia. — Clairaudience or Spiritual Hearing. — The sense of Touch. — Its general Diffusion. — Its Relation to the Love. — Communication of life by the Hand. — The sense of Smell. — Its Spiritual Action. — Taste. — Its Use. — The Spiritual Senses. — How they are opened. — Diseased Conditions in which the Inner Senses are emancipated.

IN MOST systems of mental philosophy, the bodily senses are stated to be five in number—seeing, hearing, smelling, tasting, and feeling. Some metaphysical writers have added others to the number, as the *muscular sense*, the *moral sense*, and the *esthetic sense.* Others with more reason have reduced them to three in number, the sense of smelling and tasting being viewed as only modifications of feeling, as they are excited by the actual contact of substances with their nerve fibers. In fact the sense of feeling may be considered as the universal sense underlying the action of all the others. And in certain states, as in what is called psychometry, the whole body becomes an organ of perception, and all the senses are reduced to a unity—a spiritual state it is difficult to describe.

The truth previously demonstrated, that sensation is not located in the bodily organism, but in the intermediate spiritual form, is one of great scientific value. All sensation is a spiritual phenomenon. The spiritual senses are not another set of faculties, but only our ordinary senses acting independently of the bodily organs. It has been demonstrated that there is vision, clear and far-reaching, without the use of the external eye. In somnambulism this can be proved to be the fact. The pupil of the eye is dilated to its utmost capacity, and the direct rays of the sun, or the powerful calcium light thrown upon it, do not cause it to contract in the least. The six small muscles that move the eye seem to be temporarily paralyzed and motionless. No degree of light can be made to affect the lachrymal glands, but the eye is fixed, vacant, and glassy. All this goes to show that the optic nerve is destitute of sensibility, and the external eye is of no more use than it is after death. Yet there is the power to discern objects near or remote, with far greater distinctness than in the normal state. There are certain persons who seem to have unfolded within them the power of seeing without the use of the material organ of vision. I do not refer to what is usually called clairvoyance, which is a much less spiritual state. The persons to whom I refer are in their normal state. They are not subject to what passes under the name of the trance, a magnetic sleep either self-induced or imposed upon them by another. They are not in a somnambulic state, but in perfect consciousness and wakefulness. Yet they see with more or less clearness, either with the eye open or shut, in the light or in the darkness, hundreds of miles away, so that they can describe persons, and even places, with great particularity and exactness. They perceive the complexion, the form of the countenance, the color of the hair, the temperament, and read the character, the leading traits of which they give with accuracy, though entire strangers to them, and see the objects that surround them. This state is far higher and more spiritual than ordinary clairvoyance

Their inner being has arisen above the limitations of time and space, and the bondage to material things, and the spiritual man, the interior life, has attained to freedom, such as it usually enjoys only after it has become divested of the external body. The organs of sense, like every thing else in the human body, are correspondences, or are effects of which something in the spiritual nature is the cause. The eye belongs to the intellect, or is an organ through which the understanding holds communication with the outward world. This is unconsciously recognized in the language of men. To see a thing and to know it, are used interchangeably, as when one says, the whole of a thing is greater than any of its parts, and you reply, "I *see* it is so." We at once *see* the truth of it. But seeing is not knowing, but corresponds to it, for we may see an object of which we know little or nothing. We see just to the extent of our knowledge and no further. A skillful botanist sees a thousand times more in a tree than one who knows but little of its morphology and physiology. In a purely spiritual state and world, the more the intellect is developed, the clearer is the vision. The relation of the understanding and the eye, and the sympathetic connection between them may be shown in another way. The eye sometimes silently speaks, and discloses the interior thought, which is often quite different from the language of the lips. Intelligence beams from the eye. An intense excitement of the intellect gives an unearthly lustre to the eye. The eye is oftentimes affected by the diseased condition of those organs that have correspondence with the intellectual faculties, as the kidneys and the lungs. The condition of the duodenum or second stomach, seems to influence the external eye. We have had occasion to notice that sore eyes are often accompanied with an inflamed state of the mucous surface of the duodenum. In all ophthalmic inflammations, there is found a tender spot about half way between the ear and the corner of the eye. When the sensitiveness of this part is removed, and the congestion relieved by the magnetism of the hand, it allays the inflammation of the eye and the duodenum at the same time.

It was remarked by Swedenborg that the natural eye sees only material objects, but cannot discern spiritual realities. This is undoubtedly correct. But when he avers that the spiritual eye takes cognizance only of spiritual things, and cannot perceive any objects in the material world, we think there is some mistake here, either in him or our understanding of him. He himself saw the fire that was raging in

Stockholm, when he was in Gottenburg three hundred miles from the former place. He informed his friends where it commenced, how far it proceeded, and when it was extinguished. All his statements were confirmed two days after by the arrival of a messenger at Gottenburg. It is useless to say that this was seen by the external, or what he calls the natural eye. It was only the inner sense, acting independently of the bodily organ, that became cognizant of it. Here then is a plain case of the inner eye perceiving material phenomena. There can be no doubt, that while the spiritual world, with its objective realities, is veiled in darkness to our outward senses, the penetrative vision of spirits and angels may perceive the objects and persons of this lower or exterior range of life. The spiritual may discern the material, the inner take cognizance of the outer, the higher of the lower, because this is the divine order, but the converse of this is impossible.

The sense of hearing, as a medium of communication between the mind and the external world, stands next in importance to that of vision. The ear, in its structure, is one of the most complicated and delicately organized instruments of the soul. As the eye corresponds to the intellect, so the ear answers to the affectional nature. As the eye is influenced by the states of the intellectual faculties, so the ear is affected by the varying states of the love. In the bodily organism it belongs to the vital system, as the eye does to the pulmonary. Diseases of the involuntary or vital organs affect the ear by sympathy, while pulmonary disorders, and an abnormal state of the organs having correspondence with the intellect, affect the eye. Hearing, as a voluntary act, is the result of attention and hearkening. They are the causes or prior states of the mind, of which hearing is the effect. In a state of absent-mindedness or mental abstraction, the ear becomes insensible to external sounds. Ordinary conversation is not noticed. A person may be addressed, but he hears nothing until his *attention* is excited. The mental act of listening, or hearkening, infuses into the auditory nerve a spiritual and cerebral stimulus, that increases its sensibility and renders it more impressible to the undulatory movements of the atmosphere and the ether which are necessary to the sensation of hearing. In all forms of deafness occasioned by a weakened condition of the nerve of hearing, the best remedy will be found in the frequent excitement of the mental state that is a prerequisite to the action of the auditory sense. Sometimes the very act of listening to hear the ticking of a watch, or some distant sound, will so affect the organ of hearing that the sensitiveness of the nerve will be restored. In some forms of deafness, there seems to be only a loss of the power of attention. The cause of the defect in the hearing is found in a sort of mental abstraction, and when they are temporarily aroused from this introversion of the mind, their power of hearing even ordinary conversation is restored. We have had under our care several cases of this nature. The remark is often made of such persons, that they hear with distinctness what you do not wish them to hear. When their attention is excited, even ordinary conversation becomes audible to them. This indicates with clearness that the mind is at fault, more than any diseased condition of the organ of hearing. The cause of this form of deafness is spiritual, and the remedy must be spiritual also.

There is a sympathetic connection between the ear and what is improperly called the organ of cautiousness. We have reason to suspect that the power of listening, or of hearkening, is located in this part of the cerebral structure. It will be found to be true, that the more fully this part of the brain is developed, the more acute is the sense of hearing. This is so both in animals and men. In the hare the ear, which is of unusual size, is situated in immediate connection with the so-called organ of cautiousness, and there is a remarkable power of attention, or of concentrating the mental force upon the auditory sense, and a most acute perception of sounds. What is called its timidity, is only this mental trait, the unusual activity of the faculty of attention. We have demonstrated by experiment, that by magnetizing this part of the brain, with an attempt to excite the attention, it increases the sensitiveness of the ear to sounds. We have come to the conclusion that the sense of hearing, so far as it is a *voluntary* act, depends upon this point of the cerebrum for its nerve stimulus. But hearing is also involuntary, and as an involuntary sense, the ear has sympathetic connection with the cerebellum, and by placing the hand on a point just below the cerebellum, at the commencement of the occipital portion of the spinal column, and imparting a magnetic force to it, the ear will be affected. When a person has been deaf of one ear for any considerable length of time, there will be found a perceptible depression here on one side. This we have frequently noticed.

Deafness is sometimes occasioned by an inflamed state of the *membrana tympani*, a delicate and sensitive membrane stretched across the ear passage and designed to protect the inner ear from the violence of the atmospheric vibrations. The nerve of this membrane may be affected by applying the finger just behind the *zygomatic process* of the superior maxillary bone, and in front of the ear. Beneath this place the nerve enters the ear. Here is the seat of the pain in acute *otalgia* or ear-ache. Deafness is sometimes only an inflamed and congested condition of the *membrana tympani*. It becomes positively charged with vital force, and is too sensitive, while the inner ear is coldly negative. This occasions a constant roaring or ringing sound, in its earlier stages. By cooling the nerve, the difficulty is at once relieved. This membrane seems to have a sympathetic connection with the organs of tune and time, and receives its cerebral stimulus from a point situated between them. The sense of hearing may act independently of the external organ. There are those who not only see without regard to distance of space and without the intervention of ordinary light, but also are able to hear without the vibration of the atmosphere. As light is produced by an undulatory movement of the ether, so the sensation of hearing may depend for its existence upon the motion of a still more subtle element denominated the *aura*. Certain it is, that persons many miles away are heard distinctly to speak, and even their thoughts become audible. Words, uttered at a distance of many leagues, are heard as clearly as if the person speaking were in the same room with us. This may seem even more marvelous and incredible than the interior vision above described. To this inner auditory sense spirits and angels speak. The Jewish prophets listened to voices wafted from the interior realms, and in the unruffled stillness of the soul received messages from the inhabitants of the other shore. Some in every age and nation have enjoyed the same privilege. By them the harmonies of the upper spheres have been heard through the separating vail. One peculiarity of these sounds ought not to pass without notice. They do not enter the ear by an external way, or through the auditory canal (the *meatus auditorius externus*), but they arise from within, and seem to pass up through the Eustachian tube. Whether this is real or only a seeming, we are unable to say. But the sound is as distinctly heard, as any produced by a vibration of the atmosphere, collected and thrown upon the membrane of the tympanum. Persons in whom the intellect is exalted to a spiritual plane of action, are endowed with clear-seeing, because the sight corresponds to the understanding. Those in whom the affectional nature is elevated to the same degree, so as to be in harmony with the spiritualized intellect, are not only clairvoyant, but *clairaudient* also, because the hearing corresponds to the love, and is influenced by the emotions.

The sense of touch, or feeling, is not confined to a small portion of the body, but is distributed over its whole surface. But there are certain parts, as the palms of the hand, and the lips, which possess this sense in a higher degree, in consequence of numerous papillæ, which, in addition to blood-vessels, contain nervous loops, and also peculiar ovoid bodies called "axile corpuscles," possessing gray ganglionic vescicles or cells. The touch or feeling is the sense belonging to the affectional department of the human mind. This is tacitly recognized in all languages, where we find the word feeling used to express emotions and desires, which are modifications of the love. We speak of feelings of joy, of sorrow, of want, of contentment. These are states of the affections. We also speak of various painful diseased conditions as *affections*, as a rheumatic, or a neuralgic affection. This is an instinctive acknowledgment, that these abnormal physiological conditions are caused by a disordered or unharmonious state of the affections. The sphere of our life and the states of our love, are communicable by the touch, especially of the hand

This is a truth of great practical importance. To those who are peculiarly sensitive to the influence of others, and are highly intuitional, the touch of an individual reveals his affectional states, and even his bodily condition. Such persons are like a delicate electrometer. Affection and friendship spontaneously grasp the hand of another. This is a contact of sensitive and magnetic surfaces through which there is an actual interchange of feeling. When we wish to express and communicate a more ardent state of the feelings, we employ, besides the contact of the hands, the more sensitive surface of the lips, and as Tennyson words it, "The spirits rush together at the touching of the lips." This is a thing too sacred to be deemed a mere trifle. The kiss of a mother whose whole soul goes out in loving benediction upon her child, is no empty or unmeaning form. It is an actual communication of life, and the divine magnetism of love. It is proper to remark, that the lips have a sympathetic nervous connection with the organs in the back brain that correspond to the domestic and social affections. The touch, or imposition of the hand, has the effect of actually imparting the sphere of our life, and is the natural and spontaneous expression of a desire to do good to others. Thus Jesus blessed little children, and a heart overflowing with benevolence, has often manifested its wish to communicate good to others in the same way. It has a living power, and it is the divine order of our being, that vital force is transmissible from one to another by this means. When the two blind men, who sat by the way-side begging, cried to Jesus to have mercy upon them, he *touched* their eyes, and immediately they received sight, and followed him. (Matt. xx. 34.) In this way he imparted his own life to diseased humanity, but without any permanent loss of his vital force, for it is a law as invariable as that of gravitation, that to him who gives life, shall life be given. He shall receive from the exhaustless fountain, more than he imparts. We may be conscious that "virtue" has gone out of us, but we shall be made equally certain of the reception of an equivalent potential force. The imposition of the hands always imparts life to another, and as a therapeutic agency, we may rely upon it, with unhesitating confidence and absolute certainty. It is a remedy that never fails when under the direction of intelligence and love.

The sensation of smell is occasioned by a minute exhalation of particles from the odorous body. Its anatomy is less understood than that of any of the other senses. The effluvia going forth from all material bodies, wafted by the atmosphere, affect the olfactory nerves of the nostrils. The design of the sense seems to be to give us a perception of what is agreeable to our life, spiritual and physical There are certain substances that emit to us a disagreeable odor, because they are not in harmony with our nature, yet to certain animals they pour forth a delicious fragrance.

The sense of smell may have a spiritual range of action. It may become an acute faculty of perception, and so intensified as to be affected not merely by the emanations of material bodies, but by the mental sphere of an individual. A person whom we love, and with whom we are in sympathy, gratifies all our senses, and emits an agreeable spiritual odor. While one, toward whom we feel a deep repugnance, becomes offensive to all our senses, and is a mental stench in our spiritual atmosphere. It is a law of our inner being, that whatever is out of harmony with our ruling love, should affect the spiritual sense of smell. When we hear a statement that is repugnant to our feelings, or that we deem absurd, we sometimes instinctively expel the air from the nostrils, as if ridding the nasal cavity of a disagreeable odor. The feeling of disgust toward a person, is expressed by a peculiar movement of the muscles of the nose, as if it were an effort to close the nostrils. This is sufficient to establish the correspondential relation between the mind and the olfactory sensory. They also place in a rational and philosophical light the statement of a distinguished seer, and herald of a New Age, respecting the spiritual world. He discloses the fact that in the realm above, the emanating sphere of spirits and angels is perceived as odorous, and the sense of smell becomes a means of perceiving character. When the sphere of another is in harmony with our own life, it comes as grateful perfume. When not in agreement with our affections, it is perceived as an offensive odor. This is liable to ridicule from shallow minds who do not understand the hidden laws of our being. But the statement rests on a scientific basis and is not so unlike what we here experience as to be destitute of credibility. In what we have said above, we see that the same law operates here, though not so perfectly as in the world beyond. All men know, or may be assured of it, that the perception of what is disagreeable to them ultimates itself in a correspondent movement of the nostrils. The concordant associations, into which the inhabitants of higher spheres are organized by the law of affinity or spiritual attraction, are like the "smell of a field the Lord has blessed."

On the celestial plains, where pure affections prevail and are the spring of all outward activity, odorous gales sweep over the eternal hills, and fragrant spiritual incense fills the land of everlasting spring as the fire of the golden censer perfumed the temple. The man who deems this a matter of ridicule, or unworthy the life above, to be consistent with himself ought to hold his nose, when with hypocritical sanctimoniousness he walks in a flower garden. He should put a bandage over his nostrils in the presence of the magnolia and orange-groves of the South, which fill the adjacent regions with their rich perfumes.

Taste is used in common language both in a physical and spiritual sense. It is employed to express a particular sensation excited in us by the application of certain substances to the tongue, as the taste of a grape or apple. Its office in the bodily economy is to give us a perception of pleasure in the use of the natural aliments which are adapted to promote the growth and the healthful functional action of all the organs, and to build up the various tissues. It has also for an end to furnish us with a ready means of judging what is agreeable to the life of the body. In the animal races, in whom it is seldom perverted as in man, in connection with the sense of smell, which is analogous to it, it subserves this use with well-nigh unerring certainty. It has a correspondence with a certain mental function. We have an intellectual relish for those things which are not obnoxious to our interior life, and we have a discernment or power of perceiving what is promotive of our spiritual well-being and growth. Material food serves a similar use in the outward organism to that which truths and spiritual enjoyments accomplish in the interior man. These latter nourish the inward life and contribute to the development of the soul. Hunger and thirst answer, in the external nature, to the desire of knowing, of understanding and of becoming wise. And taste, in its spiritual application, expresses the power of discerning what is promotive of such an end,—especially a judgment based on experience—and a mental relish for and pleasure in those things.

In what has been said above, we perceive that all the senses have correspondence with the spiritual nature of man. Sensation is located in the most external degree of our inner being, in something intermediate between pure mind and matter, and is the medium through which matter and spirit mutually act and react upon each other. This we have denominated the spiritual body. It is proper to remark, also, that, as the sensation of light and sound is produced by an undulatory movement of a subtle element—the ether and the aura—pervading all space, so the other senses are affected in an analogous way. And all the senses may be excited to action without the intervention of any tangible material substance. They are called into action whenever and wherever the necessary vibratory force acts upon them. They are thus capable of a range of activity independent of the bodily organs. The spiritual senses are the common possession of humanity. The opening of them, as it is called, in certain persons, or rather their emancipation from their material instruments, is apt to be looked upon as an abnormal state, or as an extraordinary, if not miraculous, vouchsafement. If, in the hour of the rending off the external covering, and the transition of the inner man to immortality, the spiritual world is unveiled before the freed vision and celestial voices and harmonies float in upon the enraptured inner ear, it is deemed proper and right, and is accepted as what ought to be. It is a consolation to surviving friends. In the funeral oration from the pulpit, which is now usually deaf, dumb, and blind to all spiritual realities, the comforting fact is dwelt upon with much solemn eloquence. But, if a person becomes sufficiently spiritual twenty-five years before his departure to a higher realm, to see, hear, and even converse with those who walk the "velvety soils" of the land of perpetual spring, he is looked upon with suspicion, sometimes treated with neglect and contempt, and his sanity seriously called in question. So inconsistent a thing is human nature. In this way the world treated Emmanuel Swedenborg, the most illumined mind of modern history.

We believe, with the force of a prophetic conviction, that the time is coming, and draws near, when men will be educated into the normal use of their spiritual senses. Then the spiritual world will no longer be like those large blank spaces on the earlier maps of Africa, marked "Unexplored Territory." The youthful imagination was wont to people this wondrous unknown region with all manner of men, animals, birds, and creeping things. To see and converse with those on the shining shore, and to pierce the hidden depths of the inner realms, will be deemed a no more extraordinary occurrence, than our every day social intercourse with those who are in this outside circumference of being. Such is the normal state of man, and may God and angels help us to return to nature and come into harmony with it. Only one thing is necessary to the unveiling of our spiritual senses, and that is the acquisition of the power of retiring behind the fleshly curtain, so that the interior man may act independently of the outward body. The main obstacle to this is the want of real faith in the actual and substantial existence of our interior selfhood—of a living personality within the material organism. Attaining this, the veil is rent and soon will be removed. As long as the outward body is viewed as the chief thing in our existence, and fills the first place in our thoughts and affections, the inner senses will be in bondage and the spiritual world shrouded in darkness. As soon as men become *assured*, that the body is no necessary part of our manhood, but the spirit is the real man, they will be able to live independent of the material shell, free themselves from its thraldom, the inner senses will be opened, and they will become conscious inhabitants of a higher world. In the devolopment of the new age, now opening before man a higher earthly destiny, this may become his normal state. The soul is sometimes freed, to a certain extent, from its bondage to the fleshly covering, and the spiritual senses are unveiled, by frequent fasting and ascetic mortifications; by an immoderate use of narcotics, as opium and hasheesh; by sickness, in which the powers of the body are gradually weakened; by loss of sleep, and drowning. These are all favorable to the emancipation and manifestation of the soul's interior powers. Whatever weakens the body loosens the soul's connection with it, and, in the same degree, gives opportunity for the independent exercise of the senses. But these are abnormal, and hence undesirable, modes of development. No method of unfolding our inner powers is to be deemed desirable which unfits a man for the duties and uses of our ordinary life.

CHAPTER XVIII.

THE MYSTERY OF LIFE EXPLAINED.

Theories Concerning the Nature of Life. — Not the Result of Organization. — The Mosaic Theory. — Electro-Biology. — The Nervous Fluid. — Definition of Life by Bichat. — Coleridge. — Schelling. — De Blainville. — Comte. — Herbert Spencer. — Swedenborg. — Its inmost Degree is Love. — Organic and Inorganic Forces. — Life a Force. — Correlation and Equivalence of Mental Forces. — Influence of the Emotive Life upon the Intellect. — Relation of Vital Force and Animal Heat. — Health is Equilibrium. — Disease an Inharmony. — Source of Animal Heat. — Heat a Form of Motion. — The Vital Movements. — The Heat of the Sun the Living Force of Nature. — God's Love an all-pervading Life. — The External lives from the Internal. — Effect of Sensation upon the Body. — Influence of the Emotions and Affections upon the Organic Functions. — Secretion. — Muscular Contractility. — The Sexual Instinct. — Its Influence upon the Involuntary Physiological Processes. — Importance of Regulating the Affections. — Impartation of Life. — Disease and Selfishness. — The Divine order of Human Existence.

THE QUESTION "What is life?" has been the unsolved mystery of ages. Some have made it identical with sensation; while others have found the "vital spark of heavenly flame" in intelligence and thought. Some have made it the result of organization. But why is life supposed to result from organization, rather than organization from the vital force, whatever it may be? Others have referred it to the contractility of the fibres. In these theories there is the error of taking effects for causes. Some have supposed it to be a certain indefinable principle superadded to the organism, and distinct from both the soul and the body,—a sort of divine Promethean spark to animate the clay image. They called this indefinable something, life, a word that has been used in Psychology and Physiology without any determinate signification. One mistake, common to all these theories, has consisted in taking certain effects or phenomena of life, for the vital principle itself. An ancient theory, dating as far back as the Jewish legislator, asserts that the life of the body is the blood, or is in the blood. The same might be predicated of all the animal fluids—the mucous, the serum, or the gastric juice. But who could tell what gave animation to the blood itself? As to the soul, if it had any vitality distinct from its own essence, who could say what it was? Some more modern theorists have referred the vital phenomena to electricity. If this were true, all that would be necessary to add to one's vital stock, would be to insulate him, and charge him from an electro-magnetic battery. A favorite hypothesis, adopted by many, is that the so-called nervous fluid is the vital element of the body. But the existence of such a fluid has never been demonstrated. Whatever life is, it is certain it is not a fluid. Bichat gives a definition of life which has been extensively adopted, viz. "Life is the sum of the functions by which death is resisted." Of this definition Coleridge remarks, that he can discover in it no "other meaning than that life consists in being able to live." Coleridge, following Schelling, makes life to be the "*tendency to individuation*," or in other words, the force which combines many qualities into an individual existence. This is true, but indefinite and unsatisfactory. We still ask, What is the power that does this? De Blainville gives a definition of the vital principle, which was adopted by Comte, viz. "Life is the twofold internal movement of composition and decomposition at once general and continuous." In other words, it is included in the phenomena of absorption and excretion. But these physiological processes are the effect of life, and not the vital principle itself. Herbert Spencer gives an abstract definition of life in the following words: "Divesting the conception of all superfluities and reducing it to its most abstract shape, we see that life is definable as the continuous adjustment of internal relations to external relations." This may involve the idea of the "pre-established harmony' of Leibnitz, or it may mean that life is only sensation.

The whole subject of life, its nature and origin, has been involved in such profound mystery, that philosophy has sometimes deemed it the part of wisdom not to meddle with it, but to pass it by, as belonging to those inscrutable matters, which, owing to the necessary limitations of finite thought, we must wait the light of a higher day to disclose. This is a way of disposing of a subject we do not understand, more convenient than scientific. A mystery is not always that which lies beyond the grasp of the human understanding, and is incomprehensible in its nature, but is something which has not been explained. There are many things, which were once classed among the secret things that belong to the Deity alone, that are now well understood. And the awful circle of mystery, into which men have been forbidden to enter, or even profanely to look, has, in the growth of knowledge during the last century, been greatly narrowed down. In the progress of the light of the New Age, things will be taken from the class of the unknown, and what is deemed the unknowable and placed among things revealed, that belong to us and our children

There is no more mystery about life than there is about anything else. More than a century ago, one of the profoundest scholars and most illuminated minds of Europe, the Scandinavian Apocalyptist, cast into the darkness the inspired utterance, *love is the life of man*. This brief sentence is like the creative fiat, "Let there be light," when light first flashed upon the solid darkness of the abyss. Love is the inmost life of the soul. It is not only the common life of the body, the vital spark that animates the outward form, the spring of all its organic movements, and the force that impels the curious and wonderful machinery, but it is the vivifying principle of all sensation and thought. Love is the highest and divinest force in the universe, and in the body is correlated to all the other and lower forces. Sensibility and intelligence, and all the psychological actions, are phenomena to which the term force is applicable. They are forces distinct from those that constitute the properties of matter, but nevertheless are forces. And all forces are persistent and mutually interchangeable. Guided by the recent results of scientific investigation, the organic forces are regarded by many distinguished physiologists of the present day as correlative of the common forces of the inorganic world. These may produce contractility, and this, sensation. Sensation may excite thought and intelligence, and the movement of the intellect, as the direction of the thoughts to an amiable object, will excite the love. And the action of the affectional nature infuses life into all below it. Thought itself proceeds from love. This may not be the *apparent* truth, but an examination of the proposition in the light of consciousness, the ultimate tribunal before which all questions in mental philosophy must be decided, will show it to be the *real* fact. One thing we know,—that in proportion as our emotional nature is excited, the more active and the clearer become our thoughts. There are moments of emotional or affectional excitement, when the flame of zeal or love burns with an intenser heat, and the intellect then emits a clearer light, and the man speaks with an eloquence and power, which, at other times, he never attains. When we think the clearest, if we turn the eye of consciousness inward, we shall perceive that the brighter light in the intelligence is the radiance of a more ardent heat of the affections. For truth proceeds from love, as light from flame. The more vehement the excitement of the sensibility, the more luminous are our thoughts, just as in nature there is a dead and cold whiteness, and a shining or living brightness. In proportion as our affections, which are forms or manifestations of the love, grow cold, in the same degree the intellect loses its vigor, and the senses become torpid. Our thoughts instead of being bright scintilations that glitter and dazzle in the darkness, fall as blackened scales from the cold iron on the anvil. Every thought and sensation, and movement either of the mind or body, has its birth in love. This is the only divine Promethean spark. Life is a flame, and the brighter it burns, the clearer the light it emits.

The inmost life, the vital force of the soul, is love. This in passing outward, according to the law of correlation, becomes heat in the outward organism. For heat corresponds to love. It answers an analogous use in the realm of matter, to that which affection accomplishes in the world of mind. When this vital heat is equally and harmoniously distributed through the entire system, there is a state of health. Disease is a loss of the proper balance. It is an inharmonious distribution of the vital force, some parts or organs having an undue share, while others at the same time are robbed of their rightful proportion. In intermittent fevers, when there is too much heat at the surface, there is not enough within, and vice versa, and the system swings from one state to the other, like the motions of a pendulum, until the lost harmony is restored, or life extinct. The heat of the body is from no other source than the love. This is the life of the soul, which, ultimated in the material organism, becomes *vital* heat. It is not a dead caloric, like that radiated from combustible bodies, though it may be correlated to it. Ordinary caloric is destitute of the spiritual element. Organic or living force does not act except at a certain temperature, which is an indispensable requisite to it. In warm blooded animals 100° F. to 102° F. is the normal temperature. Greatly below this the vital movements are weakened or suspended. The development of the germ in the uterus cannot take place at a temperature much below the normal standard.

The heat of the body is not derived alone from the combination of the oxygen of the air with the carbonaceous elements of the blood. The best physiological authorities admit that this hypothesis is profoundly insufficient to solve the mystery or explain all its phenomena. The carbon and hydrogen, contained in our food, are not sufficient to replace the heat that is radiated from the body of a man exposed, day after day, to the cold atmosphere of winter. It would require a considerable fraction of a cord of wood to do this. There must be some cause lying further back. This much we know—for it is a fact of observation and consciousness—that when we experience an increased intensity of the love or affections, the body responds with an augmented glow of vital heat, which shows itself even in the countenance. In proportion as we love, life thrills in every department of our being, and even warms the soul's tenement. How this is done, we may be able to understand in some degree.

It is accepted now as a demonstrated truth of science, that heat is a form of motion. The hypothesis of a fluid, called caloric, has been abandoned Motion and heat are correlated or mutually interchangeable, the one into the other. More than a century ago, John Locke said, " Heat is a very brisk agitation of the insensible parts of an object which produces in us that sensation from which we denominate the object hot, so that what in our sensation is heat, in the object is nothing but *motion*." This theory was maintained by Bacon, Newton, Count Rumford, Sir Humphrey Davy and others. As light and sound are occasioned by a vibration of a subtle medium pervading all bodies, so heat is caused by a similar movement. Our affectional states, by passing outward to the bodily organism according to the law of correspondence, generate therein the peculiar mo-

tion that constitutes the essence of animal heat
or the vital force. Love is the only moving power
in the universe. Do we not tacitly recognize this
in our language? Desire and affection are deri-
vations of the love, and these have received the
general name of *emotions*, a word which implies a
moving of the mind, an excitement or agitation of
the sensibility.

But by what motions are the vital processes carried
on? There are myriads of them sensible and insensible.
First we have the systole and diastole of the heart, the
contraction of the veins and arteries, and the harmonious action of the respiratory apparatus, including
the lungs, diaphragm, and the muscles that move
the ribs in breathing. In the organic vital phenomena are included digestion, assimilation, absorption,
circulation, nutrition, secretion, and excretion, and
all these are motions among the particles and atoms.
All the muscular fibres and tissues, by their irritability or excitability, respond to the movements of the
will or love, and this susceptibility they possess from
this source alone. Motion is correlated to life, and
corresponds to it. Hence the established efficiency
of the Swedish movements, both single and duplicated, as a curative agency. When the body dies,
it becomes cold and motionless at the same time.

And it is only when this is the case, that it can be pronounced with certainty to be void of life.

To recapitulate what we have said in this chapter, life is love,—a truth of far-reaching importance, and pregnant with meaning. But heat corresponds to love, and in the bodily organism is the ultimation of it, and the essence of heat is motion. All the motions of the material universe owe their origin chiefly to the heat emanating from the myriads of suns that float in the depths of space. The fixed stars are only remoter suns, and, according to Pouillet, we derive almost as much heat from them as from the center of our system. Here is the source of the motions that are constantly taking place in the world we inhabit. Were the influence of the sun's heat to be withdrawn from our earth, there would be a sepulchral stillness, and a suspension of all motion at once. The world would be a motionless and lifeless mass. But wherever there is motion, there is some living love behind it as its cause, from the trembling of a leaf in the breeze, to the revolutions of a planet; from the contraction of a muscular fibre to the victorious march of an army. In the universe all is motion, because the Lord's all-animating love and all-pervading life are in it, and all the movements of creation, from the fall of a sparrow to the ceaseless heavings of the ocean, and the flight of the viewless winds, are but the "stirrings of deep divinity within." All created things in the countless worlds that float in space, respond in harmony with the pulsations of the infinite heart of God, and motion is coeval with the divine life. Heat and light, like love and truth, are not to be classed among things created or creatable. There never was a time when space was an infinite void, and nothing stirred throughout its silent depths, and Deity dwelt alone in the solitude of his own eternity. Where He has been in time or space, there has been love, and life, and heat, and where these are, there must be motion. What has been, always will be. Ages, issuing from the dim distance of an eternity past, rush to be swallowed up in an eternity to come. In this endless procession of centuries and dispensations, each proclaims as it sweeps by with all its changes, and its voice dies away in silence, like the hush of winds at the close of day,—"God is the one and only Life." With this sublime and weighty utterance, the vail is lifted from life's profoundest mysteries. All science is drifting the human mind towards the recognition of this universal truth. If we question things created, and ask them why they exist, they answer, "Because God is love, and love is life and where that life breathes, there must be joy ous being to share the irrepressible bliss of the Divine Mind. For in him we live, and move, and have our being."

It is a truth of great practical value in a system of Mental Hygiene that every external degree of our complex being is affected by the state of the internal degrees. The external derives its vital activity from something interior to it, and the movements of the external are correspondences of the more internal or spiritual force, or, to use the popular scientific language of the day, they are mutually correlated, and act and react upon each other. To illustrate this, let us begin with the sensuous range of the mind which we have shown to be the spiritual body. Sensation is not life, for the external senses may all be closed, or their action suspended, and life not be extinct. This is the case with man in sleep, in the trance, in swooning and synocope, and with hybernating animals, during their torpitude in winter. All the varieties of sensation may be reduced to the sense of touch or feeling, which is the universal sense, and belongs to the love. It is the love, or vital force, acting upon the lowest or outermost plane of the mind. The action of the senses serves to open, or excite to their appropriate movement, the minute and invisible organic vessels of the external man, so as to render the body receptive of the influent life from the internal mind. They are an intermediate principle through which life passes outward to the external organism. It has been shown by recent physiological investigations, that sensations excite to increased activity the secreting organs in a perceptible degree; also that they affect the action of both the involuntary and voluntary muscles, for the interior spiritual forces are correlative of the organic forces, or transmutable into them. Sensations increase the action of the heart, and in a degree proportioned to their intensity, and recent physiological inquiries imply not only that contraction of the heart is excited by every sensation, but also that the muscular fibers, throughout the whole vascular system, are at the same time more or less contracted. The rate of breathing is visibly augmented both by pleasurable and painful impressions on the nerves, when they reach any intensity. It has even been shown that inspiration becomes more frequent on transition from darkness into sunshine, and the sensation of light renders the body more positively vital. It is not too much to suppose that the time will come in the progressive development of the New Age, when the action of all the organs can be regulated by means of sensation, so as either to increase or lower their vital tone. Some slight and apparently insignificant sensations, as an excitement of the nerves of touch by tickling, are followed by almost incontrollable movements of the voluntary muscles, as those of the arms or legs. Violent pains cause violent struggles and contortions, and great pleasure is attended with equally noticeable movements. The effect of sensation upon the muscular tissue, is seen in the sudden start that follows a loud sound, the wry face produced by the taste of any thing disagreeable, the jerk with which the hand or foot is snatched out of hot water, and the instinctive drawing back and turning away from an offensive odor. All these instances are illustrations of the transformation of feeling, which belongs to our inner nature, into muscular motion. There is a definite quantitative relation between them, as it is manifest that the force of the bodily action is proportioned to the quantity of the sensation. Torpidity of the senses must always be attended with a lowering of the vital force of the body, and a loosening of the connection of the mind with it. There is a sanative influence in the appropriate delights of each of the senses. They have an important hygienic value. He who understands their effect, can sometimes prescribe them as the best remedial agency. To ignore their pleasures and mortify them, under the influence of a morbid religious asceticism, is to enter the gloomy highway of disease and death. Their enjoyment, in the highest degree, is the normal state of man in the present stage of our endless existence.

If we take the emotions,—which are a more internal action of the love than sensation,—we find their effect upon the bodily organism equally marked. Emotions of only moderate intensity, generate little beyond a slight degree of the excitement of the heart and the vascular system, and this is necessarily attended with increased action of the glandular organs. Certain states of the affections or feelings change the character of the secretions. A fit of passion has been known so to affect the milk of the mother as to throw her child into convulsions. The saliva of the dog is so altered by his being enraged as to render his bite poisonous. All the emotions and passions affect, by the law of correspondence or correlation, all the secreting organs. But the emotions are a spiritual force, and in passing outward to the material organism are transmuted into physiological movements and muscular action. Certain bodily motions are only the equivalence of certain mental states. Witness the frowns, stampings, strikings, and threatening attitudes of anger, the frantic struggles of terror, the wringing of the hands and swaying of the body back and forth of grief, the smiles of satisfaction, and the dancings of great delight. To leap for joy is a common expression, but the movement of the body is the effect of the inward mental state and is only its ultimate expression. The emotion or excitement of the love, is the cause. These effects are only more visible, but no more real, than those organic movements which we can not perceive. Every change of our feelings or our affective life, is followed by a correspondent change in the functional action of all the vital organs.

There is no emotive or affectional state of more importance in Mental Hygiene, than the proper action of the sexual instinct. The cerebral organ of its manifestation is in the cerebellum. This brain is also the organ of the involuntary, or, what has been improperly called, the *vegetative* life. Comte includes all the involuntary physiological processes under the term *nutrition*, and locates its organ in the center of the cerebellum. It is evident that an inharmonious or over-excitement of the sexual emotion must draw into itself and expend too large a share of the vital force of the cerebellum, and consequently lower the tone of all the involuntary organs. Here is the spiritual root of more diseases of body and mind than can be traced to any other one source. The sexual and conjugal love is most intimately connected with the inmost life of the spirit, and is the fountain of more happiness or misery than originates with any other affection, according as it is properly controlled, or left to a disorderly activity and indulgence. The part of our mental organism that imparts life to a new human being, must be in a high degree vital, and come near the creative force. The whole train of the diseases of the reproductive organs, constituting a large proportion of the cases of chronic ailments, are caused by a want of harmony here, and their relief is only temporary and deceptive, until this department of the spiritual nature is restored to order. The superior value of the magnetic, or, more properly, the psychological method of treatment, arises from the perfect control which it has over the mental states, the affective and emotive life of the patient, and thus extends its healing force into the realm of spiritual causation, and touches' the spring of the body's vitality.

If the doctrine of this chapter is accepted as truth by the intuitive reason, it will show, in a clear light, the importance of properly regulating the affections and the whole emotional nature. A loss of harmony here is the secret spring of most, if not all, of the thirteen hundred diseases described in works or

Nosology. If life is love, then all the physiological processes must be modified by our affectional states. There are some of the noblest and purest of earth's inhabitants, both male and female, who are slowly but surely marching to the cemetery, from a blasted, withered state of the social affections—dying from disappointed and unsatisfied love. They are numbered by legions, and are found within and without the conjugal relation. This pathological mental state, lowers the tone of all the organic functions. This atrophy of the soul enfeebles the vital movements of the whole body, and the body sinks under disease, like a tender plant smitten with an untimely frost. Drugs are powerless to reach the seat of the trouble. The remedy must be spiritual.

The life of God is love. His love is an infinite desire to impart his own good to others. The life of angels is a stream from this only fountain, and partakes of the properties of its source. If we open our hearts to receive the influx of the divine and heavenly life, it will be in us a desire and conatus to impart the good, with which we are blessed, to all who are willing to receive it, and are admissive of it. Such is the true order of life, the normal state of every soul. It is evident we can never attain to the highest well-being of either soul or body, until we come into the divine order of our existence, and employ the activity with which we are endowed, according to the laws of the celestial life. We were made to impart, to be the media through which God's gifts could be transmitted to others. We are finite receptacles of the divine good and truth. We were not designed to absorb the divine rays, but to reflect them as well—to be each a center of radiation. One of the most prominent organs in the brain is benevolence. The mental feeling, of which it is the outward instrument, is a desire to impart, to share our good with others. When this divine impulse is perverted in its action, our love terminates in self, and we become the center of our universe. Selfishness is the fruitful root of more moral and physical evil and unhappiness, than any other cause. It is the perversion of the divinest instinct of human nature, a cessation of the pulsations of the central Life within us. The only true and happy life on earth, is that of love. Wisdom is divine. Truth is a ray from God. Science and philosophy are a spiritual treasure and desirable possession. Wealth, official station and power, are good in themselves. But the divinest thing in the universe is love—an all-absorbing charity. Blessed is the man in whose inner nature it is the supreme and governing principle, and who has consecrated himself to the good of universal being.

Disease is often only a state of supreme selfishness. It is a law, universal and immutable, that by imparting, we receive, and when we cease to impart, we cease to receive, and the stream of our life begins to dry up at the fountain. The candle under a bushel, soon becomes only a smoking wick. To communicate truth to another, quickens our own intellectual life, and renders us receptive of more than we give. There are those who are ever learning, but never able to come to the knowledge of the truth. They are like the dark substances in nature, that absorb all the rays, and never can become transparent and luminous. Give, and it shall be given, is a law that governs in the whole realm of mind. It has its application to every form of good.

There are many unsound mental states, which ultimate themselves, according to the law of spiritual influx, in various diseased bodily conditions, that have their root in this perversion of the true order of our being. Such persons are unhappy, and consequently unhealthy, because in the unnatural state in which they are, they think only of themselves—their own comfort and enjoyment. Insanity, especially in the form of melancholy, is often nothing but selfishness. The brain is inflamed, and there is a congestion of its magnetic life, simply because its magnetism does not flow forth in showers of blessings upon others. The waste, worn out nerve-aura accumulates, because it does not radiate around, making every thing happier and better by receiving it. Such unhappy and gloomy souls, we fondly believe, when they put off the external envelope, and wake to consciousness in the spiritual world, will be cured of their diseased mental state, and their consequent bodily infirmities. But the cure will be effected, not by the breathing of the celestial aura, or reveling in the heavenly aroma wafted by the gales that sweep over celestial landscapes, but by being instructed by angels, and guided by spiritual tutors into the true order of their life. If we deem ourselves the most miserable of human kind, and our soul the most wretched thing in the universe, it is because we have forgotten others in our insane absorption into self. The remedy is here and now. Make the heart of something outside your own being to leap for joy. Attune your soul in harmony with the Life Divine. Live to love, and then you will delight to live; and health will glow and thrill in every organic structure. Find some one whose condition is unhappy like your own. Lift up your hand and your heart, and pull down a blessing upon his head. The best prescription that man or angel can give to relieve your soul-misery, and the correspondent abnormal physiological state is, Be, like Jesus, every one's best friend. Seek to make every body and every thing happy. The good, you intend to others, will come to you in divine measure, more than you give. Get well by curing others. Impart life, communicate from your own stock of vital force to others, and life from God, its sempiternal source, and from the angel-world, will flow in to replenish your store. To love another so as to long to impart our good and our very life to him, sends a thrill of life through our whole being. It kindles anew the vital fire in the decaying body. This will seem to the world at large, absorbed in their selfish schemes, as an idle dream, a transcendental revery. Medical science, with its antiquated theories, will reject and scout so spiritual a remedy, and still cling to its senseless formulas and deleterious drugs. But we still aver there is more in it, than the science of to day is ready to admit. And is it not true, that there is more in heaven and earth, than philosophy ever dreamed of? Has science gone to the utmost boundary of all that is knowable? Is it not time for medicine to take an advanced step? Is it the province of a true philosophy, like the Roman god, Terminus, to eternally watch the old landmarks, lest the boundaries be moved? Are the limits of knowledge forever fixed, or is truth progressive in its endless evolutions? Is there not in every human soul the divine germ of an infinite development, a capacity of an everlasting unfolding? Is the stunted, dwarfish growth of the past centuries, the final goal of the mind's race-course, and the terminus of the soul in its march of endless progression?

CHAPTER XIX.

MENTAL METAMORPHOSIS; OR HOW TO INDUCE UPON OURSELVES ANY DESIRABLE MENTAL STATE.

Relation of Mental Disturbance to Disease. — Therapeutic Spiritual Forces. — Our Emotions involuntary. — Self-Conversion. — A General Law stated. — Relation of Form to Internal Character. — The Lesson taught us by the Stage. — Expression of our inward States by the Face. — How to effect a Change in our Feelings. — Hygienic value of the Law. — Inspiration and Respiration. — Soul and Breath. — Peculiar Sensation attending Psychological Influence. — Nearness of the Inner Realm. — How to be Inspired. — Breathing of the Soul. — The Respiration peculiar to all depressing Mental States. — How to relieve ourselves of them. — Usefulness of the Swedish Movements.

THE DIFFERENT states of the mind, both in the department of thought and feeling, influence the physiological manifestations. All psychological movements effect a change in the organic functions. Hence the law according to which our feelings may be changed and controlled, is one of great hygienic value. Every one who has ever had much to do in the treatment of the various forms of chronic disease, must have frequently heard the remark made by invalids, that some peculiar mental trouble, some disappointment, or unhappiness, or abnormal excitement or derangement of the spiritual nature, was the original cause of their ill health. And in every case, if we investigate their mental history, we shall find some disturbance of the spiritual equilibrium to underlie their pathological condition. But how few, either among patients or physicians, ever think of finding a cure in the removal of the interior cause of their disease, and in the restoration of the mind to a sound and healthy state. How few seem to make any practical use of those spiritual forces, that exercise so potent an influence over the external organism, both in the generation of diseased conditions, and as a therapeutic agency. Every particular case needs instruction adapted to its peculiarities, and we can lay down only some general principles, that may serve as hints in the treatment of all cases. We shall not in this chapter attempt to show how one mind may so act upon another as to change its mental state, but how the patient may effect in himself a spiritual metamorphosis, and induce upon himself any desirable mental state. For it is a matter of prime importance to teach a chronic invalid to be self-reliant, and to become his own physician.

We have seen that our thoughts and affections are not self-originated, but are the result of an influx from the world of spirit, which is interfused within this realm of being. It might, at first, seem from this, that the soul of man was only a passive recipient of the ideas and feelings of others, and that we could have no more control over our emotional and intellectual states, than over the winds that blow upon us. It is true that our thoughts and affections are involuntary, in the sense that they cannot be changed by the direct action of the will. We often struggle long and hard against them, and gain no relief from their infestation. A mere command of the volitive power cannot dispel melancholy, regret, fear, anxiety, guilt, or any affection or emotion we do not wish to nourish, and of which we would gladly rid ourselves. They cleave to us like the poisoned shirt of Nessus. Still the human soul is not like a ship on a stormy sea, driven before tempests and resistless currents, without rudder or compass. While it is admitted, that neither thought nor affection is self-derived, but both flow in from our vital connection with the all-surrounding, all-pervading spiritual world, and we are under the law of necessity both to think and feel while we live, yet if unhappy feelings or mental states flow in, why may not good ones as well? We drink in spiritual life from another realm of being; but can we not choose at what fountain or stream we will receive? Is there not a law of which we may avail ourselves, and by conformity to which, we may render ourselves receptive of any desirable mental state we may wish to induce upon ourselves, as one of calmness or joy, of faith or trust, of gentleness and lovingness? There is a way, easy and practical, by which we may loosen the hold of any unhappy feeling upon us, and cause it to give place to a better state. Suppose we find ourselves, no matter from what cause, suffering from certain disordered and depressing mental states, as anxiety, or sadness, or despair, or hurry of spirits, or the foreboding of evil, or conscious self-imposed guilt, so that we are filled with inward disquietude, and suffering the consequent derangement of the bodily functions. We desire to exchange our present mental condition for a happy one—to *convert* ourselves, to " make to ourselves a new heart and a new spirit." We would be rid of the evil and attain the opposite good. How can this be done in harmony with the truth, that our feelings are involuntary, and come to us from without, and do not originate from the depth of our being? If we are at all self reliant, we need send for neither the priest nor the doctor. They are often like the blind leading the blind, and both fall into the ditch. They are a broken reed, on which if we lean, it will pierce our hand. To struggle against our feelings, will do us no good, for action and reaction will here be equal. Our convulsive efforts to deliver ourselves from our mental sufferings, will only plunge us the deeper, like a man sinking in the mire. We are then to cease all useless strugglings and vain efforts to free ourselves by our own strength. Let the soul be calm and passive. Let it be negative and receptive towards the sphere of those who are in the state you would induce upon yourself, whether they are in this world or that above.

We lay down this general law—*that influx is always into forms that are correspondences.* We will explain this. Between external form and internal character there is everywhere the relation of cause and effect. Between the outward configuration of an object and its inward nature, there is mutual action and reaction. "It is everywhere the indwelling life, which determines the external form of things. Throughout nature, in strict accordance with this law, differences of configuration are, in all cases, found to be commensurate with differences of character and use.

Things which resemble each other in quality and function resemble each other in shape; and wherever there is unlikeness in quality and function, there is unlikeness in form; in other words, there is a determinate relation between the constitution and appearance of material objects; and the reason why any particular animal or plant assumes its own precise figure rather than any other, need be sought only in the necessity of adapting configuration to character." (*New Physiognomy, by Samuel R. Wells, p.* 83.) The relation of the outward form to the interior essence and character, is a universal one, and in living beings is a mutual one. To put an animal into a form or attitude that expresses some ruling passion, will excite it to action. This we have successfully tried. So in man, when the external is made to assume a form in harmony with any spiritual state, the emotions and thoughts constituting it flow in. It is a law of our being, uniform in its operation, that when we assume the attitude which outwardly expresses or manifests any feeling or sentiment, it spontaneously arises within us. There are many familiar illustrations of this. When an actor on the stage, by his countenance, attitudes, and gestures, outwardly manifests the feelings that belong to the characters he personates, they take possession of him in all their reality, and sometimes with overpowering force. The power of not only feigning the emotions and passions that tragic and comic acting are designed to represent, but of actually inducing them upon one's self, is the secret of the highest attainments in the art. But all this takes place in harmony with the laws of our nature, and is due only in part to a susceptible constitution. The relation of body and soul is that of correspondence, and there is a tendency in each to adjust itself in harmony with the other. The external form is under the control of the internal manhood, and obeys the dictates of its volitions. By an effort of will, it can be made to assume any attitude we please, and when it comes into the external form that manifests or expresses any feeling, it becomes as a prepared vessel to receive it from the spiritual realms. All our interior states are outwardly expressed by that most wonderfully organized instrument of the mind—the human face. Its muscles respond spontaneously to the least change of feeling, and mold the countenance into the ultimate image of every varying emotion. And melancholy cannot long reign in the mind, when the face is made to assume the form that expresses mirthfulness. So of all other depressing mental states. The muscles of the face will respond to the force of the will, and form an image expressive or representative of the opposite feelings, and the breath of lives shall be infused into it, and the outward form shall become a living soul. If one is troubled with a hurry of spirits, so common in chronic diseases of the so-called nervous type, and which quickens all its movements, the pulsations of the heart, and the respiratory action, and exhausts the nerve force, let him see to it, that all his outward motions are slow and tranquil. Become externally quiet, and soon a tranquil feeling will steal over the mind, as gently as the dews of evening descend upon the flower. If one is sad or gloomy, or fearful, or desponding, or suffers from a loss of self-respect, or is habitually impatient, let him voluntarily assume the attitude that outwardly expresses the opposite state, and the desired emotion will arise in his consciousness. Here is a principle of great practical hygienic importance and has its application to all those abnormal and pathological mental states that sustain a causal relation to the various forms of chronic disease. We can place the external man in such an attitude and form, as shall no longer ultimate the feelings we wish to remove, but which shall be the correspondence of the opposite emotional state. Then the disordered psychological condition, of which we wish to clear ourselves, having no basis on which to rest, comes to an end, like the fall of a tower when the foundation is removed, and the opposite affectional state flows in from above into the correspondent and receptive form. The wind of the spirit bloweth where it listeth, and if we spread our canvas aright, we shall catch celestial gales. When the outward man comes into correspondent harmony with the affections that prevail in the heavens, the soul will vibrate in harmony with the angels. Celestial motion will be communicated to our spirit's harp strings, and bliss shall pervade our soul, like festive lights in a long deserted mansion. For the external atmosphere will no more certainly rush in to fill a vacuum, than the all-surrounding spirit-world will flow into the outward forms that are the correspondent or ultimate expression of its states.

To receive light and love, thought and affection, from the upper or inner world, is to be *inspired*. If we would be inspired with any particular feeling, as that of joy, or peace, or hope, or faith, it is important that we attend to our respiration. Inspiration means an *in-breathing*. And there is an important connection between the manner of our respiration and our states of mind. When Swedenborg asserts that in the primeval age, the paradisiacal state, the golden age of the poets, when men were in the superior, or rather interior condition, their breathing was tacit, and not externally perceptible, it is what we should naturally expect, provided it be historically true that there ever was such an age of the world or race of men. The statement, as to the mode of their respiration, rests on a scientific basis. They thought interiorly, abstractly, intensely, and passively, and their respiration corresponded. The nearer we approach to the same state of thought, the less discernible is our breathing. The more interiorly we think, the more tacit is our respiration, as in the genuine trance. And there are states of rapt abstraction from our external surroundings, when the body seems breathless, and the spirit only respires. The breathing is internal, invisible. and in harmony with that of the spiritual world, and then the intellect is exalted to a higher plane of action. That there is an important connection between our modes of respiration, and our states of mind, is a physiological and psychological truth, not hitherto sufficiently attended to, but worthy of investigation. In all languages, the air is made representative of spirit, and it is a fact familiar to the seers of all ages, that influx from the spiritual world, is oftentimes attended with a sensation as of a cool air blow-ing upon some part of the person. Thus the word used for soul or spirit is derived from a term meaning air, wind, or breath. Thus the Latin *animus* and *anima*, are from the Greek *anemos*, wind. The old Saxon word for spirit, *ghost*, and the German *geist*, are only another form of the term *gas*, which is from the same root. In the Christian and Jewish Scriptures, there is only one word used to express the two ideas of wind and spirit. "The wind bloweth where it listeth, and thou hearest the voice thereof, but canst not tell whence it cometh, nor whither it goeth. So it is with whatsoever is generated from the spirit." The latter word is the same that is rendered wind at the commencement of the passage. The spiritual realm is within and around the material world. The sphere of the one pervades the atmosphere of the other. That sphere is composed of the emanations, or vibrations, of the life of angels. Thus we inhale the affectional states of those above and around us. While gently breathing deep and full, we may elevate the soul's *aspirations* to the upper realms. A desire for a particular state, if it be not inordinate, but calm and tranquil, is a reaching forth of the mind to grasp it. Such is the radical sense of the word. It is a negative and receptive state, a consciousness of want, a sort of mental vacuum. It renders us admissive of the mental state we wish to induce upon ourselves. With the mind thus fixed upon those above, we may *breathe through to the spiritual range of life*, and inhale purity, peace, and bliss from perennial and immortal fountains—the sphere of angels and of God. We hear people talk about the soul's breathing after purity and bliss, yet the expression has lost its meaning, and has degenerated into a cant phrase, of which no definite idea is formed. To aspire to any spiritual state, is to breathe after it, (from the Latin *ad* towards, and *spiro*, to breathe.) The very word spirit comes from *spiro* to breathe. So also the French *esprit*, the Italian *spirito*, the Spanish *espiritu*, and the Latin *spiritus*. The interior man respires, as well as the external body, but its respiration is tacit to the senses, and is not recognizable as that of the outward man is. "There is a natural body and there is a spiritual body," and the respiration of the one is synchronous and harmonious with the other. The one breathes an atmosphere surrounding the globe we inhabit, and charged with the effluvia of material objects; the other an aura enveloping the spiritual world, and pervaded with the emanating sphere of its inhabitants. The air has pneumatical or spiritual life within its serene depths. Thus while we breathe the "air of immensity," we may inhale the aura of celestial climes, impregnated with the joys and affectional states of the angels, and the spirits of the blest, who have been born into an undying life. We may be *inspired* with a bliss from above, and with spiritual delights that shall make our life a perpetual psalm of praise, and fill with unuttered hallelujahs our every day concerns. But these hints and suggestions are given only to those "who have ears to hear"—who believe the spiritual world is the *reality*, our earthly life, the dream.

All depressing, mental states are attended with a peculiar respiration, the top of the lungs only being called into action, and not the abdominal muscles. By directing the mind to the frontal muscles, and breathing naturally, and not too artificially, and with no other effort of will than the fixing of the thoughts upon the abdominal coverings, their muscular tissue is contracted in the respiratory act, and this will go far towards relieving the mind of any morbid state of the feelings, as anxiety and melancholy, and the whole class of depressing emotions. We have known this to effect, in a few moments, a surprising metamorphosis in the mental condition of a patient. As a remedial agency in a system of Mental Hygiene, it deserves consideration and a fair trial.

The motion of the diaphragm and the lungs in breathing, communicates a peculiar movement to the cerebral mass, and affects the action of the brain, and consequently the manifestations of the mind. In a work entitled "The Institutions of Physiology," by Blumenbach, it is said in speaking of the brain, "that after birth it undergoes a constant and gentle motion correspondent with respiration, so that when the lungs shrink in expiration, the brain rises a little, but when the chest expands, it again subsides." The discovery of this concordant movement of the lungs and the brain, has been claimed by some for Swedenborg, but Blumenbach ascribes it to Daniel Schlichting who described it in 1744. It shows, in a clear light, the sympathetic connection between the lungs and the cerebrum, and the effect of respiration upon the organ of the mind, and consequently upon our mental states. Just in proportion as the respiratory movements are diminished, external consciousness and sensibility are lessened. When we cease breathing, they are suspended altogether. The external manifestations of the mind are no longer possible, when the movement of the brain, consequent upon, or synchronous with respiration, terminates. It is also reasonable to suppose, that the several varieties of respiration should be accompanied with peculiar mental states, as well as with peculiar movements of the cerebral mass. This is confirmed by experience. To relieve ourselves of any involuntary and unhappy state of the mind, we have only to change the mode of respiration peculiar to it, for that which belongs to the opposite state, and the desired feeling or emotion will arise within us. The Swedish Movements are peculiarly adapted to effect the necessary change, both as to degree and character, of the breathing which characterizes all depressing and abnormal mental states. Hence their demonstrated efficiency in the cure of chronic diseases, both of the mind and body.

CHAPTER XX.

THE COMMUNICATION OF LIFE AND OF SANATIVE MENTAL INFLUENCE.

The Primal Source of Life.— Man imparts life to all below him. — Vital Force Communicable. — How Jesus gave his Life a Ransom for Many. — His cures not Miraculous in the Theological Sense. — The royal Touch for Scrofula. — Sanative Influence of the Hand. — Knowledge is Power. — Mental Conditions necessary to a Cure. — Faith a Spiritual Force. — Its Therapeutic Influence. — The Cure of a Paralytic by Davy with a Thermometer. — Effect of Fear. — Case of Hydrophobia caused by it. — Experiment with four Russian Criminals. — The Rose-Water Cure. — Vital Force and Animal Heat correlative. — How Heat is generated and transmitted. — Therapeutic Influence of Friction. — Compression. — Percussion. — Motion. — Adaptation of the Hand as an Instrument for Communicating Life. — Efficiency of the Duplicated Movements accounted for. — How to Induce upon a Patient the proper State of Mind. — Polarity of our Feelings. — Inverted Action of the Cerebral Organs. — Restoration of the Equilibrium. — Mental Vibration. — How Jesus healed the Sick. — Health is Contagious. — Spiritual Inoculation. — Mental Leaven.

THE INMOST life of all that exists is the divine Love. Creation has gone forth from this, and the life that thrills in the universe owes its origin to this primal source. Life emanates from this living center, and is communicated to all, constituting the ground of all finite existence. From this focal source, it goes out in endless and perpetual undulations, and all live by virtue of life transmitted from him. It finds its highest, completest manifestation in man, in the human soul made into the divine image and likeness. Man is a finite created receptacle of the divine love and wisdom. For as the Father has life in himself, he has given to every human being to have life in himself, and to be a reservoir for its distribution. And man is vitally positive towards all the lower degrees of creation, and they exist from God through him. His life, in its essence, is love springing eternally from the depth of the divine being. As life is communicated from God, so also is it from man, but from some more than from others. We have shown that our affectional states are transmissible, from one person to another by the touch. Life is a force, and motion and force are communicable from one body to another. It is a fact that the world has long recognized, that one person may derive vital force from another person. Thus when the monarch of Israel was enfeebled by age, they procured for him a young and healthy damsel to impart vital heat to his negative organism. It is a truth recognized by all physiologists and schools of medicine, that a young child occupying the same bed with an old person, will be robbed of its vitality, as certainly as a heated body will impart a thermal influence to another near or in contact with it. The child will pine away and sometimes die, without any apparent organic disease, but by a gradual lowering of the vital tone, while the older person becomes proportionately more vigorous, and maintains a parasitic existence. When we assert that life is communicable, that vital force is transmissible from one human being to another, we occupy undisputed ground. It was in harmony with this recognized law of our being, that Jesus cured diseased humanity. He laid down his life for men,— an expression that has no reference to his death. In the tenth chapter of John's Gospel, he calls himself the good shepherd, and affirms that he lays down his life for the sheep. One definition of the word rendered here to lay down, is *to impart, to put into or within any one.* In another place it is so used in reference to the sphere of the divine life,—as " I will put my spirit upon or into him." (Mat. xii. 18). In this sense he every day laid down, or imparted his life to diseased humanity, and he taught his disciples or scholars to do the same, "to cure all manner of sickness and disease among the people," a power that ought to have continued in the church to this day, and would if the charity or love from which it sprang had not died out. He gave his life a ransom for many, or by this impartation of sanative virtue and vital force, he delivered multitudes from diseased states of mind and body. Thus men were saved by him, not by his death, as men have blindly supposed, but as Paul avers, "much more by his life" (Rom. v 10.) He employed, in his benevolent mission to the unhappy and suffering, all the means through which life is transmissible from one person to another—the imposition of hands, the silent sphere of his mind, the going forth of his love for them in prayer, and he used the spiritual power of words. There have been those, in every age of the world, who have, to a more limited extent, done the same. His cures were none of them miracles, in the theological sense, but were effected in harmony with laws that are operative to-day. The word miracle signifies what excites wonder, from the Latin verb *miror*, to be astonished. And wonder is the child of ignorance. As soon as any phenomenon is understood, and we come to an apprehension of the laws that govern it, it ceases to be a wonder. Miracles belong only to a dark age,— to a wicked and adulterous generation. They disappear before the light of science, like birds of night at the approach of day.

The Kings of England, for many centuries, employed the vital magnetism of the hand for the cure of scrofula, and with a success that seemed to an ignorant age miraculous. No one would now suppose that the power to cure a person of a scrofulous diathesis by imparting vital force to the action of the excreting organs through the magnetism of the hands, was a prerogative confined to royality. Hundreds of others, both in civilized and savage nations, have effected the cure of disease in the same way. Love is the life of man—the inmost vital force of his organism. To apply the hands to a diseased part, or to the nerve-conductor leading to it, or to the point of the brain with which it is in sympathetic connection, with a benevolent wish to effect the necessary change, and restore it to a healthy state, by either increasing or diminishing its vital action, imparts to it a spiritual force, which affects its physiological motions, and tends to produce the desired result. This is effected in proportion to the purity and strength of the love, in which the healing effort has its birth, and of which the kind wish is only a modification. But love acts by wisdom. To attain the highest success in this mode of cure, a person must know what the pathological state of the organs is in disease, and what change it is necessary to effect in their action in order to restore the body to a healthy condition. He must have an accurate knowledge of the anatomy and physiology of the nervous system, the connection of the various bodily organs with the brain, and of the nature of those spiritual disturbances and morbid mental states that underlie all diseased conditions of the bodily organism. It is emphatically true of this system of medical treatment, that knowledge is power. Faith, both in the operator and patient, is desirable. It is a spiritual force that has accomplished wonders. The power of faith, of which we might give numerous illustrations, drawn from the recorded facts of ancient and modern times, in restoring both mind and body to a healthy state, and the law that governs its action and influence, are but poorly understood by the world at large. It is a subject worthy of investigation by thinking minds. It is an element of strength in the will,—and an essential ingredient in a sound and harmonious mental state, and thus necessary to a restoration to life and health. *It is an actual psychological or spiritual force.* To believe that we can do a thing, especially if that faith is the result of an understanding of nature's laws, empowers us to do it. To believe that we are well, or that we are becoming so, excites a spiritual force within us, that goes far towards making us so. If we firmly believe that a certain remedy will cure us of a diseased condition, though it may have no chemical adaptation to the removal of the disorder, we shall be benefitted by it. Disease has often been cured by faith alone in the patient. The familiar case of the woman mentioned in the Gospel history, who had suffered for twelve years from a dangerous uterine hemorrhage, baffling the skill of various physicians, is known to all. She undoubtingly believed that if she could touch the hem of Jesus' garment she would be restored. With this assured faith, amounting to a certainty in her mind, which comes next to knowledge, she touched the fringe of his outer robe, and her *faith*, and nothing else, made her whole. This was no miracle, but only the natural triumph of the mind over the morbid condition of the body. The same cause will produce the same effect now, for whatever takes place in harmony with the laws of our being, belongs to all ages and all lands. The lack of faith is the loss of one of the essential elements of a sound mental state, which underlies, as a foundation, a healthy bodily condition. In the magnetic or psychological healer, it is a positive mental force; in the patient, a receptive mental state. But however valuable it may be, *knowledge* is better. An undoubting belief is what we call certainty, but it should be based upon a positive knowledge of the laws by which a desired result is effected. God created and still creates the world by wisdom. Love can only operate sucessfully through the intellect. There are two things in a patient necessary to the reception of a spiritual sanative influence. One is a desire to get well. The other is a faith in the efficiency of the remedial agency. Without these two, the cure of disease by any mode of treatment, is, to say the least, if not impossible, exceedingly difficult. To put to the patient the questions, Wilt thou be made whole? and, Believest thou that I am able to do this for thee? is of more importance than to feel the pulse, or examine the state of the mucous surface of the tongue. Unless an honest affirmative answer can be given to both inquiries, the case may be dismissed, or be treated with pure water drops, or cracker pills, or homeopathic pellets. The only sure thing about the case will be the entry of the fee upon the physician's books, or into his pocket.

The influence of faith in the cure of disease is well illustrated by a fact mentioned in Paris's Life of Sir Humphrey Davy. In the early period of his Scientific career, Davy was assisting Dr. Beddoes in his experiments on the inhalation of nitrous oxide. Dr. Beddoes, thinking the oxide must be a specific for paralysis, a patient was selected for trial and placed under the care of Sir Humphrey. Before administering the gas, wishing to ascertain the temperature of the palsied man's blood, a small thermometer was inserted under his tongue. The paralytic, wholy ignorant of the process to which he was to be subjected, but *deeply impressed*, by Dr. Beddoes, *with the certainty of its success*, no sooner felt the thermometer between his teeth, than he concluded that the talismanic influence was at work, and in a burst of enthusiasm declared he felt its healing power through his whole body. Here was an opportunity to test the influence of the *mind* in the cure of palsy that was not to be lost. The gas was not used, but on the following day, the thermometer was again employed with equally marked effects; and at the end of two weeks the patient was dismissed cured, no remedy of any kind having ever been used except the thermometer. His faith made him whole, not by accident, nor by a miracle, but by an invariable law of our being. So important a principle ought not to be ignored by medical science, and left to ignorant quacks, who often perform astonishing cures by means of it.

Fear is the opposite of faith, and produces equally striking effects in the generation of diseased conditions of the body. Many facts of this kind have been collected to illustrate what is falsely called the influence of the imagination. Persons have been shot dead with blank cartridges. A familiar fact is that of the Edinburg criminal who died from a supposed loss of blood, when it was only warm water that was made to trickle over his arm after it was barely pricked by the surgeons. Dr. Moore mentions the case of a lady who died with every symptom of hydrophobia, under the mistaken notion that she had been bitten by a rabid dog, when it was demonstrable that the animal had only torn her dress. One of the most instructive and satisfactory experiments on record, showing the influence of the mind in the generation of fatal diseases, is that tried upon four Russian criminals, who had been condemned to death for political offences. It was reported in the London Medical Times. The cholera was raging at the time in Russia, and the criminals, while ignorant of the fact, were made to occupy beds on which persons had recently died with the disease. Although thus exposed to the contagion, not one of them exhibited the least symptom of the malady. After this they were told that they must sleep on beds that had been occupied by persons who had been sick with the cholera. But in fact, the beds were entirely new, and had never been used by any one. Their fear proved to be a more powerful influence than the contagion, for three out of the four took the disease in its most fatal form, and died in four hours after the attack. Such a fact, coming as it does to us well authenticated, speaks volumes in favor of the doctrine of the spiritual origin of disease, and the efficiency of psychical remedies. But the current medical science, while convinced of the truth of this, makes no practical use of it as a remedial agency. Yet it is an interesting fact, that the longer a man has been engaged in the practice of the healing art, the less confidence he has in medicinal compounds, and the more he relies upon the *vis medicatrix naturae*, and upon the principles of Mental Hygiene. An aged physcian recently informed the author of a remarkable cure he had accomplished upon a nervous patient by the potent virtues of clear water, tinged with rosemary, a few drops of which were taken before each meal. Her restoration was complete and apparently permament. Faith is so essential a condition in the cure of disease, that in Nazareth and the adjacent region, Jesus could do but few mighty works, because of the unbelief of the people. (Matt. xiii. 58.) The reason assigned by him for the disciples' want of success in curing the lunatic child, was their unbelief, showing that faith is an element of power in him who would heal diseases of body and mind by the psychological method of treatment. (Matt. xvii. 14—20.)

The life of the body, or the force by means of which the vital movements are accomplished, is heat, —not a mere dead caloric, but a heat generated by the spiritual principle. The living forces of the human system and animal heat, are now believed by physiologists to be correlative, or are mutually transmutable and interchangeable. A direct relation certainly exists between them. M. Jules, and M. Serres, Prof. Faraday, and other scientists, have demonstrated the identity of heat and mechanical force. They are correlative and equivalant to each other. In the animal mechanism the same law holds good. If the living force of the body is heat—a heat that is the correspondent of the love—then all those means by which heat is generated and transmitted from one body to another, become the means of communicating life, and are a therapeutical agency. Among these may be mentioned *friction*. If your hands are cold, you rub them till the vital action is restored. If your child's hands are cold, you use the same means to warm them. The amount of heat generated in this way is proportioned to the force employed. If we feel a pain in any part, our first impulse is to place the hand upon it. By this means the accumulation of vital heat in the tissue is soon diminished, being conducted into the hand, and conveyed to another part of the system. The hand of another person would be equally or still more efficient. In this way we have cured a burn, or allayed the most painful inflammations, in a short time. To place the hand upon any part of the body of another person, creates a tendency in the vital force of both toward the point of contact. This is perceived as an increased glow of vital heat. If the part be cold and negative it soon becomes warm, and exhibits an augmented vascular action. These are nature's remedies, prescribed by our intuitions and instincts, and are as efficient as they are natural. Compression produces heat. A piece of cold wood subjected to a powerful hydraulic pressure is immediately warmed. Percussion generates heat, or the force expended in the act is transmuted into the thermal force. A piece of cold iron on an anvil, struck by a hammer, is warmed. This principle seems to have been employed in the remotest ages as a curative agency. We have a work published at Frankfort in 1698 entitled "Curious account of how Blows will often Cure, promptly and well, all kinds of Chronic Diesases."

The prophet Elisha manifestly employed this means in the cure of disease. The Syrian general who came to him to be healed of his leprosy, supposed he was going to "smite his hand over the place" and thus cure him. But why should he have expected this treatment unless it was common in that region of country?

Motion is correlated to life. The movement of a part determines the vital force to the part moved. All motions, passive or active, generate heat. A person riding in a cold day is warmer than he would be to sit still in the open air. Water poured from one vessel to another, or made to revolve in a cylinder, is warmed. This has been shown by the thermometer. It has been estimated that the falls of the Rhine generate enough heat in one day to melt twelve thousand metres of ice. All the movements employed in the system of Ling, especially the so called duplicated movements, or those where the patient is passive—the frictions, vibrations, compressions, percussions— are efficient therapeutic agencies. We have employed the system for several years in the treatment of the various forms of chronic derangements of the body, and with a success that has sometimes seemed to those who did not understand the laws that govern it, to border on the miraculous

But we have always supposed that it owed a great part of its efficiency to an impartation of vital magnetism from the operator to the patient, an opinion entertained by the German practitioners of the art. They adopt Reichenbach's theory of the *odic force*, and assert that an influence of this kind is actually communicated to the system of the patient. The nervous energy of the invalid is thereby exalted, and the reaction of the vital powers against disease greatly increased. Dally gives a beautiful drawing of the human hand in its minute and microscopic anatomy, showing that it is an instrument skillfully adapted to perform the office, as a part of its physiological functions, of imparting something like vital magnetism to another person, and argues that an important advantage is derived by the invalid from this transmission of life. We are convinced of the correctness of this theory. It is in perfect harmony with the principles and laws unfolded in this work.

But there is manifestly an agency concerned in the cure of disease, far more subtle and potent than the semi-spiritual odic force,—a psychological influence. This acts upon the mind of the patient, thence upon the spiritual body, and through this upon the material organism. The law of its action, is from within outward. The living forces of the system are spiritual. And there is a direct and potential influence of mind upon mind. This goes to the root of all diseased conditions, and carries a remedial agency into the realm of causation. There is a variety of phenomena, passing under the names of Mesmerism, Psychology, Biology, Animal Magnetism, Pathetism, Hypnotism, and even Psychometry, that are reducible to one general principle,—the influence or action of mind upon mind, and the communication of spiritual life from one person to another, who is negatively receptive of it.

If all diseases originate in some disturbed or inharmonious mental states, which ultimate themselves in corresponding bodily conditions, it becomes a question of primal importance how to induce upon a patient, as a permanent possession, the state of mind which is the opposite of that causing the disease. Is there any law that governs in effecting such a spiritual conversion or metamorphosis? There is a sort of polarity about our feelings as well as about the different organs of the body. In fact it is coming to be recognized by science that polarity is a universal property of things, belonging to the atom as well as to the world. Even light has polarity. And by transmitting it through certain substances, as a bundle of thin glass plates or certain crystals, a change is effected in the direction of the vibratory wave, which inverts its polarity. Gravitation may be only the attraction between the positive and negative forces of things. Something analogous to it belongs to spiritual essences. There are what may with propriety be called positive and negative states of the mind, and a dual action of the feelings. There may be a loss of balance here, or an inverted action of every faculty and of its organ in the brain—as faith and fear. The one is positive; the other negative. The mind employs the same part of the cerebrum in the outward manifestation of the two distinct sentiments or feelings. Or fear and anxiety are the inverted action of faith. All the organs may undergo this transposition of their forces. In some cases of insanity, which we have had under treatment, the patients have exhibited an inverted action of the social instincts, so that those they once loved the most, become correspondingly repugnant to them. In the action of conscience, there may be approval or condemnation. There may be mirthfulness or sadness. But the same organ in the brain is used in the manifestation of both feelings, only one is a positive and the other a negative action. The same may be said of hope and despondency. The predominance of the latter over the former constitutes the negative state of the former, or its inverted action. In the case of a magnet, if there should be this transposition of its forces, how could it be restored to its normal state? Or if there should be a loss of balance and equilibrium between the positive and negative poles, how could the harmony be re-established? We have only to bring the negative pole in contact with the positive pole of another magnet, and it attracts into itself the appropriate magnetism, and becomes charged with it. So of the other pole. In a similiar way, a negative or evil mental state may be made to give place to a positive or good one. The magnetic or spiritual healer should approach the patient's mind on the side of its disturbance, and if he *desires* to be relieved, his mind will attract into itself, with all the force of a hungry sympathy, the feelings and thoughts of the operator. The good-will also of the physician, his benevolent wish to impart his own better mental states will assist and facilitate the process of spiritual induction.

Nearly every thing in science is now explained by the theory of vibration, especially the phenomena of the imponderable forces—light, heat, color, electricity, and magnetism. If two strings of equal length are set to vibrating, but not in harmony, there will be a tendency in them to a perfect sameness and oneness of movement And if they can be made to continue their motions, they will soon both vibrate at the same distance and in the same time. Further still, if two strings be stretched parallel to each other, and one be caused to vibrate, it will instantly communicate its motion to the other. In a way analogous to this, one mind may induce upon another mind its own *emotions*, its thoughts and feelings. Our love is our life, and the excitement of the love is a spiritual motion. If a patient is afflicted with certain abnormal feelings or mental states, whose depressing influence has caused his diseased condition, and if he desires to be delivered from the spiritual causes of his physical disorder, let him submit himself to the magnetic treatment of some kind and sympathetic friend. He should be passive like the unmoved string. Then the movements of the operator's mind, his *emotions* and affectional states, will be communicated to him. The effect will be permanent also. One mind may daguerreotype itself upon another. It may make an ineffaceable impression upon it, and effect a lasting metamorphosis in it. Just as certainly as one harp played upon, will cause another standing by it, to sound also, so certainly, and by an unerring law of our spiritual nature, one mind, by a sort of mysterious vibration, will communicate its mental forces tc another mind. Under the proper conditions, we need have no doubt of producing the desired result. There is no miracle here, no departure from law, any more than in the phenomena we have mentioned as illustrations. Both are natural, and we may be as certain of the desired result in one case as the other.

In this way, Jesus healed the sick, first the mind, then the body. He removed the spiritual cause of disease, and the physical effect ceased. He carried his sanative influence into both departments of our being, the inner and the outer. This was done by the law of sympathy—a law of the mind that means more than the world has ever understood. By it one mind transmits its states of feeling and modes of thought to another, and oftentimes without intending it. Jesus thus imparted to the sick and wretched the calm happiness of his own loving and gentle heart. His habitual mental condition, when communicated to the afflicted, was the panacea for all their spiritual abnormality. His mind was a perfect harmony, everywhere exactly balanced, and thus contained in itself all that any one, however wretched, needed to restore his soul to soundness and health. Hence his cures were mostly, if not always, instantaneous.

If we, who make but a distant approach to the

perfection of character exhibited by Jesus, can not instantaneously cure every form of mental and bodily disorder, we can do it more slowly, but as surely, if we are moved by the same love. The little we impart of mental good and sanative influence, will propagate and diffuse itself like leaven, until the whole mental nature of the patient is changed and becomes homogeneous with it. A little contagion, though it be but an infinitesimal amount, will multiply itself and propagate itself, until the whole system is assimilated to it. But a person may be inoculated with health as well as with disease. All contagions operate through the spiritual essence in them. Some false notion imbibed, some groundless fear, often lies at the bottom of chronic disease. It predisposes the outward organism to a state of things in harmony with it, for there is a conatus in both the soul and body to adjust themselves to each other, so as to be in agreement. One false notion, somehow acquired, will work like leaven, until the mind of the recipient is changed, and his whole life modified by it. Thus Jesus, understanding this law of mental impregnation, and the tendency of any thought or feeling to diffuse and propagate itself, charged his disciples to beware of the *leaven* of the Pharisees, referring to their false and pernicious notions. If the evil and the false work such changes, why may not the good and the true produce still greater and diviner results? "The kingdom of heaven is like leaven (as well as the false doctrines of Pharisees), which a woman took and hid in three measures of meal until the whole was leavened." But the highest heaven is only the greatest degree of love, and the most exalted range of the intellect. If heaven be in us, we may impart it to others, and it will prove like leaven in the flour —it will spread until the whole soul is assimilated to it. We may avail ourselves of these hitherto hidden laws of our spiritual essence in the cure of mental and physical disorders. As mankind become more elevated in the intellectual scale, the remedial agencies employed by them, will become less gross and material, and more spiritual. Doctrines that once were satisfactory and useful to the mind of man, cannot now nourish his inner life. So remedies, that people once used without injury, and perhaps with benefit, in the present advanced stage of the development of the race, are no longer adapted to the cure of disease. The New Age demands not only a better theology and philosophy, but a more spiritual system of medication.

CHAPTER XXI.

THE MIND NOT LIMITED BY SPACE IN THE TRANSMISSION OF PSYCHOLOGICAL AND SANATIVE INFLUENCES.

Freedom of the Mind from Spatial Restraint — Spiritual Presence. — Mental Locomotion. — Physiological Influence of Psychological Impressions. — Transmission of Mental Force. — The Model Man and Great Physician. — His freedom from Material Limitations. — The Interior State intensely Positive. — The Prayer Cure. — The Laws governing it. — Love the Healing Power. — The Mind to be first Healed. — The Mystery of the Cures wrought by Jesus explained. — How to Convert Souls without a Miracle. —Nature of the Mental Sphere. — Healing at a Distance. — The Laws by which it is Effected. — Directions given in regard to it. — Communication of abnormal States by Sympathy. — Practical Value of the Law.

IT IS one of the peculiar properties of mind, or spiritual essence, that it is not subject to the limitations of time and space. These are the essential conditions of what we call matter. It exists in time and fills space, and is limited to the space it occupies. But the human spirit is free from this confinement and restraint. In the realm of spirit, time and space are not objective realities, but subjective states, or as Kant expresses it, "forms of the intellect." It can be present, really and substantially, with those who are miles away. It is a common form of expression, not originated by Paul, but arising from an intuitive recognition of its mysterious nature and powers, that we are present in spirit with certain loved ones, though absent from them in body. Not that our souls actually leave their bodies, for the connection between them is never dissolved but once, but our mental presence and force seem to go forth to a distance, and break loose from all spatial restraints. For in another world the spirit moves not so much by a passing from one point of space to another, as by a change of state, and a transferrence of its force. In this way we may *appear* to ourselves to journey miles away, until we are present with some distant person. Sometimes the intervening objects and scenery pass in review, and may be described. We may influence the thoughts and feelings of the distant one, with whom we come into rapport, which is only a spiritual presence and conjunction of two minds, in the same way, it is to be presumed, that one spirit acts upon and into another spirit in the world above. We often feel an indefinable sense of the presence of persons, both those who are still living in the flesh, and those who have passed to the inner sphere of life. This is something most real, and not the working of what we call imagination. It usually occurs in connection with those with whom we are in sympathy. Through the impression made upon the spirit, the body, or any of its organs, may be affected. *For all psychological influences effect a change in the physiological movements.* In this way life may be infused into any weakened part, pains may be dispersed, and inflammations and congestions relieved. When examining a patient hundreds of miles away, we have sometimes been sensibly affected with their diseased state both of mind and body. Once where the patient was troubled with almost perpetual nausea, it occasioned vomiting in us. Such effects are common in psychometrical examinations. If a patient can thus affect a physician, not merely with mental impressions, but in a moment modify the functional action of the bodily organs, can he not influence the patient as well? Availing himself of this mental law and force, he can affect the physiological action of any organ in the body. We have found many cases where this mode of treatment was even more efficient than the ordinary magnetic manipulations. We devoted more than a year to the study of the laws that govern this transmission of vital force to a distance, and to experiments with it. Most of the experiments made in psychology have been of a trivial nature, and of no other value than the proof they afford of the existence of a law of action and reaction between minds at a distance. Our experiments were entered upon, not so much with the desire to establish the reality of such an influence of mind upon mind, as to see if it could not be turned to some important hygienic use. This has been satisfactorily demonstrated, and it has proved itself to be a sanative agency to an extent far beyond our expectations. Many quite desperate cases of chronic disease have been cured in this, to some incredible way, in a few days. The rest of this volume could be filled with authenticated facts in relation to marvelous cures by the use of no other remedial agency. But we have deemed it better, at least it is more in consonance with our feelings, to imitate the great Physician, and say to the patients thus healed and loosed from their infirmities, "See thou tell no man." Certificates of wonderful cures and advertisements of miraculous gifts, spring more from a desire to make money out of the sufferings of humanity, than a desire to do good to the souls and bodies of men. They are no reliable evidence of an ability to cure "all manner of sickness and disease among the people," but sometimes indicate a lack of that pure, unselfish love which is the only healing power. The great forces of nature are silent in their operation, and make but little show or noise. It does not come within the scope of the present volume, to make an encyclopedia of facts, but to unfold the principles and the philosophy of all the individual facts that could be collected under the various subjects treated of. We hold to the heresy that principles come before facts in the true order of mental growth, and the knowledge of things in their causes, is of more worth than a recognition of effects. This we acknowledge is not the Baconian method of philosophizing.

Jesus of Nazareth possessed the power of transferring his mental presence and spiritual force through any extent of spatial distance, and in a degree never witnessed before in the world. It is the highest glory of a disciple to be like the Master or Teacher. He speaks of being in heaven even while he dwelt bodily on the earth. "No man hath ascended up to heaven, but he that came down from heaven, even the son man who *is* in heaven." The import of these words is, that while on earth his soul had risen to a truly spiritual life. He inner selfhood was not in bondage to material limitations, but was subject to the laws that govern human nature in the spiritual world, and having attained to the exalted privileges of the other and inner life, was invested with the powers of a pure spirit. His interior manhood, thus made capable of acting independently of the bodily instrument, and freed from material limitations, read the very thoughts of men; told them, as in the case of Nathaniel, secret facts in their past life; and sometimes disclosed the future, by a piercing glance into the realm of causation. In a word, though possessed of a material body, the inner man was emancipated from material thraldom, and asserted its supremacy. In this state, he cured disease, often without touching the patient. His spirit acted directly upon the living spirit of the diseased, and thus acted upon the cause of the external pathological condition. Just in proportion as any one attains to the state exhibited by him, can he cure diseases of mind and body as he did. We wish to steer clear of all theological speculations and controversies, and shall enter upon no discussion as to the nature of Jesus, nor cry, Ecce Homo, nor Ecce Deus, nor Ecce Deus-Homo, though we cannot well avoid the confession of our faith in him, as the one and only God made flesh, and dwelling among us. One thing all theories and creeds admit,—and this is the only truth we care now to deal with—that he had a complete human nature, which passed through a perfectly human development from its birth to its glorification and ascension. And what the divine nature did for him, it is willing to do for us, in a degree, and we may be glorified or spiritulized with him. This is certainly the teaching of the New Testament.

The interior state of which we are speaking is not a negative one, but is intensely positive toward all on a lower plane. It is a state receptive of spiritual influx, of life and light from the celestial realms, but is positive and communicative towards those who are only in the sensuous degree of the mind's action. It is a position of great spiritual power. The lower plane of being is always negatively passive to the spiritual world. So persons, elevated or unfolded to the state we have described, are positive towards those on a lower and less spiritual plane.

In harmony with the laws that govern in the action of mind upon mind, prayer avails for the cure of disease, and would be a more common and efficient remedial agency, if there was more faith among men in the reality and power of spiritual influences. Prayer for another, in its essence, is a desire for the good and happiness of its object. It is one of the forms in which a genuine neighborly love or charity is expressed, and it always affects the mind of him who is the subject of our intercessions. It is only another illustration of the action of one spirit upon another. Among the early Christians, it was a common practice in the cure of diseased states of mind and body. (James v. 14, 15.) And no good reason can be assigned why it should not be as efficient to-day as it was eighteen centuries ago. We have known several persons who devoted themselves to this method of cure, and with a success that put to shame more material, but less rational and efficacious methods of medication. If disease has a spiritual origin, and its causes are found in preexisting disordered mental states, Proseuchopathy, or the prayer-cure, is as well adapted to the removal of the prior pathological condition of the inner man, as Allopathy, or Hydropathy, or Homeopathy. A return to the pure unselfish love and undoubting faith of the primitive church, would restore to favor again this efficient spiritual remedy for disease. The Seeress of Prevorst, characterized for her unassuming piety and ardent christian love, in this way cured the Countess Von Maldeghem of insanity and bodily disease.

The power to cure disease by spiritual forces is found in the divine principle of love. Just so far as any one receives into himself the pure unselfish love of God,—a love that in him is an irrepressible desire to communicate good,—so far there is in him a power to impart life and health and peace to others. There is lodged within him a fraction of the divine omnipotence. So far as he is calmly and humbly conscious of this divine element within him, has he power to do the works of God. Love is the life of all; it is the life of God; it is the divinest and most potential thing in the universe. If a man has attained to the life of love, having risen above all selfish considerations as controlling motives of conduct, and is filled with an all-absorbing divine longing to impart good to every human being, and has a faith rooted in love, his slightest touch is healing. His very presence is fraught with sanative influences. His sphere is a life-giving emanative energy. This healthy spiritual life is communicated by actual material contact, or the action of his mind upon others in the distance. It is a law of our being, and we cannot escape from its operation, that every time we *think* of an absent person we affect them for good or evil.

In studying the cures wrought by Jesus, one is struck with the apparent ease with which he overcame every diseased condition. The secret of this seems to be, he healed first the mind, going to the secret mental state as the cause, and on removing this, the effect or correspondent bodily condition ceased at once. The suddenness with which this takes place may be illustrated in this way. If in a fracture of the skull a portion of the cranium presses upon the brain, the patient is deprived of consciousness. The external manifestations of the mind are by this cause suspended. But as soon as the cerebrum is relieved of this pressure, consciousness is restored. Just so soon, in most cases, when the mental state, underlying any diseased condition, is changed to the normal one, the outward pathological state ceases. An effect cannot exist when its cause no longer acts. In this way Christ carried his healing power into the realm of spiritual causes. *He addressed himself as a spirit to the spirit of the patient.* If we understand all that is implied in this, and can go and do likewise, diseases of long standing will yield at once to the potent energy of our love. This may be effected at a distance, as well as in the presence of the unhappy sufferer. The greatest difficulty in the cure of a disease, is in coming to the perception of the interior cause, and in finding how to remove it. Independent clairvoyance or intuition is adequate to the first, and magnetism, using the term not merely for mesmerism, but for the law by which mind communicates its spiritual states and forces to another is equal to the latter result.

In our verbal communications with a patient, we should forget that he has any material body, and *speak as a spirit to his spirit.* Here is a source of power that is overlooked. We generally speak to each other's body, and think of nothing else. The reverse of this should be true. If we approach a patient as if he were a spirit, abstracting the mind from the mere perception of his outward organism, and approach him with our interior manhood, the living soul, as if we were a spirit, then the better mental state, which is always the stronger, will prevail over and suppress the other and weaker. This is as certain as in a combat of physical strength between two gymnasts, the stronger and more skillful of the two will overcome the other. In this way the patient is renewed in mind, the inner man. He is spiritually healed. The hidden cause of his malady being removed, the spirit being restored to health, the body with all its living, moving forces, soon becomes adjusted to the new order of things that exists within. We must induce upon the patient a new mental state, and supplant the old mode of feeling and thought. We must give him in a proper sense, a new spiritual birth, or at least impregnate him with a better interior life. We must *convert* him. Such mental changes are sometimes permanent. In the popular

revivals, *where men's souls are addressed,* and where
they almost forget that their hearers have such a
thing as a physical body, lasting mental changes are
wrought. The convert receives an impulse, an influence, an impression, that changes the whole current
of his inner life. It remains for weeks, for months,
for years, and often through the rest of his earthly
existence. There is nothing supernatural or miraculous in this, and we have nothing to say against it.
Good may come out of it. It is in perfect harmony
with the spiritual laws that govern us. The united
effort of the minister and of those in sympathy with
him, being directed to the production or induction of
a new mental state upon the "anxious" or "peni-
tent," they generally succeed in effecting the desired
result, the *conversion* or change of the soul. They
might do it much easier, if they were good magneti-
zers, and understood the laws that control the action
of mind upon mind. The most susceptible and passive natures make the easiest converts, and the men
who have the most magnetic power, as it is called,
are the most successful revivalists. There is no need
to call to our aid any supernatural influences to account for such spiritual metamorphoses. The laws of
our mental nature are adequate to produce and
explain all such phenomena. The minister and the

church induce upon the convert their own mental state. They impart their own mental life, their modes of thought and affection to him. There is nothing more miraculous in this, or out of the usual order of things in the world of mind, than there is when a bar of steel, bent in the form of a horse-shoe, is brought in contact with a powerful electro-magnet, and is made thereby permanently magnetic. All forms of religion effect such mental transformations, both the evangelical and the heretical. Mahometans, Shakers, Adventists, and even Mormons," do so with their enchantments." And the law by which it is done is available to change the habitual mental state of a patient, and is legitimately used for such a purpose. To effect such an interior change should be the first aim of an intelligent and benevolent physician. He should be a spiritual midwife to assist the inner man to a birth into a higher and happier life.

We have shown that the sphere which goes forth from every human spirit is not an emission into space of spiritual particles, but is analogous to the action of the radiant forces, heat, light, and electricity. These are now explained by the theory of vibration. When a message is telegraphed from New York to London, no imponderable fluid shoots along the wire but there is only the transmission of force, a vibra tory wave in an elastic medium called the ether. So when one mind acts upon another mind, and influences its thoughts and feelings, when the bodies they animate are separated by hundreds of leagues, the effect is produced in a similar way. There is only a transmission of mental force, and the action and reaction of one spirit upon another. This vibratory movement takes place in an all-pervading, everywhere present element far more refined, elastic, and subtle, than the ether. It is a semi-spiritual essence that fills all space, which has been denominated the aura, the atmosphere of the inner world. It is the medium through which mind acts upon mind, and also upon matter. By means of it, mental and vital force is transmissible to unlimited distances. This law of action and reaction, between mind and mind, explains the phenomena of fascination or charming, which is only the transmission of spiritual force from one being to another. When an animal is thus enchanted by another, their life becomes so interblended, that an injury inflicted upon the charmer, is felt by the other, and the killing of the fascinating animal sometimes proves instant death to the captive. When one person, by a psychological influence, is magnetized or entranced by another, any effect the operator produces upon himself, is communicated to the subject. Their life seems to be intermingled. An unseen but potent influence takes possession of the mind of the subject, and controls its actions. Here is a power that can be turned to good account, or perverted to evil. It can be made an efficient agency in the system of mental hygiene, under the direction of good men and angels, or it can be perverted to witchcraft and demoniacal obsessions. For these invisible forces are controllable by spirits either in the flesh or disrobed of their mortal covering. They may take advantage of these natural laws, and greatly aid in producing the desired benevolent result.

Let us see how this law may be employed in communicating a sanative influence, and remedial force. To think of another, interiorly and abstractly, occasions a spiritual presence, and his image seems to stand before us. Where the thought is grounded in love and good-will, it causes an interior conjunction—a mental sympathy, a state of rapport. By it they come into a living communication, as real as it would be if they reached through the intervening space and grasped each other by the hand. The feelings of each are communicated to the other. The mental state of the one who is the most positive will predominate, and take possesion of the other, for the stronger force will prevail over the weaker. Thus a healthier mental state will be induced upon the patient. This spirito-magnetic influence can be transmitted independently of spatial distance. We have experimented with it at a distance of over a thousand miles, and once between New Hampshire and Louisiana. The patient should assume an easy and quiet position, and be as passive and undisturbed as possible. The time may be agreed upon between them. It is well for him to be in a room by himself, which is to be but little lighted. For darkness, being a negative state of the surrounding atmosphere, is favorable to psychological influences and impressions, and renders the body more passively susceptible. The room also, in which the patient is, should be only moderately heated. When in the state of spiritual presence and conjunctive sympathy, any effect the operator may produce upon himself, or which he receives by influx from spiritual presences, will be telegraphed instantly to the patient. If he applies his hand to his fore-brain, as if to remove a catarrhal inflammation, it produces the same effect upon the patient. Sometimes such manipulations upon the operator's person affect the patient a hundred miles away, in as great a degree as they would were he bodily present, *and are sometimes as sensibly felt.* They affect the spiritual body, which is the seat of sensation.

Instead of applying his hands to himself, the operator may *in thought*, apply them to the person he would affect, and where and in what way the diseased condition would require. This mental act affects the spiritual organism of the invalid, and through this the physical body. It acts from within outward. It is the transmission of a mental force which produces physiological changes. Its results are sometimes marvelous to those who do not comprehend the spiritual laws that govern us. The patient will be influenced in a degree proportioned to his susceptibility, and the mental force of the operator. If the latter have great strength of will, manifested in calmness, self-reliance, undoubting faith, a peaceful desire to impart good, and confidence in the help of higher powers, the effect produced on the mind of the invalid, and the change wrought in the functional action of the bodily organs, will be decided and permanent. Thus the mysterious forces of life can be transmitted as far as those of light, heat, or electricity can be conveyed through space, and in an analogous way. We feel confident that to every ardent lover of truth the above hints and suggestions will be found to enclose a germ capable of almost unlimited unfoldment. We humbly submit them to the consideration of all such minds.

It is well known that, by the law of sympathy, certain diseased states both of mind and body become contagious. The convulsions of hysteria are often propagated among young women in this way. The same is true of chorea, and of stammering. We insensibly imbibe the tastes, manners, habits, and even the bodily condition of others. Boerhaave relates that the pupils of a squint-eyed schoolmaster near Leyden, after a while, exhibited the same obliquity of vision. Those who have the care of the insane and the sick, are more or less affected by them. All abnormal states of mind or body are, in some degree, contagious. But healthy states both of the inner and outer man are equally communicable. The law of sympathy, according to which disease is transmitted from one person to another, is available for the propagation of sound states of the spiritual and physical nature of man. The law operates with equal force both ways. A genuine sympathy, arising from a benevolent disposition, for a person in suffering, actually relieves him of his pain. There is by means of it an interchange of states. We enter, as it were, into his body, and become in some measure the same person with him, and take upon us his feelings and impart ours to him. We bear a part of his burden, and in proportion as we take upon ourselves his painful sensations and unhappy mental states, is he relieved of them. Patients feel better the moment a physician who is in sympathy with them, comes into the room. His words bring sunshine into their darkness, his presence supplies the magnetic life they need, his touch sends a thrill of pleasure through their whole frame, and his very look dispels their mental and bodily pains. Thus the doctrine of sympathy is of practical value in the treatment of the sick, and can be turned to a useful account.

CHAPTER XXII.

APPETITES, INTUITIONS AND IMPRESSIONS, AND THEIR USE.

Essential Spirituality of Man. — The Vis Medicatrix naturæ is a Mental Force. — The Fetal Growth. — Incubation. — The Nature and Office of the Appetites. — Their Prescriptions. — Illustrations. — Nutriment for the Mind. — Spiritual Starvation. — Gibeonitish Crusts. — Voices without a sound. — Spiritual Impressions. — A deep and calm Revealing. — A Law of the Spiritual Life. — The Communion of Saints. — Education of our Intuitions. — The Inner Language. — The Cogitatio Loquens. — Intuitional Prescriptions. — Mental Telegraphing. — Madam Guyon and her Confessor. — Development of our hidden Powers.

WE HAVE demonstrated the truth, that the only real thing in the life of the body is the mind, and that the organizing force is the spiritual principle. When the body receives an injury, the inner man goes to work to repair the damage. This was attributed by the earlier physiologists to what they called the *vis medicatrix naturæ*, the healing power of nature. But this healing force is evidently spiritual, as all negative, depressing mental states greatly enfeeble its action, while the positive states of the mind increase its vigor. When the system is invaded by disease, the chances of a speedy recovery depend upon the condition of the patient's mind. If he be free from anxiety, is cheerful, full of hope, and has a stubborn faith, his restoration will be far more speedy under any system of medical treatment. The mind is the hidden force that reacts against disease, and repairs the damage sustained by any of the tissues by accident. To assist the *vis medicatrix naturæ*, is the only office of the physician.

In the vital germ in the womb, the soul-principle, imparted to it, sets itself to work to complete the bodily structure. The germ in the female ovaries, is a primary form receptive of the influx of spiritual life. It attracts to itself the most vital elements of the blood, which being robbed of its spiritual essence, is cast out of the system. It is vitalized still more, or receives an additional spiritual principle from the male semen, and thus endowed with a living force, attracts to itself and around itself from the circulation of the mother the elements necessary to the growth and completeness of the fetal organism. The same process is seen in the egg of the fowl. The germ of the future chick is the yolk. When this receives the vivifying principle from the male, it goes to work to build up the bodily structure. The albumen, or white of the egg, contains in a soluble form all the elements needful for the purpose. The building materials that enter into the composition of the body, are all found in this nutritious substance, and ready to be appropriated. It diminishes in quantity, as the germ enlarges, until it is finally all absorbed.

There is something similar to this in the action of a spiritual organizing force in adult life. Action always implies waste both in mind and body. From the body the devitalized particles are eliminated by the excreting organs, and a new supply is demanded to maintain the integrity of the organization. And we firmly believe that the mind, left to itself, and unbiased by education and the influence of others, will attract to itself what is needful to repair the waste resulting from the wear of its outward machinery. It goes forth in special longings, unerring appetites, and instinctive cravings, for what the body needs. The word appetite (from *ad* and *peto*) means a seeking after something. The mind left to its natural instincts will search, through the whole range of nutritive substances, after that which will supply the needed elements. If our appetites were unvitiated, they would give us with undeviating certainty a safe guide to what the body needs. If our mental instincts and intuitions were properly educated and trusted, they would prove our best physician, whose prescriptions we might rely upon with unhesitating confidence. In most, if not all, diseased conditions, there is a lack of some particular element, the loss of which impairs the healthy functional action of the weakened organ or organs. To supply this primitive element, whether it be phosphorus, iodine, chlorine, the alkaline or acid principle, is the aim of any judicious medication, or dietetic regulations. Any prescription that fails to do this, is useless, if not positively injurious. In nine cases out of ten, the mind of the patient, in its instinctive cravings, will be the safest guide, and will give a prescription in plain English, without any unintelligible Latin or Cabalistic signs. Where there is a deficient quantity of any element entering into the composition of the human frame, the mind will be moved by a special desire and longing for that very thing, or for some article of diet containing a large percentage of it. Or if there be an excess of some organic element, the soul will put forth its feelers after something to neutralize it. In a torpidity of the liver, the alkaline bile accumulates, and the patient feels a desire for acids to neutralize the excess of alkali. For the mind, as an organizing force exhibits a perpetual conatus to keep the body in such a state as to render it a suitable instrument for the performance of the uses of the soul in this lower range of existence. We have known children to eat salt with greater apparent relish than others would sugar. This indicates a want of chloric acid, which that article supplies. In certain cold and negative states, we have known others to exhibit a special appetite for starch, which they would devour with avidity. In a large proportion of diseases there is a superabundance of the alkaline principle. In such cases the citric acid of lemons and of most sour fruits, or the lactic acid of sour milk cheese and buttermilk, become grateful to the taste. Lehmann, in his Chemical Physiology, has shown that the essential elements of the gastric juice are the lactic and chloric acids, in a free state. They also assist in the absorption of the chyle from the alimentary canal. In some diseases, as dropsy, there is a lack of the alkaline or an excess of the negative or acid element. The mind, through the sympathetic nerves, would then prescribe, as a diet, something abounding in alkali to neutralize the accumulating acid, and restore the balance between the positive and negative forces of the system. If we would learn the language of our inward oracle, and heed reverently its voice, we should discover within ourselves a temple of Esculapius, whose responses to our questionings would be a safe guide to health and longevity. But we stop our ears to its divine revelations, heed not its suggestions, and listen to the blind and senseless formulas of the drug practitioner, but too often repent our folly when it is too late.

The mind also needs nutriment to furnish the spiritual pabulum necessary to its endless growth, and to supply the means of recuperation from the fatigue resulting from long continued action in a given direction. It needs recreation, or re-creation, which is only a change in the mode of its activity. We are so constituted that whatever will heighten our spiritual activities, add to the growth and vigor of our powers, and increase our happiness, we instinctively long for, and seize upon with avidity. Many morbid mental states are only a starved condition of the intellect or the affections. There is an indefinable longing, an unsatisfied craving for something it has not. The pathological state resulting, is that of mental weakness and bodily decrepitude. If the human mind was left more to itself, and to a freer development of its individuality, the world would be better and happier. Every healthy soul is the supreme judge of its own needs. There are many in the present advanced age of society, who have outgrown the infantile state that can draw nutriment from books, sermons, essays, and the mouldy Gibeonitish crusts of cant phrases used in the current religious instruction, so called. The mental stomach loathes the innutritious and unsavory cookery of the church, which has only the power to sharpen men's appetites for something better. We rise from its table with our inward hunger unsatiated, our thirst unquenched. We crave the vital essence of truth itself, and not the external husk. Such minds turn with instinctive longing to the opening heavens, and seek, in communion with the angel-world, the living bread. This they do as intuitively as the new-born infant seeks the maternal breast. We ask our appointed teachers for bread, and get a stone; for fish, and a serpent is served up for us; for an egg—for a living germ of truth,—and are turned off with a scorpion. We run over their ancient bill of fare, worn and defaced, and find nothing which our mental instincts crave. We go through their round of outward ceremonies, their genuflections, washings, prayers, and psalm-singing, rehearse an unintelligible creed, and like a hungry man, dream we are filled, but awake, and behold, we are empty.

In such a state, it is practicable for us to listen to the voiceless instruction of the angel-world. No miracle, no departure from the ordinary laws of the spirit is required to open a living intercourse with the heavens. It is a fact, as well established as any principle of chemistry, that one mind can impress its thoughts and feelings upon another, without the intervention of spoken words. Thousands of successful experiments have confirmed its truth and reality. We accept it as a settled principle. Angelic spirits may impress our delicately sensitive inner organism, as easily as they are supposed to play upon a golden harp, and thus give us an intuitive knowledge of the truths we need. A larger proportion of our highest and best thoughts owe their origin to this source, and come to us from the upper realms, than we are aware of. We should receive vastly more from those in the inner world who love us, and long to share their celestial treasure with us, if we had not been educated to fear them, and even to believe that intercourse with them is wicked, notwithstanding Jesus set us the example of communion with the ever-present heavens. Such teachers take away the key of knowledge. They will neither enter the temple of wisdom themselves, nor suffer others, whom they can prevent, to do so. In consequence of this unnatural education, there is many a one who would be as much afraid of the spirit of his mother, as he ought to be of the mediæval devil. But the desire to communicate good and truth to man on earth is as natural for good spirits, as it is for water to descend from a higher to a lower level. It is the delight of their life. It is something like what we observe in ourselves here. If your loved and loving friend is removed from you, how he longs to see you and speak to you. If there was anything you needed to make you well and happy, if it were possible for him to speak to your inner ear, how gladly would he inform you where to find it. This longing, this pang and chasm of separation, which we feel when we are absent from loved ones, is but an expression of the same feeling that leads those above to desire to communicate their better thoughts and feelings to those below. It would be painful for us to visit one we loved, and fail in our attempts to cause him to recollect us, and to have him fly from us as from one who would do him injury. These are natural feelings, belonging to the very essence of the soul, and are carried over with us to the other life. When we outgrow our unnatural fear of our best friends, and do not fly from their love as if it were infernal hate, and welcome their return to us, and recognize them in their true character, converse with the upper sphere of being will be more frequent and elevating. We have reason to believe, that in consequence of this unnatural feeling which we owe to our want of proper education, and our dismal doubts of their real existence, our friends who have migrated to the celestial plains, feel our loss as much as we do theirs. It must be unpleasant for a child who returns home from a journey to a foreign clime, to the parents he loves, and to whom he longs to impart the rich stores of information he has gained, to have them be frightened at his approach, refuse his offered treasures, and close the door in his face.

It is remarked by one who had a larger experience of an open intercourse with the angel-world, than any man in modern history, that in the other world there is a universal communication of thoughts and affections, owing to the very nature and laws of spirit. The knowledge of an individual or association is as naturally imparted to all who desire it, as for a heated body, for instance a gold coin, to transfuse its heat into another in contact with it. Only in the spiritual world this is done more perfectly and without any diminution of light in the communicating mind. In the Arcana Celestia we are truly told, " That there is not only a communication of another's affections and thoughts, but also of his knowledge, and that so completely, as for one to think that he knows whatever another does, although before he had no aquaintance with such subjects. Thus all the attainments of one are communicated to others. Some spirits retain what they are thus made acquainted with, but others do not."

The same illumined author further observes, "Souls are surprised on their entrance into another life, to find that there is such a communication of the thoughts of others, and that they instantly become acquainted, not only with the character of another's mind, but also with that of his knowledge."

This is only a universal law and property of mind, and we may avail ourselves of it here and now, for we are only spirits clothed with a material body. It is as natural for one mind to communicate its thoughts and feelings to another, as for a flower to emit fragrance. The inner world spontaneously flows into the outer. No effort is necessary to this influx of celestial light, any more than is needful to cause the stars in a clear firmament to shine into the darkness, but only a receptive mind. We may come into a conscious communication with the light of the spiritual world, which, in its essence, is pure truth, and we may do this without intercourse with any individual spirit. We may imbibe the living light of a higher sun. The higher always gravitates to a lower level, the interior to the external. This is the established order of influx. And we have it in our power to commence a course of education, or development from within, in place of the bungling instruction we receive from without—from books and tutors. To put our spirits into harmonious conjunction with the angelic realms and the living light of a higher sky and diviner sun, is to come into a position where we may learn, in the brief space of an hour, more than by months of patient study in the schools. Blessed is the man who has been inserted into an angelic consociation, who has an all-satisfying fellowship with those who have graduated to a nearer approach to the Infinite Mind, and who finds a conscious celestial companionship in the most lonely solitude.

If we would educate our intuitions and impressions, they would become an almost unerring light. Men are influenced by them now far more than in the pride of their boasted reason, they are ready to acknowledge. What we need is the restoration of our inner life to freedom. It was made to rule the outward senses, not to be in bondage to them. Most men are in an abnormal state, an inverted position. Our inner self, by which we are placed in contact with the spiritual world, is overlaid and suppressed by our sensuous nature. To our inner man, the heavens may speak in a still small voice,—in a calm and deep revealing. Internally we are always in speaking distance with the angels. They are our nearest neighbors. Ideas, which are only the living images of things, have their home in the spiritual realm. They are an objective creation there. They are the primitives of all our mental conceptions, the soul of our thoughts, and inmost essence of vocal language. Angelic and celestial ideas flow into our thoughts so far as they are able to contain them, and spoken words are the outward expression of thoughts. *Thought in the spiritual world is as distinctly heard as words are in our social intercourse here.* For thought occasions a vibration in the spiritual atmosphere, which is conveyed to the inner ear, just as our vocal utterances cause an undulatory movement of the air, which affects the external organ of hearing. But the one is as audible as the other. Converse with those in the interior or spiritual realm is as easy to those who understand the principles and laws by which it is effected and governed, and who have passed through the necessary development, as it is for us to speak to one another in this external plane of life. There is a far more satisfying and reliable medium of communication than written or oral language. We do not attach the same meaning to outward words, hence do not understand each other fully. But our thoughts, if they were communicated to each other, would be clear and intelligible. In Dr. Brittan's recent excellent work, "Man and his Relations," he says: "The human mind in its progress employs media and methods of communication, suited to the several stages of its development. However serviceable these instrumentalities may be—each in its appropriate time and place—they may be inadequate to meet the demands of more enlightened periods. We realize the insufficiency of written and oral language to express the highest thoughts and deepest feelings. There is another—it may possibly become—a more perfect medium of communication. This language, though unwritten and unspoken, may be adequate to a fuller expression of all we feel and know. It is not unfrequently the means,—little as it is practiced and understood—of revealing thoughts and impulses to which a vocal utterance has been denied."

In the other world language is a *cogitatio loquens*, a cogitative utterance. It is the communication of thought from one mind to another. This is as perceptible to the inner auditory sensory as words are to us. When an angelic idea is received by us, the degrees of descent are these. Spiritual ideas flow into our thoughts, and these find utterance, or an embodiment, in the words that are in our memory. But our thoughts may not be capacious enough to hold an angelic idea, and our words but poorly express our thoughts. He whose mind is exalted to a spiritual plane of activity, may perceive, as Paul did, unutterable things. The soul, in the calm, loving, and living light of a supersensuous realm, may enjoy an ineffable intellectual and affectional experience.

In what we have said, there may be seen the operation of an arcane principle, a hidden and undeveloped law of our minds, of which we may avail ourselves in holding an all-satisfying communion with the angel-world, and become receptive of its light. If we are diseased and unhappy, and know not where to turn for relief, we may be assured that the light we need is shining on the other shore. Our angel guardians know, or may learn, what we need and will communicate it to us, if we will open the inner ear to receive it, as gladly as a mother would tell her child what will relieve its pains, and we may receive the needed truth as naturally as the opening flower drinks in the rays of the sun. We may rely on such impressional intelligence, and intuitive flashes of a higher light, far more than upon the prescriptions of a well-meaning, but imperfectly enlightened physician. In a calm, passive, and receptive mental state, our first impressions, before we have had time to reason, are always the safest and surest guide. What we call reason, is often only a struggle of doubt with truth, and not unfrequently throws us from the pathway of light into the dismal darkness on each side of it.

Sometimes a person attains to a state, where the thoughts of men, which are the vernacular language of the spirit, become distinctly cognizable. Jesus perfectly understood this inner language. There are those now who will answer a question put to them in thought, as readily as if it were addressed to them by the external organs of speech. We have often told what a person's thoughts and feelings were, many miles away. Madam Guyon relates, in her Autobiography, that she was accustomed to enter into protracted conversations with her Confessor, without the use of spoken words, employing only the *cogitatio loquens*, the inner language. At length they could thus converse when they were at a distance of miles from each other. This was no miracle. It was only the unfoldment of an unused power of our nature There is in every man the innate faculty of conversing with spirits in the flesh or those who have put off their outward envelope. Speech similar to that of the spiritual world is implanted in every man, but our sensual educational systems, do not unfold the hidden germ, but oftener suppress it. As soon as any one comes into the other life, he finds himself in the same speech with the inhabitants of that hitherto mysterious realm, and is able to converse with them without instruction. We could do it here and now, if we would possess ourselves of a knowledge of the laws of the human spirit, and take advantage of them. In ancient times, and all along the stream of human history, there have been those who made use of this inner language, and had communication by means of it with the spiritual world. What human nature has ever done, is practicable to-day. For in no epoch of the world have all the hidden powers and capabilities of our being been unfolded. But we are not to suppose that this privilege would be accorded to us for our amusement or that of others, but only for the accomplishment of some important use. For God always gives to every man the light he needs for the performance of the work assigned him in the plan of Providence. Guided by these hints and suggestions, we may educate ourselves to this high and holy converse, and in advanced years as well or easier than in youth. There are many persons who are dissatisfied with the mere shell of knowledge, the rind of the fruit, the cortex of the tree of life, and long for something to nourish and allay the cravings of their spirit. In harmony with the laws of their being, they may find what they need. The tree of knowledge is beginning to be looked upon as no forbidden fruit, but an enlightened science is giving us access to it, and we may eat and live. Our highest conceptions we do not get from books, but they are flashes of a purer light, undulations of the abyss of light that communicate a concordant vibratory movement to our minds, and come to us as the whisperings of a still, small voice within. Such communicated thoughts have been appropriately called impressions. If men were less sensuous, and their inner life was adjusted in harmony with the celestial realms, they would not be an unreliable source of knowledge. They are an effort of the heavens to impart to us their living ideas and share with us their intellectual and affectional treasures. For such is the nature of the divine and angelic love, that there is in it a perpetual conatus to impart its own life to all the lower degrees of existence. All that we need is a spirit admissive of it, and the light of the higher realms will spontaneously flow in. The needed receptivity consists in the love of truth for its own sake, and a desire and purpose to apply it to a benevolent use.

CHAPTER XXIII.

THE SANATIVE POWER OF WORDS.

The Words we utter embody our Mental Force. — They are the Index of Character. — How our Mental States affect our Words. — Their Permanence in the Memory. — Their lasting Influence. — Fact given by Coleridge. — Dr. Rush. — The Power of Written Words. — Books have Life. — Effect of it upon the Psychometer. — Prescriptions of Frederica Hauffe. — Psychical Remedies. — The Creative Utterances of Jesus. — Frederic Von Schlegel's Philosophy of the Communicated Word. — Therapeutic Force of kind Words. — Testimony of Baglivi.

ONE OF the principal mediums through which mind acts upon mind, is that of words, spoken or written. Words are the representatives of ideas, the outward manifestation of thought, and the ultimation of a hidden spiritual power. They are things that have life in them, which is communicable by them. They are not mere empty sounds, like the sighing of the wind or the noise of a waterfall. If this were the case, they would be of no more consequence than the breath expended in producing them. The whole soul is sometimes in the words we utter, especially when, to use a common expression, they come from the heart, that is, from the love or life. The outward material organism is not the man, and is no necessary part of humanity. It is the mind that makes the man. This is composed of the two departments of the love and the intellect, and a more outward manifestation of these is affection and thought. These are ultimated or expressed in the words we utter. Thus they are charged with the very life of man—the vital force of the soul. They affect not only the tympanum, but they sink into the interior depths of our being. They are not like the leaves loosened from the trees by an autumn wind, and strewed upon the bosom of a quiet lake to float upon its surface; but there is in them a spiritual gravity, which causes them to sink into the hidden depths of the spirit.

Words are the index of character. They enclose within them our thoughts, and the tone with which they are uttered indicates the state of the affections. In another world, the utterance of a single word reveals to the intuitions of angelic spirits the ruling love that lurks within it, and with the knowledge of this is laid open the life and character. In the effect, they perceive the cause. The heart, that is the love, is the fountain; words are the stream. If the fountain is clear as crystal, the issuing rill will be the water of life. If the heart be like the bitter well of Mara, there will not be sweetness in the words. Even idle or aimless words, and mere fashionable talk, which are like the bubbles or foam floating on the current of the stream of life, though they may assume the most beautiful forms, and steal the tints of the rainbow, will be internally like the heart whence they proceed. For bubbles are formed from the stream, and partake of its general qualities. Jesus declared a great truth when he affirmed, that "Out of the abundance of the heart, the mouth speaketh." The Greek word here rendered abundance, signifies a redundant fullness that overflows. When the heart is full of love, it overflows in kind and gentle words. When a man is full of anger, he is like the volcanic wells of Iceland, and boils over in scalding words. If there is melancholy in the heart, and the soul is full of it, there is a dirge-like strain in the tone of the voice, like the sighing of the midnight winds in the leafless trees of a cemetery in winter. If joy and heavenly peace pervade a man's inner being, the cheerful music of his voice will mix and mingle with the grand chorus of bliss in the angelic realms. We do not mean, that to the blunted perceptions of most men, a person's words will always reveal his ruling love and inward character. They may fall from the lips like spurious coin from the mint of the counterfeiter, and the gilded brass may have the ring of the genuine metal, but our angelic intuitions will penetrate the thin covering. As men become more intuitional, the personation of the good by the evil, in the drama of life, will terminate. Evil will be detected, even though it may throw around it the costume of fair words.

Words are wonderfully mysterious things. When uttered in the presence of mind, they do not waste themselves upon the illimitable and desert air, but cleave to the soul of him who hears them like nails driven into the walls of the house. Who has not been troubled by the involuntary recurrence to his memory of the vile utterances of evil doers which he heard long years ago in his youth. They light down like a flock of harpies, to pollute, it may be, a heavenly feast. They come unbidden to mingle with our holiest meditations, and perhaps even with our prayers.

> " Lulled in the countless chambers of the brain,
> Our thoughts are linked by many a hidden chain;
> Awake but one, and lo, what myriads rise!—
> Each stamps its image as the other flies."

Thus it is with the words we heard in our childhood, either good or bad. In after-life, touch but one and a whole cloud of them will arise, like aquatic birds from a lake in the mountains.

There is a lasting sanative spiritual influence in words of love and sympathy. There are coloring substances so diffusive that a minute and almost inestimable quantity will tinge a large body of water. So a few kind words will sometimes give coloring to a person's whole life. I am not speaking of that heartless sentimentality which dismisses the poor soul from its door with the hollow wish, "Be ye warmed and be ye filled," and that offers to its neighbor, who sits dumb with his overwhelming grief, its empty cant phrases committed to memory. Love is the animating soul of kind words, and through their medium we may communicate our own mental states, our inmost life, to strengthen and invigorate those that need our help. But to him whose affections are blasted and cold from some great calamity that has crushed through his heart-strings, we may say never so many times, "Be ye warmed," but if our words do not spring from a heart glowing with genuine love, there is no heat in them. They impinge against the afflicted spirit like the frost crystals of a winter's day. They may shine and glitter, but they chill the life's blood of him who speaks or hears them. In all loving words there is a therapeutic force, and a divine life. Truth, when it is the outward envelope of a living love inclosed as a vitalizing spark within it, when ultimated in words and deposited in the mind of another, never fades from his memory so that it cannot be recalled. It may for a season be forgotten, or pass from our present recollection. It may to appearance be deep beneath the accumulated rubbish of after-years. But at the quickening voice of God or of his angels, it shall start to life again, come forth from its sepulcher to consciousness, and assert its divine right to reign. It will be like characters written with invisible ink. The paper thus inscribed appears a blank, yet when held before the fire, line after line, sentence after sentence comes to view, as if penned by an invisible hand. Truth from love is divine. It is the light of a quenchless flame. Like Milton's angels, it is immortal in every part, and cannot die. It is one of those divine and positive realities that cannot be annihilated. The words that inclose it and through which it enters the memory, can never be erased from that imperishable tablet. Though sunk deep beneath the oblivious waves of after-years, they will sometime rise and float upon the surface.

Many facts are given to show the tenacity with which the mind holds the memory of words even *casually* spoken. Among them we may cite the case mentioned by Coleridge, of a servant girl, who, in the delirium of a fever, was heard to repeat long sentences in Greek and Rabbinic Hebrew, languages she had never learned, and which she had only heard without attention by the minister in whose family, many years before, she had lived as a domestic. Yet those words of a strange language were stereotyped upon the mental plate. Dr. Rush also relates that the Germans of his day in Philadelphia, when dying, usually prayed in their native tongue, though they had not spoken it for fifty years, and had apparently forgotten it. Thus our words of love and kindness will have a lasting influence. They will live in the minds of some long after the monument, that marks the resting place of our ashes, shall have crumbled back to dust.

There is a lasting power also in *written* words. A letter or a book may be charged with the divine magnetism of a spiritual life. There is an underlying truth in the apparently extravagant assertion of William Hazlitt, that "words are the only things that last forever." And some one has eloquently said, "Words convey the mental treasures of one period to the generations that follow; and, laden with this their precious freight, they sail safely across gulfs of time in which empires have suffered shipwreck." The wise and good of past ages, the noblest and holiest spirits that ever lived and moved among men, the world's real heroes and benefactors, have sometimes gathered up into a few words the rich harvest of their knowledge and experience, and launched them upon the ocean of human life to carry their celestial treasures to all coming ages. A book written by a good and wise man is not to be classed among things that are dead. A living soul seems to breathe and speak from its pages. The affection and thought of the author, that never can be separated from his living mind, still animate the speaking sentences. There is an intuitive perception of this in the veneration with which the sacred books of the nations are held. Mohammed is still in the Koran, and Jesus in the Gospels. The letter fixes in an outward form the still living thought of an author. In the cloistered stillness of the library that has gathered up these spiritual treasures, we seem to move along its silent halls among the spirits of the mighty dead. We fain would believe that this is not destitute of all reality. Place a book in the hand, or on the forehead, of a person gifted with the psychometric sense, and enough of the spiritual life of the author will be still in it, to reveal his character. This hidden influence affects the delicate sensibility of the psychometer. A letter from a person written even on another continent, will be so charged with the living magnetism and spiritual force of the writer of it, as to cause the mind of the psychometer to vibrate in harmony with it, and the authors feelings of mind and body will be reproduced, and can be accurately described. Here is a subtle force which has been turned to a practical use in the cure of disease. The psychometer is only more *conscious* than others of this influence, in consequence of the peculiar sensitiveness of his organism. For psychometry may be defined to be the *sympathetic* state, and the interior sensations, as clairvoyance and clairaudience, belonging to it. All may be affected in as great a degree. The Seeress of Prevorst used this power in delivering persons from the psychological influence of disorderly or undeveloped spirits, which is a concomitant of many diseasd conditions. She employed sentences written upon paper, which were to be carried about the person. She perhaps had little knowledge of the laws governing their action, but they were successful in relieving the patient from his disordered mental states, and thus sundered the sympathetic connection between him and similarly diseased mind in the inner sphere of being. There is a law here but imperfectly understood, and not generally recognized, but which can be turned to a good account.

There is a greater power in words than men are aware of. The creative power of God is expressed by the Platonists, and by John in his Gospel, by the term *Logos* or Word. But this power is given to every soul made in the image of God. Frederic Von Schlegel makes the distinguishing characteristic of man, and the peculiar eminence of human nature, to consist in this—that to him alone among all other of earth's creatures the *word* has been imparted and communicated. "In the idea of the word," he observes, "considered as the basis of man's dignity and peculiar destination, the internal light of consciousness and of our own understanding is undoubtedly to be included,—this word is not a mere faculty of speech, but the fertile root whence the stately trunk of all languages has sprung. But the word is not confined to this only—it next includes a living, working power—it is not merely an object and organ of knowledge—an instrument of teaching and learning, but the means of affectionate union, conciliatory accommodation, efficacious command, and even creative productiveness, as our own experience and life itself manifest each of those significations of the word; and thus it embraces the whole plenitude of the excellencies and qualities which characterize man." In proportion as man possesses this divine principle implanted in him, he approaches the divine and angelic nature. But so far as he loses that word of life, which has been communicated and confided to him, he sinks down to a level with nature, and instead of dominions over nature, becomes her vassal. (*Philosophy of History, p.* 87.)

Jesus of Nazareth possessed this divine power in an eminent degree, and nature seemed passive under his hands. He comprehended the potential spiritual force of words, as a medium of communicating life and sanative psychological influence. He employed certain formulas or expressive sentences into which he concentrated and converged his whole mental force, and made them the means of transmitting spiritual life to the disordered mind. Some of these pregnant utterances, always used according to the nature of the case, were these: "Go in peace; Be of good cheer, thy sins are all forgiven thee; Be it unto thee according to thy faith; I will, be thou cleansed; Peace be unto thee; Arise and walk." Into these few words were condensed his whole mental force, and they were made to communicate his better state of feeling and thought to the sufferer. Spiritual diseases demand psychical remedies. Thousands there are who would be better both in mind and body, if they only knew there was some one in the universe who loved them. We should demonstrate to them that God loves them, angels love them, and *we* love them. "Go to the poor sufferer, deserted and destitute, dying of despair; carry him stores of relief in your hand, love and pity in your eye and voice; and see how the sun-burst of joyful surprise breaks on his brow only just tinged with the vanishing skirts of dread. In millions of cases, no recipes of vegetable or mineral drugs can compare in value and power with such pharmaceutics as a grain of patience, a pennyweight of magnanimity, a drop of forgiveness, a draught of pure resolve, a hearty inhalation of friendship and faith. These and such as these, are—

> "Antidotes
> Of medicated music, answering for
> Mankind's forlornest uses."

Oftentimes, a physician accomplishes more toward the raising up of a patient, by his words of sympathy and encouragement, than by his medical prescriptions, for the reason that there is more sanative virtue in them, and they are better adapted to the removal of the spiritual disturbances that aggravate, if they do not originate, the disease. Baglivi was deeply impressed with the truth of this and frankly acknowledges it. He says: "I can scarcely express how much the conversation of the physician influences even the life of the patient, and modifies his complaints. For a physician powerful in speech, and skilled in addressing the feelings of a patient, adds so much to the power of his remedies, and excites so much confidence in his treatment, as frequently to overcome dangerous diseases with very feeble remedies, which more learned doctors, languid and indifferent in speech, could not have cured with the best remedies that man could produce."

CHAPTER XXIV.

THE RELATION OF MENTAL FORCE TO PHYSICAL STRENGTH, AND HOW TO CURE GENERAL DEBILITY.

The Amount of Force' generated in the System.— Whence Produced. — The Abnormal State Called General Debility. — What is Strength ? — Case cited to show its Mental Origin. — The Mental Faculties that influence the Will Force. — Their Importance. — The Cerebral Organ of Muscular Motion — The Relation of Respiration to Muscular Force. — What is Swooning ? — The Force of the Bodily Movement proportioned to the Mental Energy. — The Effect of Respiration upon the Vital Processes. — Nervousness a Mental State.— Its cure — Relaxation of the Abdominal Muscles.— Misplacement of the Internal Organs. — Depressing Mental States the Cause — How to get rid of the Supporter and Body Brace — Relation of the Mind to Diseases of Diminished Vitality. — Dr. Combe.

THE AMOUNT of mechanical force generated and expended in the human system in the daily working of the animal machinery, is far beyond what would be conjectured by one who had not investigated the subject. For the performance of the functions of respiration and circulation, the amount expended every day is not less than several thousands of pounds. To this we must add the amount necessary to the ingestion and digestion of the food and the expulsion of the excretions. The aggregate amount of force expended in labor and locomotion, has been estimated to be not less than two millions of pounds a day, or one thousand tons. We have seen that heat and mechanical force are correlative. But the heat necessary to the generation of such an amount of force cannot be produced by the oxydation or slow combustion of the carbon and hydrogen of the blood. This is wholly inadequate to meet so great a demand, and to replace the amount radiated from the body. We must look to some other source for the generation of the muscular power of the system.

Let us look at the phenomena exhibited by that pathological condition called *general debility*. These words are in common use to express a state of the system with which every medical practitioner frequently meets. A very large fraction ot chronic diseases, at least three-fourths, come under this general designation. There seems to be but little, and sometimes no organic disease, but only a general weakness in the action of all the organs, a lack of vital force everywhere, a negative state of the body.

The favorite prescriptions for it include quinine protoxide of iron, and various tonics and stimulants. But drugs have no adaptation to the cure of such a state of things. A more subtle chemistry must be brought to the aid of the enfeebled and negative organism. Strength is not in the body, the muscles are not a force. These are only the instruments of a spiritual force. We have seen a girl, weak, pale, and apparently possessing but little muscular power, who, when under the excitement of a certain form of Hysteria, would exhibit almost gigantic physical strength, requiring the force of two men to hold her. After coming out of these attacks, she did not seem greatly exhausted, not more than ordinarily followed a walk of half a mile. This almost superhuman power, this Titanic force, was not in her physical system. It was not a property of the bodily organism, it was purely a mental state, and the augmented muscular strength was the resultant of increased mental force. What we improperly call physical strength is always in the mind. The body has no force but that of gravity and cohesion, which belong in common to all solids and fluids.

But what is that mental condition which makes one strong? A consciousness of strength, of what we call physical power, if not synonymous with health, is closely allied to it, and is correlative of it. Ling based his movement cure upon the truth, that perfect health and physical power were convertible terms. But what goes to make up the spiritual state that is the cause of muscular force? The opposite of that which underlies a state of general debility. In this there is a lack of mental force—of will energy. Neither the muscular nor the nervous tissue is diseased. In paralysis there is a softening of the nerves of motion, and they become imperfect conductors of the will-force. Nothing of this kind is found in general debility. The lack of mental force may be, and often is, the result of *discouragement*—a state of mind made up of a want of faith, an inactive or inverted condition of the organ of hope, and a negative action of the sentiment of self-esteem. It is the office of this latter faculty to give us the sense of our personal identity, our peculiar individuality, and to cause us to feel a respect for it, and to place a proper value upon it. It inspires us with the feeling of self-reliance, and of freedom, which is favourable to the manifestations of muscular force and virtuous activity. It gives that confidence in the use of our powers which is necessary to success in every department of human labor, and to the efficient discharge of the functions of every office. Its office seems to be to add force to all our volitions. It imparts a positive influence to the mind, and gives the power of controlling both ourselves and others. The lack of this quality causes a negative condition of the mind, which by influx into the body, weakens the tone of all muscular action. What we call self-esteem, for the want of a better name, has much to do with physical strength. The persons most remarkable for muscular power, exhibit a large and active development of it. The part of the brain where all *voluntary* motions originate, is in close proximity to it, being situated at a middle point between firmess and self-esteem. This part of the cerebrum supplies the necessary stimulus to the diaphragm and all the voluntary muscles. It is the seat of the will, the self-determining power of the mind. Surrounding it are the organs whose office it is to give energy to our volitions, as faith, firmness, self-esteem, and continuity. When these organs are in a normal condition, there is seldom found a state of general debility. A judicious magnetic treatment of this part of the brain accomplishes wonders in restoring the strength of a patient. When a person has the feeling, "I am strong; I can do a great thing; I can do what man has ever done," it is an excitement of the sentiment of faith, firmness, and self-esteem, and the increased vital action of their cerebral organs extends instantly to the organ of voluntary motion. Under the stimu'us of these feelings, the body spontaneously assumes an erect attitude, and the person exhibits the conscious dignity of his manhood. The shoulders are drawn back, the chest enlarged, and the breathing is deep and full. Whatever mental state will increase the amount of respiratory action will increase the strength. And nature has provided that when we are about to exert great muscular force and feel adequate to it, whether it be lifting or striking, we shall precede the effort with a deep inspiration. Let any one try the experiment. The more one breathes, other things being equal, the stronger he is. The size of the lungs, indicated by breadth between the shoulders, and deepness and fullness of the chest, is the measure of a person's muscular force. The less one breathes, the weaker he is. In swooning, which is accompanied with a loss of all voluntary motion, there is only a suspended respiration. On recovering or rather the cause of the restoration to consciousness and muscular power is, a deep breath is drawn, and with it comes back the lost physical force. The best restoratives are magnetism of the part of the brain that is the seat of the will, and alternate pressure of the abdominal muscles and the chest, to create an artificial breathing, as is done in cases of drowning and asphyxia. This is often successful in a few minutes. We have thus restored a patient in one minute. In cases of general debility, there is always a feeble respiration, in fact, it is physiologically a partial and chronic swooning. The breathing is short and quick, and the pulse correspondingly feeble and rapid. For nature maintains a rythmic harmony between the movements of the heart and lungs. All depressing mental states, as we have before shown, are attended with an imperfect respiration, the lungs only being called into action, and no movement being communicated to the abdominal muscles. The muscular membrane, called the diaphragm, separating between the thoracic and abdominal cavities, whose contraction supplies the respiratory force, loses its nervous power, and its convexity. It must be restored to a healthy tone, and its contractility increased, for its action is prior to all muscular motions, and voluntary exhibitions of physical force. But there is no medicinal compound in the endless list of pharmaceutical preparations, that can effect this change. There must be a return to a natural respiration, a normal breathing, which must not be a momentary exercise, but become an habitual bodily state.

We have shown, in a previous chapter, that the action of the heart and lungs are primary motions on which all the physiological movements and processes depend. The effect of respiration extends beyond the substance of the lungs and the thorax. Motion is communicated by it, not only to the abdominal coverings and to all the organs within the abdominal cavity, but to the smallest blood vessels, and promotes the circulation of their fluid contents. There is not only a rising and falling of the mass of the brain, synchronous with the contraction and relaxation of the diaphragm, and the expansion and shrinking of the pulmonary substance, but the same movement, though not so perceptible, is communicated to the cerebro-spinal axis and all the nerves, which are only the continuation or ramification of the brain into the body. Its effects extend to every fiber and minute vessel of the organism, and are consequently promotive of all the vital processes and functions. Too much importance cannot be attached to a proper respiration, as being intimately related to a normal manifestation of the mind, and a healthy functional action of the various organs.

It is evident that the stimulus of any mental state, that causes a normal action of the diaphragm, the lungs, and the abdominal muscles, and thus increases the breathing force, will alone permanently increase the strength, restore the lost tone of the vital movements, and cure the prevalent state of the system called general debility. To breathe is to live and the more we breathe, the more we live. Strength is not a property of our material organization, but is more a mental state. The body moves with a power proportioned to the mental energy. Motion in the body is an effect, of which some spiritual force is the cause. It does not originate in the body. There is a force distinct from all material organization, which is the motive power of the machinery. The power of the motion is ever proportioned to the degree of the spiritual force. To strengthen the body, if such a contradiction were possible, does not demand the use of tonics and stimulants, but we must increase the mental force. If we can by any means arouse the mind to a vigorous tone, and become "strong, and of a good courage," our general debility will soon disappear. The patient is always under the influence of certain depressing mental states, which sustain a causal relation to the trouble, and the so-called bodily weakness. It is of no use to try to relieve symptoms, and doctor effects. The remedial agency must be less superficial. We must attend to the fountain of bodily life, and minister to a mind diseased. We need not filter the stream. We must purify the spring. Remove the spiritual cause, and the bodily effect will cease.

One of the concomitants of the state of general debility, is what is called nervousness. But nervous disorders are wholly mental. The patient often suffers more than in cases of great organic derangement. A disease is none the less real because it is mental, as the soul is the most real element of our complex nature. Nervousness is nothing else but a morbid state of the mind, and only spiritual remedies are adapted to its cure. The sufferings of the patient arise not so much from the absolute amount of pain, for this is usually very trifling, but from the extreme sensitiveness of the mind to all uneasy feelings. There is a morbid dread of disease, a tendency to watch their shifting symptoms, and perhaps an unusual acuteness in their sensations. When a patient can be made aware that his disease is wholly mental, an important point is gained in the process of recovery. For a knowledge of the cause of disease is half of its cure. To tell a nervous invalid that his troubles are all in his mind, need give no offense, if we at the same time exhibit a true sympathy for his sufferings, and show him that they are not less important because they arise from a pathological state of the inner man. To say that a patient's disease is in the mind, is quite a different thing from an assertion that nothing ails him. These are not equivalent propositions. What are called nervous diseases, are among the most real of the ills to which man is subject. An unsound state of the mind is more to be deprecated than the fracture of a limb, or dislocation of a joint. All remedies except those of a generally hygienic nature, are ineffectual. Relief is soonest found in the ministry of mind to mind. A spiritual magnetism is a specific for all the Protean forms it assumes. Its unutterable horrors, its morbid dread, its sensitiveness to trifling pains, its melancholy and despair, are made to give place to the influx of faith, hope, and peace. The remarks we have made above in relation to the treatment of general debility, are equally applicable to the cure of the nervousness attending it.

In ninety-nine cases out of a hundred, that come under the appropriate name of general debility, there is a mechanical misplacement, or falling downward of the internal organs, owing to a relaxation of the muscles of the abdomen which constitute their natural support. There is a series of organs located within the trunk mutually supporting and influencing each other. Within the thorax or chest, we have the heart and lungs filling its entire cavity.

Then comes the diaphragm, a muscular membrane, separating between the organs in the thorax and abdomen, and curving upward, forming the floor of the chest, the heart and lungs resting on it. Its contraction draws its convex surface downward, forming a partial vacuum, and the air, by the force of its pressure, rushes in and fills the lungs. The more convex the diaphragm, the deeper and fuller is the breathing. The lungs are wholly passive in both inspiration and expiration, as much so as a sponge in absorbing water and yielding it up when pressed. In cases of general debility the diaphragm does not come back to its proper convexity, and consequently the heart and lungs gravitate downward. Underneath the diaphragm are the liver, the stomach, the spleen, and the pancreas; below these the duodenum, and the intestinal canal in a sort of spiral column; then the organs in the pelvic cavity. As a displacement of these organs interferes with their healthy functional action, it becomes an important question, What holds them in position, and counteracts their gravitating force? They evidently cannot rest on nothing. They are all held in their appropriate place by the walls of the abdomen which consist almost entirely of muscular tissue. There is a series of muscles so arranged as admirably to adapt them to the support of the truncal organs. We have first the transverse muscle, extending across from side to side over the abdomen; then the oblique muscles, one of them extending from the hip or fan bone and back, obliquely upward, and inserted into the lower ribs, the other extending from the lower edge of the ribs, and also from the back, obliquely downward and fastened upon the pelvic bone and the white line of the abdomen; next the pyramidalis muscle, arising from the projecting bone of the hip and running up about half way to the navel, where it terminates in a point; and lastly, though not least in importance, the rectus abdominalis muscle. It is shaped somewhat like a suspender, and performs a similar office. It runs up the front of the abdomen and is inserted into the lower extremity of the sternum or breast-bone. These muscular bands are so contrived, that when in a healthy condition, *and the body is in a perfectly erect attitude*, they hold up in their proper place within the trunk all the internal viscera. When in a relaxed state, all the organs tend downward toward the pelvis, and by their superincumbent weight crowd the pelvic organs down— the bladder, the rectum, and the uterus. Then the animal machinery works wrong, like a watch when the wheels are moved out of place. This misplacement interferes with their physiological functions. The cure consists in bringing the organs back into place. Any artificial support, as the great variety of body braces and supporters, affords only a temporary relief, but aggravates the trouble in the end. The duplicated movements applied to the muscles of the abdomen, afford a better remedy, and those gymnastic exercises that call them into action are also of use. But no relief can be *permanent* until the spiritual cause of the trouble be removed. *All depressing mental states destroy the healthy tone of the abdominal muscles.* This is so manifestly the case, that mankind have instinctively recognized its truth in their common forms of speech. When we speak of one who is *bowed down with grief*, we express a physiological fact, and not merely a figure of speech. It is the natural attitude of a man in sadness and melancholy, which destroys the contractility of the muscular coverings of the abdomen. Fear in all its forms, as anxiety, melancholy, and a want of faith, relaxes the diaphragm. It weakens the epigastric nerves, and deprives their organs of their proper cerebral stimulus. We speak of depressing mental states, and a sinking of the spirits,—forms of speech arising naturally from the bodily sensations which they originate. Depression is the act of pressing down, and when applied to the mind signifies a lowering of its tone below the normal and healthful standard, and, by weakening the muscular support of the organs within the trunk, they obey the law of gravity and press downward. When a person is bowed down, he feels as he looks It is the natural language, the ultimation, of *dejection* of spirits. All that is needed to restore the abdominal muscles to a healthy state, is habitually to exercise them. The appropriate nerve-stimulus, or rather spiritual force, that is infused into them by use, will harden them as certainly as exercise strengthens the arm of the blacksmith. *They are always called into action by the respiration attending all happy and exhilarating frames of mind.* If a patient can be recovered from his *depressing* mental condition, the body will become erect, without any other mechanical support than nature supplies. His weakness, his lassitude, his languor and fatigue will disappear. On the influence of depressing mental states, Dr. Andrew Combe justly observes: "The tendency of grief, despondency and sorrow is to produce *meditative inaction.* These emotions require no exertion of the bodily powers, and no unusual expenditure of vital energy : but rather the reverse. This is a condition incompatible with a quick supply of blood, *or a high degree of respiration*; for if these were conjoined, they would only give rise to an amount of bodily activity at variance with the absorbed and inactive state of the mind. The nature of the exciting passions is to impel us vigorously to action; but action cannot be sustained without a full supply of highly oxygenated blood, and hence a manifest reason for the quick respiration and accelerated circulation which attend mental excitement. Great depression of mind thus leads naturally to imperfect respiration, a more sluggish flow of blood, and the various diseases of diminished vitality; while excessive excitement induces full respiration, quickened circulation, and the various diseases of exalted vitality. These principles show the paramount importance, in the treatment of disease, of carefully regulating the mental state of the patient, according to the object we have in view."

CHAPTER XXV.

SLEEP AS A MENTAL STATE, ITS HYGIENIC VALUE, AND HOW TO INDUCE IT.

Sleep Defined. — Its Influence upon the involuntary Physiological Processes. — Nutrition. — Circulation. — The Excreting Organs. — Its Remedial Value. — The Obstacles to it. — Cold Feet. — Tea and Coffee. — The Law that governs in Inducing it upon Ourselves. — Position of the Eye. — Its Effect upon the Cerebrum. — The Respiration in Sleep. — In the Magnetic Trance. — The moral Influence of Sleep. — The Order in which the Senses lose their Susceptibility to Impression. — Practical Directions based upon this Law. —

SLEEP MAY be characterized as an involuntary and passive state of the mind. The cerebrum, as we have shown above, is the organ of our voluntary life; the cerebellum of the involuntary vital movements and passive states of thought and affection. In a state of sleep the cerebrum is quiescent, and the cerebellum is the organ through which the physiological processes are carried on. Sleep is one of the most important remedial agencies in nature, and a knowledge of the laws that govern it, and by which we may induce it upon ourselves, is of sufficient practical value to justify us in devoting this chapter to its consideration. It being a passive state of the muscles of voluntary motion, the no inconsiderable amount of vital force thus expended can be employed to increase the action of the involuntary processes. In the period of childhood we spend much more time in sleep than in after-years, in old age much less than in the middle of our existence. This is one reason why the functions of the entire nutritive system are carried on with so much more vigor in the morning of our existence than in subsequent years. The state of somnolence facilitates the circulation of the blood and all the fluids of the system. This is owing to the withdrawal of the forces expended in our voluntary activities, and their employment in increasing the vigor of all the involuntary functions, and also to the usual position of the body in sleep. In wakefulness and in the upright position, the circulation of the nutritive fluids is opposed by their gravity, which tends to retard their flow. The horizontal position being that which diminishes their gravitating force the most, is one which is the most favorable to their circulation. The diminished action of the ganglionic nerves of motion and of sensation, affords an increased supply of cerebral stimulus to the excretory organs, and the waste worn out particles are thrown off from the system in greater profusion than during our waking hours. These fill the atmosphere of the bedroom, so as to be more recognizable to our senses than they would be if we were confined for the same length of time in the same apartment while awake. Sleep is consequently peculiarly adapted to the relief of a dry and feverish state of the skin, and to all diseases whose secondary causes are found in a defective action of the excretory functions. There is much of physiological truth in the reply of the disciples to the statement of Jesus that his friend Lazarus was asleep: "Lord, if he sleep, he shall do well." The rabbins regarded sleep as one of the most important of the "six good symptoms" of disease. We feel convinced that in a great variety of pathological conditions, especially most cases of nervous debility, it will be found among the best of nature's remedies. In the early stage of all febrile disorders, if the patient could induce upon himself a sound and normal sleep, it would prove the most efficient means of cure. But the sleep must be natural and not that resulting from the stupifying influence of narcotic drugs. There are those who have the power of commanding sleep at any time; and such are seldom diseased. It is their only resort in sickness. They sleep for any length of time, and when and where they please.

But is sleep under the control of our volitions? Not directly, but only indirectly so. It cannot be induced by the active or positive state of the will, but only by the passive or negative position of the volitive power. The more a nervous patient *tries* to sleep the less he feels of the somnolent influence. The effort to sleep is a voluntary state of the mind, while sleep is an involuntary and passive condition of both the brain and the soul. Any active volition is wakefulness. If we remove all obstacles to sleep, it becomes spontaneous, and steals over the excited mind and wearied powers, like the cooling breath of a summer evening, and we enter the pure and tranquil dream-land as softly as flowers close at set of sun. There is a powerful magnetic sympathy between the feet and the brain. If the feet are cold and negative, the head is pressed with an accumulation of the nervous and vital forces. Restore the circulation to the extremities, by immersing them in water below the temperature of the blood, rubbing them dry with the hand, and smiting them until they glow with vital heat. This relieves the brain of its congested condition and throws it into a state favorable to repose.

Rub the back-brain with the left hand, also the back of the neck, so as to attract the cerebral force towards the cerebellum. Use your own hand or that of a sympathetic friend. Avoid the intemperate use of tea and coffee. The former, by the semi-spiritual essence it contains, stimulates the fore-brain to action, which is the organ of voluntary thought, and sleep becomes difficult, and sometimes impossible under its influence. The latter acts upon the cerebral organ of voluntary motion, and its effects are equally unfavorable to sleep. Every article of food or drink tending to throw the mind or body into a positive state, should be avoided for the evening meal. Removing these hindrances, the induction upon ourselves of the state of somnolency, with its quieting, invigorating and restorative influences, will be easy. We will now proceed to unfold the laws by conformity to which, sleep may be self-induced at any time.

We shall have to avail ourselves of a principle previously stated and illustrated, that when the body is made to assume the attitude and condition that externally manifests any mental state, it spontaneously arises within us. This is the key to the whole mystery of going to sleep. Let the patient assume a reclining position, with the head but slightly elevated so as to bring it only a little above a level with the shoulders. Then elevate the ball of the eye, rolling it up as it is called, as if attempting to look toward the back-brain. This inversion of the eye is its natural and fixed position in sleep, as is easy to prove by an examination of any person, who has passed from the realm of external consciousness to the dreamland. This upward and backward movement of the eye, which must not be too strained or artificial, inverts the action of the cerebrum, and suspends all active thought, terminates the voluntary states of the mind, which passes from the active to the passive state. The vital force of the cerebrum flows back to the cerebellum, and this, physiologically, is a state of sleep. The patient may not instantly become unconscious, and the mind may not immediately be withdrawn from the bodily senses, but he will soon sweetly lose himself to all external perceptions and surroundings, and be in the care of the angels, who, in a less sensuous age of the church, when it was animated by a higher spiritual life, and a more childlike faith, were supposed to guard our defenceless slumbers when the "Lord gave his beloved sleep." The great obstacle to sleep is a want of ability to suspend active thought. The best way of doing this is to put the brain into the inverted and quiescent state it exhibits in the passive mental condition that constitutes somnolence. Various methods have been employed to effect the necessary suspension of thought, such as counting, but they only change the direction of the thoughts. This may have its use in facilitating the process of going to sleep, but is not so much in harmony with nature as the course we have recommended above.

It is proper also to remark, before we leave this subject, that the respiration in sleep is different from that which accompanies intense and active thinking. In sound and healthy sleep the breathing is deep and full, calling into action the muscular coverings of the abdomen, while in abstract voluntary thinking, only the upper portion of the lungs is slightly moved. We have frequently had occasion to observe also, that when a person in passing into the magnetic coma or trance, he precedes his loss of external consciousness with a few deep inspirations. In inducing upon ourselves the mental state that constitutes the essential thing in sleep, we do well to imitate nature in this respect. We have known some who have resorted to nothing else but this, when they wished to counteract the tendency to prolonged wakefulness, and with them it was found uniformly sucessful. But this form of respiration need not be too artificial, but only such as is naturally produced by simply directing the thoughts to the frontal muscles. One object to be aimed at is the cessation from all active volitions. For sleep is only a natural, healthful, and temporary suspension of the functions of the two hemispheres of the cerebrum, which is the organ of the voluntary life of the mind and body. It is the natural rest or repose instituted by the Author of our being to restore the exhausted energies of both the inner and outer man. In this state of passivity and abstraction from the bodily senses, we become inhabitants, in a degree, of a better world, and recipients of elevating and purifying influences. So that sleep has its moral as well as hygienic uses. It is a mental state, that belongs to another world as well as this. It is one of the established means of mental progress, both here and hereafter.

The withdrawal of the mind from the bodily senses in sleep, takes place progressively, and may exist in different degrees. In its first stage it is called drowsiness. When this is habitual it is denominated lethargy. The senses become oblivious to impression from external things in a fixed order or succession. The sight ceases to receive impressions first. The sense of taste is the next to lose its susceptibility, and then the sense of smell. The hearing is the next in order, and last of all the sense of touch or feeling.

In drowsiness, which is an incipient sleep, the eye becomes dull and heavy, and involuntarily closes. To prevent the further progress of somnolence, persons are seen instinctively to rub the eyes, to take something into the mouth of a strong taste, and to smell of something pungent, and if circumstances permit, to call into action the muscles of voluntary motion. For drowsiness or lethargy affects only the three senses mentioned above, together with the part of the cerebrum which the mind uses in voluntary motion. These three senses are the most external, and are at the outpost as sentinels. They are the most voluntary of the senses, and if sleep passes them, the others will soon surrender. In inducing upon ourselves a state of sleep, let the eye be closed, and turned away from the light, as light will affect the eye even through the eye-lids. If inclined to wakefulness, the face should not be turned toward a window of the sleeping apartment. The mouth must be free from every thing which can excite the sense of taste, and the atmosphere of the room must be free from all perfumes and the effluvia of medicine, and from anything that can affect the sense of smell. The invalid must be removed from all unpleasant noise or sounds that can excite the sensation of hearing. Though listening to certain agreeable and monotonous sounds, as the roaring of the wind in a forest, or the sound of distant music, facilitates the induction of sleep. It draws away the activity of the three senses, which are affected by drowsiness, and serves to induce that state. And lastly the body must be in an easy position, with as little weight of clothing as will serve to prevent the sensation of cold, and not enough to excite a sensation of heat. Observing these simple directions, in connection with those before given, there are few cases where natural and healthful sleep may not be self-induced.

It is proper to remark, that in awaking from sleep, the senses come to conscious activity in the inverted order in which they lose their susceptibility to impression. The sense of touch first awakes, and that of sight last. Sometimes a slight touch will arouse a person, when our voice is unheeded by him.

CHAPTER XXVI.

THE WILL-CURE, ACTIVE AND PASSIVE.

Connection of the Organs with the Mind. — How to affect their Functional Action.— The Will-Force and the Stomach and Intestinal Canal.— Cause of Coldness and Weakness. — The Cure. — The Passive Will-Cure. — A general law of Health Stated. — Voluntary Movements Fatiguing. — The Involuntary Actions not so. — How to take up thy bed and walk. — How to walk a hundred miles a day. — The Interior State. — Its healthful Influences.—Passive Knowledge. — Influx of better Emotional States. — The Spirit with which to approach the Inner World. — Importance of our Relations to it.

THROUGH THE grand system of ganglionic and sympathetic nerves, each organ in the body is connected with every other, and the whole with the mind. There is no part or function which cannot be affected just as certainly, though perhaps not as sensibly, by the will-force, as the muscles of the arm. To do this requires no straining, no struggle, as if we were going to lift a mountain from our condition, any more than it does to move one finger without the others. The pneumogastric nerve, which is distributed to all the organs within the cavity of the trunk, is the appointed conductor through which the mental force is communicated to them, and influences their functional action. This important nerve seems to be in sympathetic connection with the organ of vitativeness, which, when fully developed and normally active, renders one tenacious of life, and affords a healthful cerebral stimulus to the vital organs. We have only to concentrate the mind's force upon any of the internal organs, as the stomach, liver, or intestinal canal, and through the pneumogastric nerve, its vital movements will be influenced. It is the divine order of our existence, that the mind should be the body's sovereign. Spirit is superior to matter; it is a higher and diviner force. The one is positive; the other negative; one is an active principle; the other a passive recipient. The will and the love we have shown to be identical, and love is the life of man. To direct the will, therefore, to an organ, determines the vital force to it, and increases its sensibility. It is a truth demonstrated by our experience, that the more our thoughts can be diverted from a part that is the seat of a painful sensation, the less we feel of it. On the other hand, the continual concentration of the mind upon any portion of the system in a state of inflammation, increases the sensibility and adds to our sufferings. The successful practice of the will-cure must be based upon a sufficient degree of the knowledge of our pathological state, to enable us to judge when it is desirable to concentrate the mind's action upon a diseased part, or when to divert the spiritual force from it. If the stomach has become exhausted of its nervous force, so that its vermicular movements have ceased, and the food in it is a motionless and fermenting mass, it can be made to obey the behests of the sovereign mind. Concentrating the mind upon it, converging our spiritual force to a focus, we may calmly and powerfully will it to proceed to business and attend to its proper work, and it will obey us as readily and as promptly as a good servant yields to the orders of his employer. The same effect may be produced upon the action of the intestinal canal. If the blood and vital heat do not circulate through the extremities, which feel a deadly coldness, it is because the spiritual life does not permeate the tissues. We may send the spiritual principle there, by the will-force, to distribute to the negative parts their share of the vital flame. For it is ever to be borne in mind, that the negative, weakened state of an organ is not caused so much by a want of blood in it, as it is by the absence from it of a more subtle element. The spiritual principle does not circulate freely through it. The active will-cure is peculiarly adapted to all negative, devitalized states of the organism. But the mind should never be directed to any organ of the body while under the dominion of depressing emotions and feelings, as those of fear, anxiety, or melancholy, but we should convey to a diseased part only the healthy life-giving current of our positive and normal mental states. A little practice will render the will-cure easy and natural, and we can become our own physician. Blessed is the man, who, in sickness or trouble, has a skillful and sympathetic physician for soul and body, in whom he may trust. But he has attained a far higher blessedness, who, by his knowledge of the laws that govern the action of the mind upon the body both in the generation of health and disease, is able to do without both physician and medicine.

There is a less active state of the will-power which we have often found equally efficient, and even more so, in the removal of diseased conditions, especially with those whose nervous energies are much exhausted. Many patients exhibit a morbid inclination to watch their symptoms and sensations. The general law of health requires that the thoughts should be abstracted as much as possible from the action of all the organs which perform their appropriate functions involuntarily. They should be left to act in their own way without any interference with their movements. In all forms of dyspepsia attended by a too sensitive condition of the reticular membranes and mucous surface, the mind should not be directed to the stomach. The attention should be diverted from any uneasy sensations in that region. The reason of this we will explain. In addition to a principle previously stated, that to concentrate the mental force upon an inflamed part intensifies its sensibility, we may observe that all involuntary movements and processes are attended with no fatigue, or loss of nervous energy. Illustrations of this may be seen in the respiratory movements, and the systolic and diastolic motions of the heart. When we breathe involuntarily and without directing the mind to the act, the movement, though continued day and night, occasions no weariness, for then the spiritual force, which impels the respiratory apparatus, is received by influx from the all-surrounding spiritual world, with which we are in vital sympathy. But when we direct the attention to our breathing, and it becomes aftificial and voluntary, it is fatiguing. It is less wearisome to ride in a coach, than it is to draw it ourselves. The same law operates in regard to the stomach and all the involuntary organs. When we direct the attention to an involuntary organ, it exhausts its force and makes the discharge of its functional action all the same as a voluntary movement. Persons can walk a great distance in a day if they are not thinking of their movements. They then walk spontaneously and involuntarily, and the more they approach an involuntary action of the muscles concerned in their march, the further they can go without fatigue. This is the main secret in walking a hundred miles a day, a feat some have accomplished with less weariness than others experience in going the same number of rods. Availing ourselves of this law, we have sometimes walked many miles with invalids, and they have returned from their seemingly miraculous feat of pedestrianism more invigorated than when they started. By constantly diverting the attention of the patient, so that he takes no notice of his movements, nor the distance gone over, he can be made to go for miles, when before he has not thought himself able to leave the confined limits of the court-yard of his dwelling.

There is a *passive* cure of diseased conditions of the body and inharmonies of mind. We may become quiescent, assuming an easy position, perhaps reclining with the head to the north, to bring the body into an attitude agreeing with the magnetic poles of the earth. Then we may transfer our mental life to the organ of the involuntary thoughts and affections, as we have directed in inducing sleep. This is the middle state between sleeping and waking. In it the senses become unusually acute, especially that of touch or feeling, and become in a degree independent of their bodily organs. It is referred to by Paul, (2 Cor. xiii. 3), and he describes his experience while in it. In this state we become receptive of the better spiritual life of a higher sphere, which flows first into the interior organism and through this into the body. By inverting and suspending the action of the cerebrum, we are brought to that mysterious borderland situated between the two realms of being. Taking position on the mystic boundary-line between the material and spiritual worlds, the soul suspends active thought, and becomes the recipient of passive knowledge or intuition. This is a thousand times more accurate than that which is the result of active thought and reasoning. Knowledge becomes a spiritual instinct —an influx from the superior range of life. A bee will construct a cell with perfect mathematical exactness, so as to contain the greatest quantity in the smallest compass. Yet it knows nothing of geometry. Its knowledge is an instinct, or a passive intelligence, received from the spiritual world. We can become the recipients of passive knowledge. Then we gain truth not by the slow and laborious process of reason, but as the diamond imbibes the light of the sun. In this state, the mind becomes perceptive of the spiritual causes of our diseases, and of the laws of life and health—a return to which is a necessary prerequisite to a *permanent* cure under any method of treatment. This condition of the brain and mind has been denominated by some the "superior condition," but we choose to call it the *interior state*. The Swedish seer speaks of it as the "self-evidencing reason of love." It is eminently a spiritual and happy state. Anxieties, griefs, regrets, fears, doubts, self-condemnation, and all disturbances that have their seat in the external degree of the mind, are left behind, as the soul retires inward upon itself. For what men call evil, never invades the interior degrees of the mind. All unhappiness exists on the lowest plane of our spiritual nature. It becomes admissive not only of the light of the celestial climes, but also of the affectional states of the angels. Their sphere of peace, purity and love, their calm and tranquil bliss, the soul imbibes, and is made to vibrate in concord with heavenly harmonies. In the interior state, the spirit retains its consciousness, and its memory, and on its return to the external condition it brings down its higher knowledge, and the recollection of its exalted perceptions, and comes back laden with celestial spoils, as the spies returned to the desert encampment of Israel bearing with them the rich clusters of the grapes of the promised land. The tranquil soul drinks in life from perennial fountains. Oftentimes in the interior state, which is so sensitive to psychological impressions from the land of the blest, the lost harmony in the distribution of the vital forces, which constitute our pathological condition, is in a few minutes restored, and all morbid affections of mind and body are dispersed by the influx of a healthier spiritual life. Before thus approaching the boundaries of the other realm of being, it is important that we be in charity, the love of use, and in purity of intention. For like attracts its like in the spiritual world. Approaching that realm in any other moral attitude, we shall expose the susceptible inward man to the peril of imbibing the miasm of the Stygian pool, and the poisonous effluvia of disorderly spirits. The foul emanations of their surrounding sphere will serve to make our condition worse, mentally and physically. But no evil spirits, in this world or the next, can do us harm, if we approach them in the moral attitude of charity, and with a desire to do them good. Jesus went and preached to spirits in prison, or to those who were in bondage to disorderly and unharmonized passions, and the purity of his soul received no stain. And a good man might explore that mythic region, called an orthodox hell, and remain as uncontaminated as a sunbeam in an infected hospital. When we approach the higher realm of being, where all is calm, and pure, and loving, and the outward scenery seems pervaded with the life of its inhabitants, and to be only the chrystalization of their thoughts and affections, carrying with us an immortal desire to bless all mankind, and a consecration of all our activities to the good of universal being, our individual soul mingles its spark of vital force with the abyss of life in the heavens, and we receive back more than we contribute to the common stock. We come into vital sympathy with all that is pure, and healthful, and living, in the land where sickness and sorrow, pain and death are unknown. The interior state is one in which, like healthful sleep, the spiritual world comes consciously near, and angelic influences are thrown around us, and we return to our usual external condition better in mind and body. Men are only just beginning to entertain some feeble conceptions of the value and importance of our relations to the inner world, both in the generation of disease and its cure. In the interior state, when the mind retires inward upon itself, and becomes abstracted from all sensuous images and impressions, it rises to a higher plane of activity. Its intuitions are quickened, and nobler thoughts are evolved. The profoundest problems are solved by an intuitive flash of a higher light, and the deepest mysteries are unveiled. It feels a more vivid consciousness of its relations to the inner world, and of our vital connection with its immortal intelligences. It is rendered more sensitive to psychological impressions and influences from the supersensuous realms. It becomes receptive of the intellectual and affectional states of the angels. It is temporarily an inhabitant of the spiritual world, and so appears to those who dwell above. The spirit thus abstracted is actually seen by the angels, as if it had come among them by the normal process of death, which is only a complete and permanent state of introversion. This appearance of the soul among the angels, when in a state of abstraction, takes place in harmony with the same laws by which men have appeared visibly to their friends at a distance, in this world. Many well authenticated facts of this kind are on record. This temporary insertion of our partially freed spirit into the society of the celestial plains, must be productive of the happiest results, and an efficient remedy for those mental inharmonies, and spiritual disturbances, that are the cause of our bodily diseases. And many persons, while in a complete trance, have been cured by the reception of the angelic sphere of life, when their friends have deemed them dead. With the inner nature harmonized and renewed, and its spiritual forces augmented, it has come back to consciousness in the body, which soon receives the influx of life from the restored spirit, and many years of health and usefulness have been added to their earthly existence. The spiritual world is real and living. Its objects and inhabitants are not like the fantastic creations of a dream, unsubstantial and transient. It is not the abode of shadows and phantoms. It is the home of life, the seat of causation, the habitation of reality. To approach that healthful shore, is to inhale the atmosphere of immortality.

CHAPTER XXVII.

THE INFLUENCE OF THE SPIRITUAL WORLD UPON MENTAL HEALTH AND DISEASE

A Self-Evident Truth. — The Law of Sympathy. — How Jesus bore Men's Sicknesses. — Obsession. — Its Influence in causing Disease. — How cured. — Experiences of Swedenborg. — What is a Demon? — Psychological Laws stated. — Scriptural Statements respecting Destroying Angels. — They could Save Life as well. — The Medium through which Mind acts upon Matter. — Ponderable Bodies moved by Spiritual Forces. — The Release of Peter. — Paul and Silas. — The rolling away of the Stone at the Entrance of the Sepulcher. — The Availability of such unseen Forces. — Their Useful Employment. — The Plates of Copper and Zinc. — Positive and Negative Mental Forces. — Angelic Influence in the Cure of disordered Spiritual States. — The Nature of Goodness. — The Angelic Ministry. — Vital Connection with the other World. — Nearness of the Unseen Realm. — Longfellow.

THE SUBJECT introduced into the preceding chapter leads us naturally, and by an easy gradation, to the consideration of the laws that govern in the transmission of sanative spiritual influences, and psychological forces, from the inhabitants of the inner world, for the cure of pathological states of the body and mind. We take it to be self-evident, that all the effects that can be produced by one mind acting upon another in this world, can be produced, in a still higher degree, in accordance with the same laws, by the intelligences who have graduated to the superior range of life. But the question may be asked, Is it allowable and in agreement with the divine order, for good spirits to use the powers they manifestly possess for the relief of the sufferings of men? It is an axiomatic truth, that a good deed, an act of benevolence, being in harmony with the ruling principle of the divine nature, is always in order. An opinion is current among religious people, that it would greatly mar the happiness of those in the heavenly world to have any knowledge of the affairs of this world, and to feel any sympathy with the ills and the pains of those they have left below. Supposing it had that effect, what then? We have a thousand times, by the law of sympathy, taken upon ourself the diseased feelings of a patient, both those of his body and mind, and thought it a far happier, as it certainly was a more useful life, than singing psalms, or selfishly seeking the enjoyment that arises from the activity of the devotional sentiments of our nature. Jesus sometimes even cured disease by taking it upon himself. "Himself took our infirmities, and bore our sicknesses." (Matt. viii. 17; Isa. liii. 4.) This did not destroy the calm happiness of his nature, although for doing it an ignorant world afterwards "esteemed him smitten of God and afflicted." From this sympathetic bearing of human griefs and carrying the sorrows and pains of men in his own person, sprang up in a subsequent age the great theological error of a vicarious atonement for sin. He was the physician of soul and body, and used nature's most efficient remedies, but never administered medicines, not even so much as herb drinks nor homeopathic pills. He sometimes relieved the sufferers by sympathetically taking upon himself their diseased condition, and assured all his followers who were willing to do the same, that if they should "drink any deadly thing," or imbibe any morbid influence, "it should not hurt them." The effect upon the magnetic healer is sympathetic and transient; but the benefit to the invalid is permanent. Whatever Jesus did, a Christian man might reasonably believe was proper for us and even angels to do. If Jesus is viewed as the highest revelation of the Godhead to the world, and was God manifest in the flesh, and in this character went about doing good to the souls and bodies of men, "healing all manner of sickness and disease among the people," the highest angel ought not to deem it beneath his dignity or out of order to follow his example. All those who worship Jesus as a God, as an incarnation of the Divinity, as the Word made flesh and dwelling among us, ought to deem it the highest moral attainment of a worshiper to be like the Being he adores. He spent much more of his time in healing the sick, and ministering to minds diseased, than in the devotional exercise of singing hymns and saying prayers. He did both these, but it was evidently a secondary matter, to be attended to when no higher use was to be accomplished. And it ought not to be improper for redeemed spirits to lay aside the golden harp, on which they are supposed to play so skillfully, and exchange the pleasures of music and devotion, for the higher and diviner enjoyment of relieving the ills that their earthly friends are subject to. To do the works of Jesus, cannot be deemed an impossibility by any one who has faith, though like a grain of mustard, in his plain promise and declaration, "The works that I do, shall ye do also, and greater works than these shall ye do, because I go to my Father."

We take it to be a maxim, that no man should ever undertake by magnetic treatment to cure disease alone, and by his own unaided strength. He should be humbly, trustingly, and passively negative toward the higher realm of life to receive, and intensely positive toward the patient to impart. He should be in a state of vital sympathy with Jesus, and the angel-world. Without divine and angelic aid he will be as inefficient in imparting sanative influence and vital force, as was the staff of the prophet, in the hands of his servant, to bring the apparently dead child of the Shunamite woman to life.

At the commencement of the Christian era, spiritual obsessions, or as they have been called, demoniacal possessions, were of frequent occurrence in Judea and in other parts of the world. By psychological influences disorderly spirits gained control over the subject, and so conjoined themselves to him, as to use his body as the instrument of their own will, and for the expression and manifestation of their thoughts and feelings. They spake through his vocal organs, and acted through his members. This originated, or at least aggravated, the diseased tendencies of the unfortunate sufferer. Many of the diseases, healed by Jesus, were thus caused, and the cure was effected by releasing the patient from the chains of this disorderly psychological influence. Similar phenomena have been exhibited in every age One of the most illustrious instances is found in the so-called Salem witchcraft. In fact all morbid conditions of mind and body, by the great law of sympathy by which we are more or less controlled, connect us with disordered mind in the other world, and the cure of disease is a casting out of devils.

In the Arcana Celestia (5711—5727), the author affirms that all diseases have correspondence with the spiritual world, and he gives an interesting account of his experience of the effects of the sphere of certain spirits upon his own system. Those whose conscience was over-scrupulous affected "the part of the abdomen beneath the diaphragm," that is the duodenum. Adulterous spirits occasioned pain in the *periostea*, or membranes investing the bones, and also in the loins or small of the back. Some induced a sense of oppression in the stomach, and numbness in the members and joints. Others caused an extreme weakness of the muscles. The sphere of ·some spirits acted upon the excrementitious matter of the brain, aggravating its deleterious nature. Hypocritical spirits affected him with a pain in the teeth and jaws. This is what might reasonably be expected. The teeth and jaws receive their cerebral stimulus from the organ of secretiveness or from a part of the brain in immediate connection with it. In the animal races, which are characterized by the largest development of it, we find the greatest strength in the teeth and jaws, as the lion, and the feline species generally. Hypocrisy uses the organ of secretiveness for its manifestation, and it is easy to believe that the sphere of such spirits would affect the teeth. The whole chapter is suggestive to one who would investigate the connection of disorderd mental states with disease. This diseased spiritual influx was found to affect the bodily tissues, not directly, but indirectly. Its first effect was upon "the smallest and altogether invisible vessels which are continued to a man's interiors." This vitiation of the spiritual organism, when continued, occasions disease and death.

We would put the question to every man's intuitive reason, that if Providence has deemed it proper to allow such unhappy psychological influences, as must, from the vital relation subsisting between the mind and body, either generate or intensify a diseased condition, if it would not be far more allowable to permit angelic spirits to influence men, in as great a degree, in the direction of a sound mind in a sound body? For a truthful solution of this query, we would send every man, for the answer, where Jesus himself directs him to go — to the oracular response of the divine light within "Why judge ye not from yourselves what is right?" Would it not be as much in harmony with every attribute of God, and as consistent with the principles of the divine proceedure, to permit and empower good spirits to employ a psychological force to heal both mind and body? It is worthy of remark that the term improperly rendered devils by king James' translators, is from a Greek word meaning happy or prosperous, and primarily signifies good and happy spirits. In the crucible of a false theology many good things have been transmuted to evil. A demon, which originally was a term expressive of an angelic human spirit, has been transformed into a devil, with all the mythic attributes of such a being. In the superstitious alchemy of the church, the finest gold has often been basely alloyed, or even changed to a valueless lump of earth. The first definition of the word *daimōn* or demon, in your Greek lexicon, will be found to be the Divinity, the Godhead, and the next, a guardian spirit. To be influenced by a demon is necessarily no bad thing. Socrates had a demon, but was very far from being possessed of the devil. Angels or demons came and ministered to Jesus, and may they not to our humanity as well? If not, why?

There are several ways, in harmony with the laws

that govern psychological influences, in which they may greatly aid in the cure of disease. In experiments in magnetism, and in inducing upon a subject the mesmeric sleep, it is found that when several persons direct their mental force to the operator, with a wish to aid the process of induction, it facilitates and increases the effect of his manipulations. This is among the things proved. May not angels do as much in increasing and intensifying the transmission of sanative influence and vital force to an invalid under treatment by a magnetic healer? Where is the impossibility of this? Who can assign a reason why they either cannot or would not do it? The benevolent end aimed at in the cure of disease, would justify the employment of all their powers, and it is characteristic of them that they "excel in strength." It is recorded in the Jewish Scriptures, that an angel, in one night, smote, with the blast of death, one hundred eighty-five thousand men in the camp of Sennacherib king of Assyria. Also in the reign of David, a destroying angel was let loose upon the Jewish population, and by three days of pestilence caused the death of seventy thousand people from Dan to Beersheba. If credit is given to these statements as historical facts by any one, he ought to find no difficulty in believing that celestial intelligences and the principalities and powers of heaven were adequate to cure here and there a patient of a fever or a consumption. And would it not be more in harmony with the known character of Him who takes more delight in saving men's lives than in destroying them, to permit them to do so? We present these statements in the Jewish annals, in order to use them as an *argumentum ad hominem,* rather than as either crediting or justifying them ourselves. Such angels, surely, ought not to run at large in the universe, if it be true there are any such in it.

There is a hidden semi-spiritual principle that operates within the body of nature, which is the cause of all its visible phenomena. What we call causation is always unseen, at least it cannot be cognized by our senses only so far as it is ultimated in effects. The visible world is the region of effects; the unseen world is the realm of causes. The subtle essence to which we refer, is everywhere present and pervades all things, as the soul the body, and is the life of nature. It is the *animus mundi,* the soul of the universe. It is the intermediate essence through which mind acts upon matter. It is manifestly under the control of spiritual intelligences, and may be so concentrated upon ponderable bodies, as to enable them to move them by their will-force. Or it may be detached from the living organism of certain persons, as it was from the Seeress of Prevorst, and by means of it enable them to move solid bodies, as articles of furniture. A multitude of well attested phenomena of the kind find here a rational explanation, as those occurring in the Wesley family. In the early history of the church, it is recorded that, while the apostle Peter and the rest of the twelve were engaged in healing great numbers of the sick in Jerusalem, they were arrested by the Jewish authorities and put in prison. But at night (for darkness has been proved to facilitate the action of psychological force) an angel opened the doors of the prison, took off the chains from the apostles, and brought them forth from their confinement. In a similar way and by a like instrumentality, Paul and Silas, while in prison at Philippi, with their feet in the stocks, were released at midnight. The foundations of the prison were shaken, and the doors were opened. Angels also are said to have rolled away the stone from the mouth of the sepulcher in which Jesus was placed. We have no hesitation in crediting these things as veritable facts of history, and many others chronicled by ancient annalists, for the law by which they could be done has been discovered, and taken them out of the class of miracles. But the idea which we are most desirous of impressing upon the reader's mind is this: Here is an exhibition of a spiritual force that could be made available for some higher use. A force adequate to remove a ponderous stone from the entrance of a sepulcher, might just as easily reduce a dislocated joint. If an angel can open a prison door, and take a man's feet from the stocks, and release him from chains, why is not the same power equal to the restoration of the lost equilibrium of the organic forces in disease? To take off a man's handcuffs is not a more benevolent work, nor more in accordance with the angelic nature, than to loose a man from his bodily infirmities and mental unhappiness. A being who is supposed able to do the one, ought to be believed adequate to the other. The subtle, imponderable force of which we have spoken, is available to spirits, and even to the truly spiritual man, for the cure of mental and physical disorders. The organism that is animated by an enlightened mind and loving heart, and vigorous will, may become receptive of it, the organ of its diffusion, the reservoir of its distribution, and the radiating center of its communication. It can be controlled by angelic spirits, as well as we can direct the flow of water, or cause light and heat to be reflected from polished surfaces. It can be directed to the inner and outer organism of a diseased person, just as well, and far easier, than we can turn a rivulet into the parched ground of a garden to revive its withered vegetation, or admit a ray of sunshine through an opening into the dampness and darkness of a dungeon. All the imponderable forces, which are now deemed correlative of the organic forces of the human body, may be controlled by spiritual agencies.

It is practicable for us to call to our aid invisible powers, and the intelligent living forces of the spiritual world, in the cure of disease, or, more properly, we can co-operate instrumentally with them, in the relief of suffering humanity. Let us illustrate this by tangible representations. If you conceal in the earth a plate of copper, which is electrically positive, and a hundred miles away, another of zinc, which is a negative substance, and then connect the two by a wire, there will pass from the one to the other a constant current of magnetic or galvanic influence, which will operate as long as the conjunction of the two substances continues. A vibratory circuit is thus formed between the positive and negative poles. To multiply the number of the plates, thus connected, increases the effect. So between the operator and patient a conjunction may be formed analogous to this. The operator is represented by the positive plate; the patient by the negative. Both may be *passive*, or exert no mental force except to direct the thoughts to each other. They may be miles away or in the same room. Along the invisible cord, the odylic bond of connection, a spiritual therapeutic influence and force may pass from angelic beings. A circuit of the living forces of the spiritual world may be formed. And he whose inner vision is purged, so that to him "the invisible appears in sight," this vibratory current may be seen passing from one to the other, resembling a mild light. It is an essential property of spirit to communicate itself, its life, to others, and of good spirits to transmit their good to all who are admissive of it. The positive and negative distinction exists among them as well as among the inhabitants of this world. This is not merely a difference of sex, but there are those in whom the love-principle predominates and controls their activities, and others in whom the intellect is the governing force. If those who are vitally positive should conjoin themselves to the operator, and those who are negative with the person at the other end or pole of the odylic line, the psychological influence would be greatly intensified and the effect increased. And it must never be forgotten that all psychical forces directed to any part of the organism, cause a change in its physiological movements. Under the direction of intelligence any desired result can, in this way, be effected in the action of the vital forces.

But would good angels and spirits do this? It is implied that they would in the fact that they *are* good, for goodness is only a desire to impart happiness and promote the well-being of others. It is benevolence, that is, as the word signifies, *good-willing*, or wishing well to the neighbor. This point being settled, we have only further to ask, "Is it possible?" He who has but an imperfect knowledge of the arcane forces of nature, both in the realm of matter and of mind, and believes in the Scriptural and rational doctrine of their subjection to angelic powers, and their passiveness under their hands, will not hesitate for an answer. But whatever is possible, such is their benevolent nature, they will do for the benefit of mankind, whom they love and serve. They are all ministering *spirits*, who have passed through the discipline of this first stage of human development, and have graduated to the higher life. We need have no more doubt of their aid in curing disease, than in the accepted account of the New Testament of their ministrations to us in general. In the writings of Swedenborg, it is affirmed that every man is attended by *at least* two spirits and two angels. These correspond to the two departments of the mind, the intellectual and affectional. Our connection with them was viewed by him as a vital one. If they were withdrawn from us, consciousness would be suspended, and even life become extinct. A man is allowed to believe the doctrine of the angelic ministry or service to men, always taught by the church, and found in all religious systems, Pagan and Christian, without subjecting himself to the odious charge of heresy, provided he does not consider it too *real* a thing, but accepts it by faith as an undemonstrated proposition, or an unimportant item of a creed. The heresy consists in the demonstration of the truthfulness of the creed. For men are supposed to be saved much easier by faith, than by knowledge. Suppose it was asserted for the first time in the history of the world, that infancy and childhood were accompanied by an angel guard. We might ask, "Is it consistent to suppose that an angel would lay aside his golden harp, and permit his endless round of devotional exercises to be suspended, to guard the cradle of a sleeping infant?" Ask the love of a fond mother, and she will answer. Jesus also responds to the question. "See to it, that ye undervalue not one of these little ones, for I say unto you, that their angels in the heavens do always behold the face of my Father in the heavens." (Matt. xviii. 10.) We give the correct translation of the passage, which implies two things,—that little children will be unfolded into angels, and that angels watch over them. To wipe a tear from an infant's eye is not a work beneath the dignity of the loving nature of the most exalted finite intelligence, nor even of the Deity. There is no room to doubt, that what is possible, they will do to heal our mental and bodily maladies, relieve our sufferings, and add to the sum total of our happiness. They are *human* spirits, not *disembodied souls*, for we have shown that souls are never destitute of a substantial body. They feel an interest in all that concerns the welfare of humanity. And we may more certainly and unhesitatingly rely upon their aid in any work of love and mercy, than upon the feebler assistance of good men and women in this world. We may place the same confidence in them that we do in the forces of nature in any mechanical operation. It is no more natural for water by its gravitating force to run down hill and carry the mechanic's wheel, or for steam to expand and do the same, than it is for a pure unselfish love to impart all possible good to others, and save them from all possible evil. In calling to our aid the laws of nature, we have no misgiving, no doubt, no unbelief. Why not have the same confidence in spiritual aid? In the one case as in the other, knowledge is power. To know how a thing is done in harmony with nature's laws, is to be able to do it. And to all who are sick and in trouble, in body and mind, may Jesus, according to his promise, "come to you in the glory of the Father, and with his holy angels." It is one of the principles of the divine government, that God imparts good to men through the mediation of angelic human spirits. The spiritual world is not far off in the unsympathetic distance of the milky-way, nor separated from this by distance of space.

> "Some men there are, I have known such, who think
> That the two worlds—the seen and the unseen,
> The world of matter and the world of spirit—
> Are like the hemispheres upon our maps,
> And touch each other one at a point.
> But these two worlds were not divided thus,
> Save for the purposes of common speech.
> They form one globe, in which the parted seas
> All flow together and are intermingled,
> While the great continents remain distinct."
>
> ——"The spiritual world
> Lies all about us, and its avenues
> Are open to the unseen feet of phantoms
> That come and go, and we perceive them not
> Save by their influence, or when at times
> A most mysterious Providence permits them
> To manifest themselves to mortal eyes."

www.ingramcontent.com/pod-product-compliance
Lightning Source LLC
Chambersburg PA
CBHW020828160426
43192CB00007B/564